THE HISTO
WORK

Pan-European
and transnational
youth organisations
The overall lessons learned
from the history project

Volume 7

Howard Williamson
and Tanya Basarab (eds)

Council of Europe and European Commission

Cover design: Documents and Publications Production Department (SPDP), Council of Europe

Cover photo: Archiv der Arbeiterjugendbewegung, Germany – PB Ziberg, Rosette 6

Layout: Jouve, Paris

Council of Europe Publishing F-67075 Strasbourg Cedex http://book.coe.int

ISBN 978-92-871-8965-3 © European Commission and Council of Europe, December 2019 Printed at the Council of Europe

Contents

PREFACE   5
Tanya Basarab, Hanjo Schild and Jan Vanhee

INTRODUCTION – THE CHAPTERS AND SOME OVERARCHING OBSERVATIONS   9
Howard Williamson and Filip Coussée

CHAPTER 1 – AIESEC   17
Tanja Dibou

CHAPTER 2 – EUROPEAN FEDERATION FOR INTERCULTURAL LEARNING (EFIL)   29
Elisa Briga

CHAPTER 3 – THE EUROPEAN CONFEDERATION OF YOUTH CLUBS   43
Ioana Şurubaru

CHAPTER 4 – DON BOSCO YOUTH-NET – DEVELOPING A EUROPEAN YOUTH WORK ORGANISATION THROUGH YOUTH PARTICIPATION AND HISTORICAL RESEARCH, 1841-2000   51
Rein Meus

CHAPTER 5 – WORLD SCOUTING: A CENTURY OF WORK FOR YOUTH EMPOWERMENT   63
Eduard Vallory

CHAPTER 6 – HISTORY OF THE RED CROSS AND RED CRESCENT YOUTH   91
Vesselina Valcheva Dimitrova

CHAPTER 7 – INTERNATIONAL YOUNG NATUREFRIENDS   103
Petre Mrkev

CHAPTER 8 – THE DUKE OF EDINBURGH'S INTERNATIONAL AWARD   111
Amy Pearce and Melek De-Wint

CHAPTER 9 – INTERNATIONAL FALCON MOVEMENT – SOCIALIST EDUCATION INTERNATIONAL (IFM-SEI): A HISTORY OF THE MOVEMENT IN THE CONTEXT OF THE POLITICAL AND SOCIAL INFLUENCES OF THE 20TH CENTURY   127
Sabine Troitzsch

CHAPTER 10 – EUROPE IN THE INTERWAR YEARS: YOUTH ORGANISATIONS OF AUTHORITARIAN REGIMES   139
Eli Pilve, Marti Taru, Simona Sglavo

CHAPTER 11 – THE KOMSOMOL AND YOUTH ORGANISATIONS IN BELARUS   153
Olga Khabibulina

CHAPTER 12 – THE TURBULENT HISTORY OF YOUTH WORK IN BOSNIA AND HERZEGOVINA   159
Lana Pasic

CHAPTER 13 – YOUTH WORK IN UKRAINE: FROM SOVIET MODEL TO INTERNATIONAL INTEGRATION   175
Yevgeniy Borodin

CHAPTER 14 – REFLECTIVE TRIALOGUE: CONCLUSIONS FROM THE HISTORY PROJECT – 12 TRILEMMAS FOR YOUTH WORK   191
Howard Williamson and Filip Coussée

NOTES ON CONTRIBUTORS   211

Preface

Ten years and a community of people building the grounds for an informed youth work identity

Tanya Basarab, Hanjo Schild and Jan Vanhee

Over the past 10 years we have been exploring with fervour and passion the history of youth work in Europe and beyond. This project has encouraged people to think about the roots of youth work and to look for "the" history of youth work in their own country. As we know history is very much a product of subjective interpretation and there are always many angles to it. It is a continuous search for facts, stories, sources, reasons and narratives around which individuals advance their own arguments and perspectives. In addition to the search for individual histories, an attempt was made to trace or clarify some trends that transcend boundaries. This work yielded seven volumes of knowledge books with the country stories as well as stories of institutions, associations and movements. We have attempted to understand the roots and reasons at the foundation of youth work initiatives, what connections were made to the context in which youth work structures were born and developed at country or international level. We looked at how youth work has evolved in relation to social work, social pedagogy, formal and non-formal education and learning, all the while exploring the pull and push factors that have sometimes provided youth work with a more autonomous identity and shape or, at other times, subordinated it to wider agendas of the time.

The project has also coincided with, and contributed to, an important opening in the European policy field to shaping an open and inclusive European discourse around the identity and purpose of youth work. The History workshops provided critical knowledge for the two European Youth Work Conventions and hopefully the knowledge base of the overall history project will make a similar contribution to the third convention. In addition, that knowledge has also helped to build common ground for some transformative European youth policy frameworks, including the Council of Europe Recommendation CM/Rec(2017)4 on youth work and the European Union Quality Development of Youth Work. The merit of the history project lies in, among other things, the fact that we brought youth workers, researchers and academics, and policy makers together to reflect jointly with us on critical issues that shape, influence and develop youth work. Despite the lack of a rigid definition and thanks to its inclusive and incredibly resilient and adaptable nature, youth work has galvanised some of the most humanist, caring, inspiring and purpose-driven communities throughout times.

The work of recording the way those groups came together and added their piece to today's story of youth work is anything but complete. Systematic knowledge on youth work in Europe has only recently started to be analysed and further investment is needed in working with the knowledge already collected to anchor youth work practice in evidence and theoretical approaches – a crucial process for developing fields of professional practice. We invite policy makers, academics, practitioners and their associations and, critically, young activists themselves to continue the work that we started. For example, we dream that PhD students will further investigate this topic and, together with us (youth workers and policy makers), consider which lessons can be learned from the past that help to develop and advance youth work today, what are the unique features that have made youth work so resilient and attractive to young people, how youth work has responded (or not) to the critical experiences and questions young people have faced in different times and how we can share with society at large the importance of continuing to support this community in its free spaces to experiment in democracy and in its social and educational purposes. It is also to be explored where youth work has failed, where it was instrumentalised by policy, and where it did not attract or reach out to more young people.

The history of youth work in Europe is so diverse and closely related to what is going on in society. The ability to remember people as well as facts or circumstances, to touch items that have been (nearly) forgotten or were at risk of getting lost or excluded are crucial elements for social groups, social processes and humanity in general. Memory helps to open eyes and to see horizons for future perspectives. "People without memory have no future, no vision forward," says the German sociologist Oskar Negt in a speech on learning democracy, entitled "Maulwurf und Schnecke" [Mole and Snail] (2012). Thus, it is necessary, every now and then, to stop time and to critically look into what is happening around us and what happened before us. Only with a historical awareness and knowledge of where we come from can we master the challenges of the future and find answers to relevant questions of today.

In a 1992 essay, Francis Fukuyama wrote that as the communist regimes traded in their totalitarian systems one by one for fledgling democracies, capitalist, liberal-democratic state organisation had taken the upper hand over the authoritarian, state-led model. And even if Fukuyama warned then that the attachment to authoritarianism had not disappeared, no one still doubted that the whole world would soon be democratic.

How different the world looks now, around 30 years since that essay was published. Of the Arab Spring revolutions, only in Tunisia did the democratic experiment seemingly come to fruition. In the eastern European countries that cast off the shackles of communism in 1989, authoritarian leaders have found a second breath. And in almost all Western countries, populist parties are on the rise and voters question the democratic system.

The question is: what did we learn from the past, what does history teach us? How immune are we to authoritarian, nationalist and xenophobic answers to insecurity, well-justified fears and untreated challenges in today's world? As stressed above: we need a historical consciousness to find forward-looking answers for current challenges, not backward-looking ones.

Youth work and youth work development have a role to play in this regard. Youth work must contribute to democratic, social and inclusive solutions by knowing its roots and its histories. It must also remember how fragile it is and how often it has been manipulated and instrumentalised for undemocratic and nationalist purposes. We see in both history and today many positive ways in which young people and civil society organisations unite for the preservation of the planet, for rights, for equality and for other progressive agendas. World leaders refer to the courage of young people to mobilise against discrimination, precariousness (for example, Movimiento 15-M, Occupy) or the latest schoolchildren's marches for climate change.

Are these phenomena new or have there been other important youth mobilisations in history? Do they create lasting effects? How do they relate to youth policy or youth work agendas? How vulnerable are they to ideology, context or political influence? What are the features that persist in time? These were some of the questions that we explored in detail in the last history seminar, looking at the history of transnational youth organisations and their relation to youth work today.

We have tried hard to lay the foundations for systematically recording and gaining insight into how youth work and youth work organisations originated and developed in the different countries as well as at European and international level. Now we invite practitioners, researchers and policy makers in member states as well as in the Council of Europe and the European Union to continue this work. There is a growing community of people interested in the history of youth work in European countries and beyond. We are optimistic because, just as an example, the History volume 6 publication reached an audience of more than 10 000 users on social media. Young people and youth sector stakeholders recognise the contribution of this project as an important reflection point in the multitude of puzzle pieces that make youth work today. They know that now, more than ever, history can unlock more clues for a positive way forward. The commitment and insights identified can help us develop a clearer vision and direction for setting a youth work agenda in Europe.

Lastly, we owe an enormous amount of gratitude to everyone who has contributed to this project and brought all those written country and organisational (hi)stories to light, and especially to those who analysed the patterns, lessons, connections and disconnections emerging from the contributions throughout this series of publications for the benefit of stronger youth work throughout Europe. On behalf of the EU–Council of Europe youth partnership and of the youth work history project team, thank you all and may the good work continue!

Introduction – The chapters and some overarching observations

Howard Williamson and Filip Coussée

Introduction

This book is the seventh and final volume in the *History of youth work in Europe* series. For that reason, it brings together two further country histories (there have been 68 country and regional histories in earlier volumes), the contributions of most of those who presented the histories of their transnational youth organisations at the final seminar in Slovenia in October 2018. We start this chapter with some overarching reflections from the seminar itself and then introduce the chapters in the book, which culminates in a reflection on the history project as a whole.

The seventh history seminar

The final History of youth work in Europe seminar had, in its Concept Note and Call for Contributions, invited transnational youth organisations to participate from the perspective of one of a number of thematic clusters:

- *a.* Those designated as the "Big 6", having secured a global reach, though their roots were often within Europe.
- *b.* Youth work organisations and initiatives reflecting and addressing the sustaining "grand narratives" of discrimination and inequality: race, gender, class and geography. Here the focus will be on international youth work concerned with ethnic, sexual and other minorities, including rural youth.
- *c.* Those engaged in a "struggle for ideas": belief-driven youth work through faith-based organisations, the youth wings of political parties or the youth strategies and structures of authoritarian regimes.
- *d.* Issue-focused youth work development that has emerged in response to new European and global challenges: ranging across but not excluding such themes as housing and homelessness, environment and ecology, tolerance, mobility and conflict.
- *e.* Transnational youth work advocating or defending particular methodologies of youth work: self-governed youth organisations, club-based, street-based, project-based, information-based and more.
- *f.* Institutions and NGOs whose institutional and professional role incorporates the promotion and support of youth work.

Space would also be made at the seminar for the histories of youth work in European countries that had not yet been told; hence the contributions from Bosnia and Herzegovina and from Ukraine.

All the other contributions came from long-standing, established transnational youth organisations, though – as is evident from the chapters gathered in this volume – they had very different (hi)stories to tell. At the end of the seminar, we took on the responsibility both to capture some of the generic issues that seemed, to us, to have emerged from the seminar itself, and to locate the input to the seminar within the overall history project and to draw some generic conclusions from that as well.

To start with, we provided a brief résumé of the essential framing themes from the history project, though without going into the complexities that are now articulated and elaborated in the final chapter of this volume. We highlighted six aspects of the history debate:

1. that youth work serves young people both as a forum and as a transit zone;
2. that youth work has to navigate between the risks of institutionalisation, on the one hand, and individualisation on the other;
3. that youth work is characterised by both unity and diversity;
4. that youth work is shaped significantly by its political context – both right and left;
5. that youth work has always to be attentive to relationships within wider youth policy: paradoxically, greater autonomy may often be secured through some dependency on other youth policy agendas;
6. youth work is often both an educational and a social (work) practice.

The contributions at the final seminar largely reinforced these perspectives, though with some twists in the tale. As with earlier country histories or the histories of youth work projects in different European countries, transnational organisations had often twisted and turned through the turbulent times of the 20th century, sometimes to the extent of rebranding themselves and revising their objectives in response to external forces and opportunities or internal changes in leadership, sometimes forcefully retaining the values and mission on which they were established.

Most were focused on providing some measure of supplementary education, protection or welfare (safe havens), leisure activities (breathing spaces) and citizenship education (civic ideals). Some were more explicitly concerned with promoting more robust political engagement by young people. All, at least implicitly in our view, seemed to be concerned, to some extent at least, with health, rescue and inclusion. Within that starting point, however, the explicit goal was invariably concerned with the fulfilment of young people's potential. Whatever practices they had developed (exchanges, camps, clubs, hiking in the hills), they were all viewed as tools for the empowerment of young people, and pathways towards what might be described as responsible autonomy. All the organisations laid claim to an educational methodology, one that created robust learning environments that stretched young people's horizons and sense of possibility. With such self-belief, it was no surprise that most of the organisations engaged in advocacy work relating to their (different) visions and missions. Over time, if not from the very start, they had put youth participation at the heart of their structures, both in terms of "starting where young people are at" and, with one or two exceptions, ensuring that young people's voices and aspirations were represented at the very heart of decision making within the organisation.

Not that it was always clear about how decisions were actually made. Beyond some inevitable variation and evolution over time, organisations were differentially self-organised or self-directed by young people, shaped through adult guidance and ideological conviction, infused with adult support, mentoring and instruction to different degrees, and sometimes subjected to some level of adult determination and assessment. All organisations talked with commitment and enthusiasm about the benefits of experience. Slightly flippantly, we depicted this as a passion for "experiential therapy", as presenters waxed lyrical about experiential learning, learning by doing, non-formal education and non-formal learning. And all the time, other participants in the seminar – coming from very different traditions of youth work – demanded to know whether it was really youth work.

It was certainly "working with young people" in responsive and usually democratic and participative ways. Indeed, the ubiquitous claim made by all contributors was enshrined as follows: anchored in some foundational, often viewed as fundamental, values and principles, their organisation served a diversity of young people through a diversity of practice, and this in turn produced some level of transcendence in the form of personal, community and social change.

These three proclaimed outcomes clearly lie at the core of what transnational youth organisations (perhaps all youth work organisations) believe they do; it is their central *raison d'être*. As in so many definitions of youth work, the idea of "personal development" looms large: there was recurrent reference to the values, skills, morality and attitudes that are engendered in young people through their participation in these (often very different) organisations. Beyond that, however, many also laid claim to their origins in and continued commitment to service to others, through community involvement and civic participation. And on top of all this was the assertion by many of the organisations that their work constituted what might be called "little democracies". Through the provision of space and opportunity for the participation of young people, they contributed to societal development through the renewal of a democratic imperative.

Yet despite their lengthy track records and, usually, commendable adherence to some core principles over a long period of time, all of these organisations had necessarily faced persisting dilemmas as they had sought to adjust and adapt over that time. They had sometimes had to walk the tightrope between maintaining independence and becoming more incorporated (or subordinated) within wider youth policy agendas. They had often had to prove their continuing contemporary relevance, having been founded in very different times (and often for very different reasons). They faced the perennial issues of attracting and commanding the resources necessary for their sustainability. Simultaneously, even when there might have been the attraction of strengthening resourcing, these organisations seem to have endeavoured not to respond to moral panics and to avoid knee-jerk reactions, instead seeking to sustain their established priorities. Throughout their histories, there has been frequent attention to both maintaining continuity and considering change, all within a context of remaining faithful to the spirit of the organisation and trying to avoid adaptation simply because it might have been expedient at the time.

All of that was primarily at a strategic and management level, mapping the direction of the organisation within the context of both internal deliberations and external pressures. In terms of delivery, most organisations have continued to tread a fine line between the open and active transmission of particular values and what might be called a more "trojan horse" approach, where it is hoped that the core values of the organisation will steadily be internalised simply through participation. Nearly all the organisations have attempted to balance their "political" goals with youthful imagination, seeking to build a dynamic between top-down ideology and bottom-up engagement.

Most of the organisations whose (hi)stories were presented at the seminar and which appear in this book are now over 100 years old. Yet they still seem to be moving forward. But how confidently? Are they dying dinosaurs, more suited to another age, or a vanguard of social renewal for the 21st century? It is quite possible to argue both positions. Listening to the presentations, it sometimes sounded as if these were stories from a disappearing world, with the battles fought in the past not needed any more. On the other hand, it is perhaps time for their resurrection; some of these organisations have risen from the ashes before (notably after the Second World War) and perhaps it is time for them to do so again.

On the other hand, there were many striking similarities in the history and evolution of some of the organisations, and one wonders whether they all need to continue to tread their separate paths. There could be arguments for greater convergence and association, if not completely, then at either strategic or more local operational levels.

We did wonder exactly what kinds of young people are drawn to these organisations, irrespective of their diversity of values and activities. There was often a sense that they were primarily, though certainly not always, for the privileged and motivated. And if we are right about that, the youth engagement and decision making, through the "youth sections" some of them established long ago or through other mechanisms, may in fact be vehicles for continuity rather than engines for change. Indeed, despite glimpses to the contrary, we found many of these histories pointed to organisations that continue to operate in rather splendid isolation, with rather limited connection to, and influence on, a European or other international youth work policy agenda. Such engagement may have emerged in recent years, but it is still relatively thin, given the depth of experience and expertise that is clearly inherent in their backgrounds.

International youth work presents particular challenges, not least around resourcing. It is usually an expensive business. We were curious about its sustainability in modern times, especially given its many different strands. In some respects, however, transnational youth organisations appear to be ahead of the game, already diversifying their funding base (so still seeking public money but also using crowd funding, membership fees, participation charges, philanthropy and more), embracing technology and cultural change and harnessing it to their objectives, and broadening the age range of the young people they serve in the context of changing youth transitions. Readers will discover a range of innovation taking place in their projects and programmes (though not usually their principles): a case of learning to fly, or die. Yet we return again to their constant celebration of diversity, which may be proclaimed as a strength but, in straightened times, could also be an ultimate weakness. The history project may have helped to put youth work on the map but it is still in a precarious position in Europe and beyond; expensive international youth work could easily be accused of "fiddling while Rome burns", arguing recurrently over definitions in order to avoid a more pressing agenda for convergence and collaboration.

That would be a depressing note on which to conclude the seminar series. These organisations also epitomise everything that is to be commended about youth work – their diverse origins, their adaptation over time, their capacity to absorb new pressures and circumstances without sacrificing their central rationale or capitulating to the expectations of others. In their different ways, they have maintained a youth work commitment to association, dialogue and guidance, and to the spaces/bridges dichotomy that was the outcome Declaration of the 2nd European Youth Work Convention in its quest for common ground.

At a deeper level, the final seminar reinforced what we had already concluded from the earlier seminars. Time does not stand still! Youth work has always had to adapt to changing times and changing challenges – navigating a place and role between political expectations and the lives of young people. Contemporary Europe in recent times has had to contend with, *inter alia*, the credit crunch, austerity, populism, the refugee crisis, Brexit, youth unemployment, the rise of the right, and violent extremism. We have passed through the Arab Spring, the Occupy movement and the Indignados and encounter different perspectives on social media and the digital economy. There was much more before those times and there will be more ahead. But youth work is still here, in one form or another, roving across social groups, invoking a diversity of theories and methods, addressing a variety of issues and taking place in many different contexts, at local, regional, national and international levels. Arguably, it is now more firmly on the map in Europe, with political resolutions and recommendations, professional conventions and declarations, and a host of ancillary activity at local and transnational levels. The history project has illustrated the myriad ways in which youth work has connected with economic, social, cultural and political change, with differing levels of success, support and recognition.

Conclusion

And so we ask a final question deriving from the history project. Even though it has no answer, it is more than rhetoric, for it is not a question that we want left hanging in the air, but one which we want other generations of youth work practitioners, youth work educators and trainers, those who research youth work, and those who formulate youth policy and the place of youth work within it, to address.

Even though youth work in Europe may, right now in 2019, 30 years after the fall of the Berlin Wall and the "end of history", be more firmly on the map, its position is by no means secure. There is always a risk that a strong framework for youth work in any country (and there are only a few that have ever had it) may be diminished. Youth work is always vulnerable to being reduced to atomised, local, recreational responses to young people's leisure needs, supported only by parents, volunteers, young people themselves, community groups or faith initiatives.

Should youth work be embraced by public authorities, there is then a risk that some corrupted idea of youth work will be co-opted and enslaved in the interests only of other wider "youth policy" agendas, targeted only at certainly groups of (probably problematic) young people, tightly framed and required to deliver prescribed results over a specified timescale. Or, as we have learned from the history of "youth work" under authoritarian regimes, it could come to be used solely for the purposes of ideological renewal.

Alternatively, youth work may be acknowledged, developed and sustained across national borders as a public commitment to democracy, service and personal development, to be delivered as a value-based practice accessible to a diversity of young people and openly focused on a process that can accommodate both continuity and change.

For this to flourish, however, youth work itself requires space – "wild zones" for experiment and experience, places for autonomy and association, pockets of intimate democracy – that is not prescribed and pre-defined but that is a platform for orientation by young people, providing them with a sense of direction through dialogue, for the benefit of both themselves and the communities and societies in which they live.

Which is it to be?

The chapters in the book

We start with one of the younger, though perhaps better-known youth organisations, AIESEC (Chapter 1), established just after the Second World War to provide exchange opportunities for students in a number of European countries to foster better understanding between those nations. In a similar vein, EFIL (Chapter 2) had been started after the First World War to promote intercultural learning. Both organisations were focused essentially on students.

The European Confederation of Youth Clubs, ECYC (Chapter 3), established in 1976, was established to provide for working-class youth who did not have the same opportunities as European students. In that vein, it was following in the footsteps of Don Bosco Youth-Net (Chapter 4) which, though specifically established only in this millennium, was embedded in the traditions and philosophy of the Don Bosco Movement from the 19th century.

The most ubiquitous international youth organisation in the world is, of course, Scouting (Chapter 5), which has sought to empower young people for over 100 years. Less well known as a youth organisation (because it is much more than that) is the equally ubiquitous, and older, Red Cross and Red Crescent, RCRC (Chapter 6). Also emerging as a youth organisation from a parent body established in the 19th century, International Young Naturefriends (Chapter 7) celebrates outdoor activities and environmental responsibility.

The Duke of Edinburgh's International Award (Chapter 8) was, in contrast, founded very specifically for young people, to address what were seen as some of the "declines" in youth after the Second World War. Established by Britain's Prince Philip in 1956, it was designed to provide a "do-it-yourself guide to civilised living" by certificating a range of activities chosen by young people themselves. With very different roots, the International Falcon Movement-Socialist Education International (Chapter 9) was founded in 1922 and intended to challenge capitalism and promote a socialist way of life.

The interwar years (1918-39) saw the emergence or development of many transnational youth organisations but they were not all emancipatory or democratic. On the political right, in Italy, Germany, Spain and Estonia (Chapter 10), state-controlled youth organisations were established to regulate the lives of young people in the interests of the state. Nowhere was this more evident than in the work of the Komsomol across the countries of the Soviet Union and which is still thriving in Belarus (Chapter 11).

Such variations in forms of youth work are rather well reflected in the national history of Bosnia and Herzegovina (Chapter 12), as the political winds of change blew youth work in different directions. Similarly, youth work in Ukraine (Chapter 13) was dramatically reconceptualised following the collapse of the Soviet Union.

The book concludes with a comprehensive and reflective conclusion to the history project overall (Chapter 14). This chapter conveys forcefully that youth work has little choice but constantly to navigate and defend its position within a constellation of interconnected triangles – balancing the pressures and expectations or legacies from each corner – without ever being pulled or acquiescing to be pushed into any of those corners. For if it does get sucked into a corner, youth work as we know it, and as we have learned from history, is lost.

Chapter 1

AIESEC

Tanja Dibou

Introduction

The impact of international youth organisations on the development of global, national and local youth work cannot be underestimated, as many activities in the youth field have arisen through the initiatives of international actors. International youth organisations play an important role in the development of key competences of young people. Also, such organisations increase the participation of youth in the community by supporting them and involving them in the activities of the organisation through non-formal learning, which helps to promote civic and political engagement among all young people.

This chapter provides an example of such impact from the world's largest non-profit international student-run organisation, AIESEC. It aims to present briefly the history of AIESEC, describing the organisation's vision and mission, its main activities and its relations to youth work. Additionally, it illustrates how experiences in AIESEC have had an impact on the development of competences of young people in general. I argue that AIESEC has contributed indirectly to youth work through raising the role of youth participation, youth volunteering at national and global levels and impacting young people's personal and professional development through non-formal education, as youth participation, youth volunteering and non-formal education are basic principles of current youth work in many countries.

AIESEC organisation and programmes connected to youth work

AIESEC is an international non-political, non-governmental and non-profit organisation, present in over 125 countries and territories with more than 47 000 members across 2 600 universities. Taking into consideration that the definition of "youth" in the EU is 13-30 years old, AIESEC can be confidently described as a youth-led organisation, as it is exclusively managed by students and recent graduates. A large majority of members are students at an average age of around 18-23 years old, while the maximum age among employees of AIESEC is around 30 years.

AIESEC's activities, aims and mission are strongly related to the main principles of youth work. AIESEC's mission is to place its confidence in youth to become the leaders of tomorrow, and the main aim of the organisation is to develop young people's leadership skills in cross-cultural contexts. It seeks to give its members integrated development experiences, consisting of three main attributes: leadership opportunities, international traineeships and the global learning environment. AIESEC, through its activities, attempts to develop young people who have the knowledge, skills and determination to build a world with more respect for others. The cross-cultural activities of the organisation open young people's minds and help them to under-stand the different cultures, religions and other aspects that differentiate human life, in order to avoid conflicts.

Concerning youth work and AIESEC activities, the connection between them is more than obvious, as youth work can be carried out in many settings. Youth work carries a more profound purpose than simply providing leisure and recreation-based activities, care or diversionary services. One of the main principles of youth work is encouraging young people's educational development and promoting equitable social change (Sapin 2013). The activities and objectives of AIESEC are closely aligned to the EU youth work framework, as the EU also stresses that youth work aims to help young people open their potential and encourage personal development, autonomy, initiative and participation in society (EU Council 2013). AIESEC stands for the devel-opment of youth initiative-led projects around the world. Its activities include not only working for and with youth but also considerable social networking involving universities and other educational institutions, government, non-governmental and private organisations, and individual professionals. AIESEC provides young people with opportunities to make a positive impact on society. All AIESEC programmes are run under a set of core values: Striving for Excellence, Demonstrating Integrity, Activating Leadership, Acting Sustainably, Enjoying Participation and Living Diversity.

As youth work is strongly "justified" and explained through non-formal learning (Kiilakoski 2015), it is essential to mention that AIESEC's methods have much in com-mon with non-formal learning. This is because the students participating in AIESEC programmes have different tasks, which helps them put into practice the knowledge acquired in school. In other words, AIESEC creates a connection between the formal knowledge offered at universities and real working life. Being part of an AIESEC pro-gramme, young people learn to take the initiative, to work better in groups, to take decisions, to be independent and to become a leader. Being a member of the student organisation helps youngsters to develop better both personally and professionally. The organisation also helps young people's entry into the labour market (Nicolae 2016).

Young people learn new skills and gain new knowledge through "learning by doing" activities as they follow AIESEC programmes:

> ▶ **Volunteering** has two levels: local volunteering and global volunteering. The programme allows the volunteer on a project or in an NGO to address one of the emergent issues in society. Participants may work in an organisation, school or other institution, or take part in a project, as long as their experience both supports their personal development and has a positive impact on society through its contribution to the UN Sustainable Development Goals.

> ▶ **International traineeships** enable young people to contribute to the goals of the organisation, complete a job description requiring special expertise or skills, and receive supervision and evaluation in relation to their professional development.

> ▶ **Entrepreneurial international traineeships** provide an opportunity for young people to contribute to the goals of a business start-up, work with multiple job descriptions usually in diverse fields, and receive mentorship and evaluation in relation to their entrepreneurial development.

All programmes incorporate the aims mentioned above as central objectives of youth work: young people's personal development, their active participation and their preparedness to be active citizens through making a positive impact on society.

These days in the EU, youth work is focused on the development of so-called "soft skills" that can help young people to adjust in many spheres of life. In the EU context, soft skills are stressed through a framework of key competences that are defined as a combination of the knowledge, skills, attitudes, values and critical understanding that each individual needs for personal fulfilment and development, active citizenship, social inclusion and employment (European Commission 2007). The emphasis is on improving young people's chances in life and giving them better opportunities in the labour market and in education. Therefore, youth work is also about building bridges for better transitions of young people from school to working life. AIESEC opportunities are also directed towards giving young people their first experiences of employment, which raise their competitiveness in the labour market in the future. Youth unemployment is an issue in most parts of the world, often at higher rates than average unemployment. At the same time, employers are having difficulties filling their junior-level positions. AIESEC's work is about creating bridges between young employees and employers. More than 1 500 diverse organisations provide placements for international traineeships and volunteering opportunities to young people. AIESEC has promoted the view, through various organisations, that young employees are not a threat for companies but a resource for new ideas and new ways of thinking in the organisation. AIESEC strongly believes that youth unemployment can be tackled through youth international mobility, as experience in other countries gives young people new skills, which compensate for the lack of practical experience that is provided at current educational institutions.

AIESEC stands for the active participation of youth in decision-making processes. This is one of the priorities for youth work in many countries. AIESEC has built the platform YouthSpeak Forum to promote a structured dialogue between young people and politicians and senior leaders from diverse fields. YouthSpeak Forum is a forum run by youth, where young people can take an active part in discussions and where their voices are heard.

However, youth leaders from AIESEC do not much relate themselves to youth workers, the role of youth leaders in AIESEC activities having much more in common with the role of the contemporary youth worker. For example, Coussée (2010) found that youth worker roles have moved away from social pedagogical questions on the conditions in which young people grow up and have to find their way in society, towards the positive and harmonious development of individual young people and their participation in society. Bamber, O'Brien-Olinger and O'Brien (2014) argue that youth workers have carried roles such as leader, expecting young people to follow them, and it was then replaced with the role of teacher, where the active position of young people in the process of youth work was also minimised. From the 1950s we can see the shift from passive young person to someone who is actively involved in youth work, while the youth worker is open to the better engagement of young people in society, and also paying attention to the personal development of youth in the light of social change. Youth workers took on the role of facilitator in the period 1950-75, and from 1975 onwards, social critic and activist. Butters and Newell (1978) (in Bamber, O'Brien-Olinger and O'Brien 2014) provided a youth work framework that traces three major approaches in terms of: character building (focusing on moral development); social education (involving cultural adjustment, personal development and empowerment); and self-emancipation (involving social change). Smith (1988) argues that youth worker roles are multiple and overlapping and that the role is largely associated with the moral and personal development of young people.

AIESEC members and youth team leaders' role as youth workers is to help young people to explore themselves and their abilities and apply their potential to working constructively in society. Leaders are also young people and peer learning is common within the activities. The methodology of AIESEC training is directed towards empowerment and character building of young people, through raising their awareness about youth opportunities to impact society and increasing young people's leadership skills to make positive change in the future.

To sum up, AIESEC as a youth-led organisation has common features with youth work. First of all, it works with and for the best for young people, secondly it values youth personal development and participation in society, and thirdly the methodology of the activities of AIESEC is based on non-formal learning that is directed towards developing the soft skills and empowerment of young people.

History and structure of AIESEC

AIESEC was originally a French acronym for Association Internationale des Étudiants en Sciences Économiques et Commerciales (International Association of Students in Economic and Commercial Sciences). Nowadays, AIESEC is no longer used as an acronym but simply as the name of the organisation. It was founded in 1948 when a group of young students from seven countries (Belgium, Denmark, Finland, France, Netherlands, Norway and Sweden) wanted to carry out traineeships in other countries with the idea of fostering better understanding between various nations, increasing tolerance and joining the ties between countries after the Second World War. The students strongly believed that cross-cultural traineeships would give the opportunity to young people to become open-minded, that such support would help to avoid prejudice and prevent conflicts between people from various cultural backgrounds and keep peace in the world in the future. AIESEC was founded on a vision of friendship and unity of nations. Such a vision is shared with other international organisations that were established after the Second World War. It is, for example, the basis of the UN and the EU. However, AIESEC's vision was also different from that of other international organisations. The idea of international student experience was quite new at that time. In contrast, the well-known EU Erasmus students' programme was established only in 1987, almost 40 years after AIESEC established its own initiatives for students' international traineeships.

In 1949, in the first year of AIESEC's existence, 89 students took part in exchanges among seven countries. In those first years, AISEC provided mostly internships and study tours for young people. The organisation then dramatically expanded internationally during the period 1955-89. During those years, all the world's continents joined AIESEC's programme. The development of exchange programmes grew by 22%. In 1966, AIESEC launched the Summer School Training Programme, which expanded the opportunities from just student exchanges to the unique training programme for participants. Also at that time, traineeships were divided into two types: short-term up to three months and long-term traineeships of more than three months. In 1989, despite the Cold War, the highest number of traineeships was recorded. From the 1990s, AIESEC put effort into involving young people in United Nations (UN) programmes and intensified its co-operation with the UN. AIESEC gained international recognition at the UN Earth Summit in 1992 in Rio de Janeiro, at the World Summit for Social Development in 1995 in Copenhagen, and at the World Habitat II meeting in 1996 in Istanbul (AIESEC 2019). Nowadays, AIESEC has consultative status with the United Nations Economic and Social Council (ECOSOC), is affiliated to the United Nations Development Programme (UNDP), is a member of the International Co-ordination Meeting of Youth Organisations (ICMYO), and since 1953 has had co-operation status with the United Nations Educational, Scientific and Cultural Organization (UNESCO). Since the 1950s, and until now, AIESEC has taken part in many social projects that attempt to tackle various issues such as poverty, inequality and climate change. In 2015, AIESEC leaders and representatives gathered at the UN headquarters to promote the role of young people and youth participation in the implementation of the Sustainable Development Goals (SDGs). AIESEC have common projects with UNDP in Asia-Pacific, and UN Volunteers in West and East Africa to advance youth contribution to SDGs. AIESEC is working in close co-operation with the United Nations Industrial Development Organization (UNIDO) with a focus on SDG 4 on quality education, SDG 9 on industry, innovation and infrastructure, and SDG 13 on climate action.

In 2001, AIESEC also opened its programmes for all students from various fields of study. In the beginning, its programme had only been for students of business and administration. AIESEC proposed four different types of traineeships concerning management skills, technical skills, development objectives and educational traineeships.

Table 1.1. An overview of the history of AIESEC

The start of AIESEC	1948 – AIESEC was established.
	March 1951 – First International Congress of AIESEC in Stockholm
	Main activities:
	traineeships and study tours
	Mission:
	improve international understanding

The global expansion of AIESEC	1953 – AIESEC achieved co-operation status with UNESCO
	1955 – more than 1 000 traineeships
	1956 – USA joins AIESEC
	1958 – South Africa joins AIESEC as the first African country and Venezuela as the first in South America
	1961 – establishment of permanent secretariat in Geneva
	1963 – AIESEC extends to Asia with the inclusion of Japan and Korea
	1965 – Australia joins AIESEC. AIESEC now in all inhabited continents and Czechoslovakia joins AIESEC as the first country from behind the Iron Curtain
	1966 – AIESEC Summer School Training Programmes were introduced
	1989 – the highest number of traineeships ever recorded (7 029)
	1992 – AIESEC was involved in almost every UN conference as a youth sector representative
	2001 – traineeships divided into four pools: management, technical, development and educational traineeships
	Main activities:
	traineeships and study tours
	social projects
	Mission:
	improve international understanding and co-operation of countries and communities
Currently	2015 – AIESEC's youth leaders from 126 countries in collaboration with the Office of the Secretary-General's Envoy on Youth gathered at the United Nations headquarters to promote and drive youth participation in implementing the Sustainable Development Goals (SDGs)
	July 2015 – AIESEC was recognised for the ninth time on the WorldBlu list of "Most Freedom Centred Workplaces"
	Main outcomes:
	AIESEC annually offers over 27 500 leadership positions and delivers over 500 leadership conferences to its membership of over 100 000 students
	Mission:
	looking for new practical ways of building a better world
	educating future responsible leaders

In terms of structure, AIESEC can almost be compared to a multinational company. The president works with a global committee made up of global vice-presidents: one for each region (Europe, Asia-Pacific, the Americas, the Middle East and Africa) and one per key function (marketing, finance, account delivery, information systems, and partnership development). The global committee is located in Rotterdam and consists of 21 members who oversee the operations of all committees worldwide and lead the accomplishment of the five-year plan. They supervise member committees who are the presidents and vice-presidents of each country. The member committees are responsible for organising more than 500 training and leadership development conferences every year. The member committees supervise the local committees, which are the AIESEC structures at university level. Local committees at university level are responsible for the recruitment of new members and the delivery of traineeships and volunteering programmes. The country and university levels benefit from the operation support teams, which act as coach/consultant and bring their experience of a specific field (partnerships, account delivery, talent management). All committees are renewed every year through elections. AIESEC members of each university elect a local committee president. These, in turn, elect their national president, and the national presidents elect the global president (AIESEC website, Jadoul 2017).

The members of the global committee and member committees have full-time paid jobs, whereas local committee members work voluntarily while completing their university degrees; and being part of the AIESEC allows them to build their first professional experience. Young people working in local committees at university level receive a stipend that cannot be considered a salary. They work for passion, firmly believing in the purpose of the organisation: that of creating a more peaceful society through the cultural understanding and diversity it offers through its programmes.

AIESEC recruits its members from universities. These students become volunteers and form part of AIESEC's global membership. Some of the members stay in the organisation even after university graduation and continue to contribute to AIESEC's various social projects. AIESEC attracts students from various backgrounds. Students who join AIESEC are mainly interested in gaining work experience, diversified academic knowledge, cross-cultural experience and the opportunity to participate in global programmes. The selection criteria for newcomers are based on whether young people are committed to the AIESEC vision, values and mottos.

When students become members of the organisation, they receive training on the programmes of AIESEC. They are also involved in induction projects, which are activities that intend to measure their proactivity, leadership potential, resilience, responsibility, learning capacity, open-mindedness; this is a kind of evidential test to make members consider whether AIESEC is what they really need. It is not unusual that at the end of the projects some members do not remain within the organisation. These projects are usually about events organisation on social issues. After their induction, members are allocated to one of the areas of the organisation, and they begin to "formally work" in AIESEC (Velez 2015).

The impact of AIESEC on youth and youth work

In the year 2018, AIESEC celebrated 70 years of experience in providing young people with opportunities for mobility, volunteering and traineeships with the objective to develop leadership and entrepreneurship skills, and to raise cross-cultural and global awareness. During these years more than 1 million young people have participated in AIESEC programmes. The organisation has grown from 7 countries to 126, from 7 members to 70 000, and it has a high retention rate, with more members aspiring to join every year. What are the reasons for its success?

According to Velez (2015), analysis after the second month of involvement in AIESEC shows that most individuals feel encouraged to continue because of the friendship within the work environment, the support everyone provides to each other, and the great network they get through contact with other members from other cities in their country and from the whole world. The skills that young people have the opportunity to acquire during their time in AIESEC include public speaking, event management, sales, project management, finance management, time management, resilience, public relations, communications, marketing, human resources subsystems, negotiation skills, conflict management, training skills, commitment, flexible thinking, coaching, mentoring, global mindset, entrepreneurial outlook, social responsibility, emotional intelligence, proactive learning, languages (learning or improving), and information systems management. In fact, members generally think about AIESEC as a personal and professional preparation for "life out there".

The role of AIESEC activities as non-formal education was analysed by Elena Nicolae (2016) in Romania. Young economist students, who have been involved in AIESEC activities and compared to students who participated only in formal education, consider themselves to be better at solving issues, developing new products and services, to be able to efficiently communicate with others, to have leadership abilities, to be creative, and also to be capable of making professional contacts.

AIESEC also contributes to the key skills that were stressed in the European Union framework of eight key competences (European Commission 2007). How soft skills are learned and practised within youth programmes in AIESEC was studied in Estonia through focus groups with AIESEC members in 2018 and interviews with Estonian young AIESEC volunteers in a 2016 survey (Tael 2016). The main objective of the survey was to discover the role of volunteering in AIESEC for personal development, how volunteers themselves assess their key competences and how these competences have improved young people's everyday lives.

Figure 1.1 – Youth scores (average scores) for key competences development after membership of AIESEC and after being a member of AIESEC

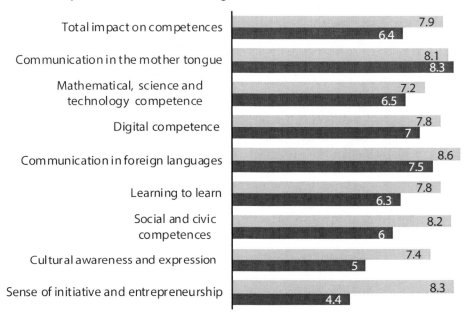

As a result of the research, it was found that all respondents saw their personal development in the context of key competences improved through AIESEC activities. Initiative and entrepreneurial competence were the highest rated. The development of cultural awareness and expression and social and civic competence was also highly valued. Skills were mainly developed through the organisation and planning of social projects and events. In addition, sales, marketing campaigns and participation in social events contributed to development. From the perspective of their own development, the initiative and entrepreneurial spirit, social skills, learning skills and cultural awareness, and expression gained from AIESEC were valued. Young people appreciated the ability to plan and organise social projects and events that ensure a more stress-free daily life and an understanding that there can be a solution to all problems. It also increased their ability to produce new ideas and find innovative solutions to various problems. Social skills acquired at AIESEC, which help people communicate more freely and courageously in everyday life, were considered important. The participation in the activities of AIESEC also had a positive impact on time-management skills.

The impact of the AIESEC organisation can be summarised on three levels. At a macro level, this has implications for society as a whole. One of the roles of international youth organisations is the popularisation of important values such as democracy, human rights, peace and tolerance. Young people participating in international youth programmes gain an idea of the most common problems and ways to analyse and solve them. Discussing the world's problems teaches young people to understand the complexity and diversity of today's world. Generally, AIESEC contributes to preventing and solving societal problems, facilitates youth participation and non-formal learning. The voice of young people becomes audible and young people have more opportunities to participate in learning, where they are no longer in just a passive consumer role, but are actively teaching others (learning from "young to young"). From an educational point of view, it is very important that AIESEC provides young people with a wide range of knowledge that will enable them to adapt well in different situations in today's society and to meet various challenges.

The micro level refers to impact at the level of the organisation, such as the impact on a specific institution engaged in the network of AIESEC. By exchanging experience and good practices between organisations in different countries, AIESEC brings new perspectives to local youth work and makes communities better.

At the individual level, there is the impact on a particular young person. International co-operation gives them good experience for the future. This will enable them to acquire the skills needed both in the labour market and for personal development. It provides a unique opportunity to get to know people from different cultural backgrounds and find friends from other countries. In an international environment, it is possible to take on new tasks for yourself and test yourself in a different role than usual, which in turn enriches life.

Conclusion

AIESEC is an international youth organisation that plays an important role, and an increasing role, in supporting youth participation in society. It provides an opportunity to increase the involvement of young people in the community by engaging them in volunteering and traineeship programmes and in the organisation's activities through non-formal learning, which helps to promote civic and political inclusion among all young people. It appears that through its activities it is possible to contribute to the multifaceted development of young people and so-called soft skills, which are lacking nowadays in the system of formal education. The results of the study in Estonia about the impact of AIESEC on the development of young people's key competences have provided confirmation that membership of an international youth organisation provides young people with the environment for personal development. Although AIESEC activities and programmes are mainly voluntary work, the skills of the participants will increase.

With globalisation, it is important to ensure openness and acceptance of other cultures among people. Through international youth organisations such as AIESEC, it is possible to ensure transnational co-operation and intercultural learning, which makes young people more aware of what is happening in the world. International youth organisations also deal with the problems and needs of young people at an international level, and today AIESEC organises a youth-initiated forum, where young people can make their voices heard and stand up for their interests.

To conclude, AIESEC has impacted youth work indirectly, by improving the possibilities for youth voices to be heard and for youth development through non-formal education in traineeships and volunteering programmes. Also, AIESEC's role in the empowerment of young people cannot be diminished. AIESEC's values and working principles with young people are very similar to youth work.

Hopefully the impact of AIESEC as an international youth organisation creates a broader understanding of the role of international organisations in the positive development of young people and creates further understanding of the contribution of international organisations in the youth field. Such a contribution must not be underestimated, particularly because many activities in the field of youth have started with international initiatives. Knowledge of international initiatives is often a driving force for the development of local youth work. Knowledge of documents issued by international organisations concerning young people's lives will help to better understand the principles and values of youth work at all levels, from the international to the local, and encourage youth workers to use these principles in their daily work.

References

AIESEC (2019), *The history book of AIESEC*, available at https://issuu.com/aiesecinternational/docs/aiesec_history_book, accessed 26 July 2019.

AIESEC website: https://aiesec.org/.

Bamber J., O'Brien-Olinger S. and O'Brien M. (2014), *Ideas in action in youth work in theory*, The Centre for Effective Services, Dublin.

Coussée F. (2010), "The saint, the poet, the lord and the cardinal: learning from youth work's history", *Coyote Extra*, First European Youth Work Convention, EU–Council of Europe Youth Partnership, Strasbourg, pp. 10-15.

EU Council (2013), Council conclusions on the contribution of quality youth work to the development, well-being and social inclusion of young people, available at https://eur-lex.europa.eu/legal-content/EN/ALL/?uri=CELEX:52013XG0614%2802%29, accessed 26 July 2019.

European Commission (2007), *Key competences for lifelong learning: European Reference Framework*, Luxembourg.

Jadoul T. (2017), "What are the key success factors that lead AIESEC global virtual teams to higher performance?", AIESEC case study, MA thesis, Louvain School of Management, Belgium.

Kiilakoski T. (2015), "Youth clubs as spaces of non-formal learning: professional idealism meets the spatiality experienced by young people in Finland", *Studies in Continuing Education* Vol. 37, Issue 1, pp. 47-61.

Nicolae E. (2016), "The role of nonformal education in shaping young economists", *Cactus Tourism Journal* Vol. 13, Issue 1, pp. 29-40.

Sapin K. (2013), *Essential skills for youth work practice*, 2nd edn, Sage, London.

Smith M. (1988), *Developing youth work: informal education, mutual aid and popular practice*, Open University Press, Milton Keynes.

Tael N. (2016), "Võtmepädevuste arendamine rahvusvahelises noorteorganisatsioonis vabatahtlikuna osalemise kaudu" (Lõputöö), Juhendaja Tanja Dibou [The development of key competences in international organisation through volunteering (Diploma), Supervisor Tanja Dibou, Tallinn University, Tallinn.

Velez E. (2015), *Organizational analysis of AIESEC*, New York University, New York.

Chapter 2

European Federation for Intercultural Learning (EFIL)

Elisa Briga

Introduction

In its 100 years of history, AFS Intercultural Programs have been transformed from a wartime humanitarian aid organisation into a groundbreaking international exchange, volunteer and intercultural learning organisation aimed at building a more peaceful world by promoting understanding among cultures. AFS organisations are present in 59 countries and operating in 98 countries worldwide, involving more than 12 000 participants and more than 53 000 volunteers every year, raising US$28 million for scholarships. Since 1949, 500 000 participants and 400 000 families have been involved.

The AFS mission today is to:

> empower people of all ages and all backgrounds with the intercultural knowledge, skills and understanding required to take action and make a positive difference at home and around the world.

This mission is pursued mainly through a specific type of educational programme, namely the immersive long-term (3 to 10 months) intercultural exchange for 15-18-year-old students, host family and host school-based, supported by non-for-mal education experiential learning activities before, during and afterwards. Today, AFS also promotes intercultural learning through other programmes such as short-term exchanges, volunteering and internships abroad for 18+ students, and teacher exchanges.

In order to ensure quality, for each of these exchange programmes AFS has set clear educational objectives and developed its so-called "Learning Journey" where these are matched with methods for achieving them. Moreover, Learning Journeys have also been designed to shape and guide the learning experience of volunteers, host families and schools involved in the AFS programmes.

From the 1970s, AFS organisations in Europe started a closer co-operation by creating the European Federation for Intercultural Learning (EFIL), which has played a key role in the development of European youth work and mobility programmes. More recently, AFS organisations in other parts of the world have also established similar regional co-operation: AFS Asia Pacific Initiative (AAI)[1] in 1991, AFS in Africa (AiA) in 2015,[2] Alianza Latinoamericana de Educación Intercultural (ALEI) in the Latin American region in 2017.[3]

An overview of the history of AFS and EFIL

AFS began as the American Ambulance Field Service (AAFS), a volunteer ambulance corps created in 1915 by A. Piatt Andrew as an initiative within the spirit of French–American friendship. It was established in order to treat wounded soldiers returning from the war front in France. During the war, 2 569 ambulance drivers transported 600 000 wounded soldiers and 127 of them lost their lives. An American woman living in France, Anne Vanderbilt, contributed enormously to the creation of AAFS with her financial support and the donation of the first 10 ambulances (Chinzari and Ruffino 2014: 28-31). Her role in the early and crucial days of the organisation reflects within the history of AFS the change in women's role in society that was triggered by the First World War.

The AFS Association was established in 1920 to co-ordinate reunions among former ambulance drivers and to administer a university student exchange programme, the American Fellowship for French Universities, between the USA and France: the objective was 127 fellowships a year, and former ambulance drivers were a key source for fundraising and for keeping the memory alive. However, the Great Depression obstructed the vision and only 45 students took part in the exchange programme between the two world wars. However, to perpetuate the memory of the First World War and the French–American friendship that had been established, in 1938 the Volunteer Pavilion dedicated to AFS was inaugurated at the Musée Franco-Americain in Blérancourt, France.[4] Then, in 1941, AFS was reactivated as a volunteer ambulance corps under the leadership of Director-General Stephen Galatti. AFS officially aligned itself with the British military and Free French Forces and as the war progressed the ambulance drivers served alongside the allied troops all over the world – 2 196 ambulance drivers carried more than 700 000 wounded combatants "no matter what uniforms they were wearing".

In 1946, inspired by the student exchange programme run between the two world wars and the international exposure that the ambulance drivers had during the Second World War, Stephen Galatti and former ambulance drivers revived the university exchange programme with students from all over the world, with the intention to perpetuate international friendships in peacetime. From 1946 to 1953, this programme involved 177 university students who were hosted in AFS volunteer families during the holidays and supported by them in the new and exciting

---

1.   AFS Asia and the Pacific Initiative (AAI): https://prezi.com/kbgeg1myorkq/afs-asia-and-the-pacific-iniative-aai/.

2.   AFS and Africa: https://afs.org/2017/10/13/afs-and-africa-engaging-with-youth-on-the-fastest-growing-continent/.

3.   Organizaciones de AFS en Latinoamericana Formalizan el nacimiento de La Alianza Latinoamericana de Aprendizaje Intercultural ALEI: www.afs.do/2018/05/23/la-alianza-latinoamericana-de-aprendizaje-intercultural-alei/.

4.   https://museefrancoamericain.fr/.

experience of living abroad (ibid.: 89). Moreover, in the period 1949-51 the American State Department entrusted the US–German exchange programme to AFS, aimed at offering to German 16-18-year-olds the opportunity to "live democracy" (ibid.: 109).

Just one year later, in 1947, AFS also started running a secondary school programme in boarding schools thanks to an exchange programme with England through the English Speaking Union (ESU) (ibid.: 90), and shortly afterwards some secondary school pupils from France were sent to the USA. Soon the majority of students coming to the USA on fellowship programmes with AFS were from secondary schools. In the academic year 1949/50 pupils were hosted for the first time in host families for the whole period (ibid.: 91).

In 1951, the first students from the USA spent a period abroad living with families in Europe: 24 secondary school pupils from the USA spent their vacations in France hosted by AFS volunteers, contacts of the ex-ambulance drivers. The following year, the German students who had been to the USA on the programme funded by the US State Department and managed by AFS, decided to invite 54 American peers to Germany for the summer holidays. The number of students from the US spending an exchange period in the rest of the world steadily expanded, as well as the variety of hosting countries. This happened thanks to the work of AFS students from all over the globe who, after spending their exchange year in the US, helped develop exchange programmes in their home countries.

During the period 1950-67 AFS exchanges boomed, reaching about 2 000 students hosted in the US every year (ibid.: 102). These were years of expansion and consolidation of the bilateral exchange system: the perspective was purely American – to and from USA. At the time, AFS was mostly known as a "Year in the USA programme", albeit for groups of pupils who were more and more international.

Stephen Galatti died in 1964 and the leadership passed to Arthur Howe, who had to deal with a request for the internationalisation of the organisation, moving beyond exchanges solely between the USA and the rest of the world. In the same year, on the occasion of its 50th anniversary, the AFS chapter in Torino, Italy, had the idea to invite delegates from every AFS organisation in Europe for an informal meeting to discuss how AFS could develop common activities across the continent. At this first meeting the leadership of Roberto Ruffino emerged, to guide the development of a European network of AFS organisations. This meeting led to the establishment of a "European Information Committee". Other annual informal meetings followed in 1965 and 1966, and in 1967 this initiative became the "European conference". AFS International supported this voluntary co-operation movement in Europe and in 1967 it opened the European Coordination Office in Brussels. Thanks to the co-operation between the European Information Committee and the AFS European Coordination Office in Brussels in 1971, AFS Europa was founded during the AFS World Congress in Lake Mohonk and, as from 1975, the organisation was renamed as the European Federation for Intercultural Learning (EFIL 2011: 1). EFIL forged its first contacts with the department of education and youth of the European Economic Community and was invited to define their policy on student mobility (ibid.: 3). At the same time, links with the Council of Europe and its European Youth Foundation were also built.

While AFS Europa was taking shape, in the academic year 1971/72 the AFS multinational programme began, allowing students to travel to and from countries other than the USA: it started with 19 students, and today 7 000 are choosing destinations that are different from the USA. In 1971, at the AFS World Congress, the organisations of various countries sought independence from AFS as a US-based organisation, expressing the desire to move towards legal, financial and logistical recognition of national AFS entities (Chinzari and Ruffino 2014: 113). As a result, the congress changed the name of the organisation to AFS International Scholarships (then, as from 1978, to AFS International Intercultural Programs, and later, until now, to AFS Intercultural Programs). In these years, the process of transforming AFS into a network of partners, namely independent national organisations, linked to AFS International through the partnership system, began, though it was completed only in 1989.[5]

During the 1980s, the term "intercultural" became popular, and AFS formally defined its Educational Goals,[6] which continue to be the foundation of its activities. In this period the focus of EFIL widened, aiming at expanding the number of partner countries in Africa, in co-operation with AFS International, by establishing a joint office in Rome for this purpose and organising several colloquia to provide a different approach to the North–South relationship and a better understanding between African and European cultures. The federation also embarked on events to promote East–West co-operation within Europe, and new projects for students, young workers and migrants (EFIL 2011: 6). None of these initiatives survived over the long term. In the late 1980s and 1990s there were many changes in EFIL staff and boards, and while AFS was focusing internally due to the process of restructuring as a network of partners, the European Union accelerated the citizens' integration process through large investment in youth mobility schemes, which threatened the role of organisations such as AFS that had initiated them. At the same time, Europe had to deal with the end of the East/West division and AFS welcomed new partners in the former Eastern bloc (Russia, Hungary, Slovakia, Czech Republic, Latvia) and had to regain a presence in the new countries that emerged from the dissolution of Yugoslavia (ibid.: 8). Moreover, the internal restructuring completed in 1989 caused turbulence in many AFS organisations, which had to focus on their internal stability with regard to finances and governance rather than on European projects (EFIL 2011).

In 1993, at EFIL's General Assembly, participants even raised the question of whether EFIL should continue, as many of its early priorities became part of the AFS International strategic plan defined together by what was now a network of partners. Despite these tensions and challenges, in 1994 the federation was revived with new statutes (ibid.: 2011) and from then onwards EFIL supported its members in implementing the AFS strategy in Europe, creating meaningful links with the related policies of the European Union and the Council of Europe. One of

---

5. *The AFS story*: https://afs.org/about-afs-old/our-story/.
6. AFS Student Learning Journey & Curriculum: https://afs.org/education/the-afs-student-learning-journey-curriculum/.

the first initiatives of the renewed EFIL was to run the European Secondary School Student Exchange (ESSSE) from 1998 to 2002, an initiative by the Council of Europe to promote East–West dialogue in Europe through trimester exchanges (Council of Europe 2012: 72). Thanks to this new beginning, EFIL had developed into a respected organisation by the end of the 1990s (EFIL 2011: 8).

From the mid-2000s, thanks to a stable secretariat and committed board, EFIL had the chance to make an important contribution to the development of EU programmes, starting with the pilot project on Individual Pupil Mobility in 2007-08, while engaging more broadly in youth policy and youth work. The European Year of Intercultural Dialogue in 2008 provided the opportunity for EFIL to initiate several new annual initiatives, such as the European Citizenship Trimester Programme, the Volunteer Summer Summit and the Berlin conference Moving Beyond Mobility, whose winning format of bringing together researchers, practitioners and policy makers was continued thanks to the now yearly Forum on Intercultural Learning and Exchange. In the meantime, EFIL started developing new AFS organisations in east and southeast Europe, and also established internal structures such as the European Pool of Trainers and the European Pool of Representatives.

In those two critical years of 2007 and 2008, EFIL expanded its activities considerably, profiling itself as a key actor in the field of learning mobility and becoming what it is today: an organisation which offers to its members support in four main areas to achieve the AFS mission: advocacy, training of volunteers and staff, innovative programmes and projects, and organisational development.

The developments of the past 10 years would not have been possible without the support of the European Youth Foundation and the EU programmes in the field of youth. At the same time, being an organisation operating exchange programmes within the school system, recent years have also seen EFIL committed to engage with the school education sector and build links between formal and non-formal education. For this purpose, EFIL joined the Lifelong Learning Platform in 2013 and remains strongly focused on supporting its members to build links with schools and ministries of education.

In 2014 AFS celebrated its centennial and established a partnership with UNESCO and the OECD, starting a process of evolution towards profiling itself more and more as an educational organisation for the promotion of global competence and active citizenship. This direction has been confirmed by the Future AFS Strategy that was launched in November 2017. This is based on three pillars:

1. Develop Active Global Citizens
2. Globalise Schools and Institutions
3. Expand Access to Intercultural Education.[7]

AFS aims at reaching these objectives through learning programmes, volunteering, educational resources and advocacy. During the same period, the European Union

---

7. New strategy advances the historic AFS peace and justice mission through three bold impact goals: https://afs.org/2018/01/25/afs-releases-new-strategy/.

launched the European Education Area,[8] with a focus on funding for pupil mobility and recognition of learning periods abroad during secondary school.

Currently, the latest internal and external developments show an increased capacity of AFS and EFIL to promote intercultural learning within society, and a political will by international institutions to promote global competence as essential for living and working in today's society as well as the future, with mobility as a key tool for fostering it.

Key moments of influence: internal and external

The development of AFS was strongly influenced by historical events. The First World War led to the birth of AFS, and the Great Depression meant that the "hopes of the veterans" were somewhat dashed as it was very difficult to raise scholarships for the American–French student exchanges (Chinzari and Ruffino 2014: 56-7). However, the Second World War resurrected the vision of AFS and expanded its horizons beyond the USA and Europe.

The reconstruction of Europe by the USA and the ideal of American democracy were the triggers for youth exchange after the Second World War: the exchange between young people was seen as a political tool for reconciliation and

> the American government offered German youth a chance that could turn out to be the dawn of a new era. It was necessary for them to come to America and be immersed in the water of a new culture for a significantly long period. (Ibid.: 84)

President Eisenhower observed that "AFS is helping to spread the real concept of American democracy throughout the world and to create a true international understanding of our country" (ibid.: 108).

The financing by the US government of university exchange programmes (Fulbright), and other universities offering fellowship similar to those of AFS (ibid.: 90), encouraged AFS to move away from university exchanges and pursue its mission through secondary school exchanges.

The Cold War and decolonisation influenced the range of countries with which exchanges were possible. AFS exchanges expanded beyond Europe, to Latin America, Asia and above all the Middle East and also Afghanistan. In the 1960s, African countries were involved. The countries of the Soviet bloc, however, stopped taking part in the AFS exchanges, as well as many African countries, Afghanistan, Saudi Arabia, Lebanon, India, Pakistan (ibid.: 101). By the end of the 1960s some governments were also embarrassed to have unilateral exchanges with the USA, the "realm of capitalist imperialism" (ibid.: 108).

At the end of the 1960s, the American model was creaking, with the Kennedy brothers and Martin Luther King assassinated, the massacres of the Vietnam War and racial conflicts. The United States was no longer the social-political ideal of democracy and

---

8.   Communication from the European Commission: "Strengthening European Identity through Education and Culture", 14 November 2017, https://ec.europa.eu/commission/sites/beta-political/files/communication-strengthening-european-identity-education-culture_en.pdf.

American culture was no longer a series of dreams to follow but often considered the expression of a new cultural colonisation (ibid.: 107). In contrast, national AFS associations grew in all countries with which AFS was running exchanges and this created a network of volunteers and offices. These organisations involved young people aged 15-18 and, as teenagers, they started asking questions, including, "What is the true mission? Going to and from America? Or creating a movement of international education?" The political crisis of those years in the USA cast doubts on the motivation that was originally behind the AFS scholarships. The main requests by young people were:

1. to open and internationalise exchanges creating a multinational programme;
2. to transform the worldwide organisation into a network of independent partners not dependent on the USA;
3. to begin studies to monitor the educational content of the intercultural experience that involved pupils, families, schools and communities in AFS exchanges (ibid.: 109).

In the 1970s, the construction of Europe deepened and the mandate of the European Communities began to grow beyond agriculture and trade: in 1973 a division on education and research was opened (EFIL 2011: 2). The Council of Europe started exploring the topic of youth policy in the mid-1960s and established its European Youth Foundation in 1972. EFIL was created in 1971, at the same time as European supranational entities were starting to be interested in learning mobility and this "perfect timing" shows how AFS organisations in Europe embraced the political ideal of European integration of those years; and at the same time how EFIL succeeded in profiling itself from the beginning as a key interlocutor of European institutions on the topic of intercultural learning through exchange programmes.

In line with this increased focus on internationalisation of education and exchanges in Europe, as from the 1970s the topic of intercultural learning became more and more prominent: Marshall McLuhan developed the concept of the global village and the UN launched the project of a world university. It became clear that enabling people from different countries to meet and interact was not enough to construct world peace. In fact, mass tourism, international business and better communication did not prevent wars and social tensions in those years (ibid.). The rise of multicultural societies and the ability of common citizens to have easier contact with the rest of the world led to the creation, especially by the end of the 1980s, of multiple organisations dealing with the topic of intercultural dialogue. This also attracted strong attention from governments, which tended to link this topic to the integration of migrants in multicultural environments. Today, political institutions are looking more and more at the promotion of democratic citizenship in diverse societies and the development of global competence through "internationalisation at home", with no need for physical mobility. AFS and EFIL have had to find their place in this evolving world with a multitude of actors talking about "intercultural learning" from different perspectives. Within this environment, AFS identified itself as an educational organisation and a large international movement of volunteers that promotes intercultural learning experiences which are immersive and deeply rooted in the community thanks to the host families and host schools.

Another external factor that contributed to the development of AFS is the Kennedy-Lugar YES programme[9] launched in 2002 by the US government as a tool for peace after the events of 11 September 2001 (9/11). The programme provides scholarships for secondary school students from countries with significant Muslim populations to spend one academic year in the United States (and vice versa). AFS organisations in the USA and in countries such as Turkey, Egypt, Malaysia and Indonesia are running the programme, which has a strong focus on "Changemaking". This co-operation between the YES programme and AFS led to greater attention to active citizenship and social impact within the AFS network.

The evolution of AFS through the intuition of its leaders

The AFS leadership understood from the very beginning the key role of returnees and volunteers in keeping up the operations of the organisation, not only in terms of spirit but also financially: fundraising through former ambulance drivers has often been crucial for the development of AFS, especially in the post-war periods. Even today, AFS alumni are donors to scholarships.

Another intuition has been seeing the potential of secondary school exchanges and host families, while involving volunteers and local communities as key tools for the achievement of the mission (Chinzari and Ruffino 2014: 91). In fact:

> the AFS recognised very soon that it was no longer an issue of courses for university specialization, the issue was something else, the objective was to give the young people of various nations, a real understanding of America as they could get in a year. AFS wanted them to be ambassadors for their countries ... At the same time they would learn about America and could take this understanding back to their families and friends at home. (Ibid.: 90)

Stephen Galatti wrote in 1947 that, "I feel that the graduate student is more tied down by his work, and therefore less able to mix with fellow students and others" (ibid.: 90). Exchanges were considered to be "a life-changing experience, turning places into people". Pupil exchanges by AFS soon boomed, with claims about their impact on the surroundings likened to "stones thrown in ponds" (ibid.: 93), with key partners in this development being the host families, the host communities and the host schools. Volunteerism took root as the most important element of participation in the organisation, through the idea of "hosting". The power of hosting and opening up their homes redesigned AFS in the space of just four years, from 1946 to 1950, going from perpetuating the memory of war to promoting exchange programmes. The "maternal component, the aspect of being taken care of" shifted from saving lives on the war front (a task performed mainly by men) to home hosting a foreign student – a task to be performed by a family (ibid.: 93).

In the same post-war years, another stroke of genius came about: the bus trip at the end of the exchange experience (ibid.: 92). In 1947-48 most students were hosted on the East Coast of the USA and at the end of their courses they embarked together, by bus, on a 24-day discovery of another America. They were hosted by

9. www.yesprograms.org/.

ex-ambulance drives and friends of AFS. The bus trip was intended to convey the essence of AFS internationalism: it brought together young people from different countries in one unique experience and gave space for international dialogue. In 1963, the bus trip ended at the White House where the 1 827 pupils were addressed by President J. F. Kennedy.

In 1964, there was a drastic change of leadership in AFS. As noted earlier, Stephen Galatti died at the age of 76 after having dedicated 49 years to AFS. He was an incredible fundraiser, a gentle and intuitive man who had a great talent for solving problems and who got everybody to do what he had in mind (ibid.: 103). Arthur Howe, an ambulance driver at the battle of El Alamein, took over. He was described as a serious educator, who aimed to rationalise resources, apply principles of delegating authority, understand how idealism could dialogue with the changing reality, and open the door to diversity and internationalisation (ibid.: 106), which was the primary request starting to arise within the network.

The process of renewal of the organisation started in 1971, and the leadership changed again, as Arthur Howe dealt with two hot issues: social diversity in participation in the exchange programmes (felt mainly by Americans) and internationalisation (felt by AFS organisations outside the USA). For the first time, the role of president was given to someone who had not been an ambulance driver: the 29-year-old former exchange student Stephen Rhinesmith (ibid.: 110).

At the same time EFIL was born, not without tensions with AFS. The birth of EFIL can be seen as the first step in the internationalisation of AFS, due to the loss of image of the USA, the hope for a united Europe and the process of decolonisation.

For many years the old American AFS looked at EFIL with suspicion as a "power block" – and EFIL's first decade was full of battles and antagonism (EFIL 2011: 2). Moreover, in Europe AFS had an identity crisis when approaching the European institutions in Brussels and Strasbourg, which were asking "What is AFS standing for?": the federation was perceived as an American entity, and this is why the name was changed in 1975, to better reflect the purpose of the organisation. Looking back, EFIL played a positive role in the evolution of AFS and introduced the ambition of being present in all cultural areas of the world with a focus on educational content.

In the 1970s and 1980s the overall AFS network faced internal economic crisis and discontent not least through restructuring, and also competition from other youth exchange organisations (Chinzari and Ruffino 2014: 110). This period in the history of AFS mirrors the instability of changing times. Within EFIL many initiatives started and were discontinued:

> EFIL ran the risk of wanting to do too many things for too many people and of losing sight of its specificity; at the end the Federation diluted its identity in an attempt to be something for everyone. (EFIL 2011: 6)

As a result, the ties among its members became looser. Moreover, the changes in staff and boards brought a lack of continuity and expertise at times when the European Union was more and more active in the field of educational exchanges. EFIL suffered from a loss of image (ibid.: 8) and also some AFS organisations in Europe discontinued their membership.

Since the 2000s, however, thanks to stability in EFIL and AFS Intercultural Programs, the organisation has launched several initiatives aimed at ensuring the quality of learning mobility and profiling itself externally as an educational actor: the AFS 100th anniversary, the focus of UNESCO and OECD on global competence, and the EU and the Council of Europe on common democratic values have supported these developments. Now, as stated by Roberto Ruffino,

> we have to take into account the current characteristics of society when shaping exchange programmes and education projects to offer to young people, families and schools. We must keep the eyes wide open to avoid any kind of rigidity in our educational mission, while aiming at improving the quality of the experience even more. (Chinzari and Ruffino 2014: 146)

The contribution to youth work

Since the time volunteer host families started hosting university students and then secondary school pupils and supporting them during their international experience, AFS has been doing youth work. A key milestone in youth work development within AFS was, as noted, the legendary bus trip in the summer of 1948, bringing young people from different countries together to reflect on their exchange and discuss their perceptions. Since then, AFS organisations have supported the learning and development of young people through, first, so-called "orientation camps" for exchange students before, during and after the exchange (the objective is to prepare them for the experience abroad and help them reflect on their non-formal and informal learning) and, second, individual counselling and support. All activities are based on experiential learning and clear educational goals.

Volunteering, which lies at the core of AFS, is also a key element of youth work. Within AFS, the ratio of staff to volunteers is 1:100. Volunteer development takes place through non-formal education and learning by doing, and being in positions of responsibility; this is the heart of AFS's organisational mission. On account of this, both AFS and EFIL organise regular training of youth workers (both staff and volunteers) at regional, national, European and international level, and also, occasionally, at large-scale events).

EFIL has made a great contribution to the AFS network in terms of shifting its focus towards the training of staff and volunteers in order to ensure the quality of exchange programmes, educational goals and research in the field.

Connection and disconnection in
European youth work structures and debates

In the 1970s, intercultural studies were very alive in the USA and, albeit on a modest scale, EFIL introduced new theories to Europe especially within the European institutions, youth organisations and schools (EFIL 2011: 4). EFIL received consultative status at the Council of Europe in 1976 and joined the European Coordinating Bureau of IYNGOs (later the European Youth Forum): as Inge van Gaal, EFIL's European Coordinator at the time, said, "it was the first time institutions were giving the youth a voice – both through the establishment of the Youth Forum and by listening to us". (Ibid.)

EFIL organised several colloquia at the European Youth Centres and contributed to defining elements of quality for intercultural exchanges – such as training of volunteers, staff and participants – which influenced European policies and funding programmes. This process started with the colloquium "Youth mobility and education" in 1978 at the Council of Europe (ibid.: 2). This event brought together researchers in the field of pedagogical science and culture with governmental and non-governmental representatives to discuss existing research on youth exchanges.

EFIL supported the European Commission in developing and running the pilot of the first exchange of young workers in 1977 and drafting the guidelines for the programme Leonardo in 1979, and the following programmes Erasmus and Petra.

The outcomes of the pilot of the ESSSE programme initiated by the Council of Europe and run by EFIL was taken as a model and example of good practice in the European Quality Charter for Mobility in education and training (European Parliament and Council 2006) adopted by the European Union in 2006.

Since 2000, EFIL has run a number of projects funded by the European Youth Foundation and the EU programmes in the field of youth and education. Moreover, EFIL contributed actively to youth policy debates, in particular in relation to the definitions of intercultural competence,[10] the recognition of learning outcomes from non-formal education, and specifically the assessment of intercultural competence,[11] while providing evidence of the impact of learning mobility, resulting from the studies conducted by AFS.[12] Since 2011, EFIL has been involved in the work of the European Platform on Learning Mobility in the field of youth, a much needed initiative co-ordinated by the Partnership between the European Commission and the Council of Europe in the field of youth. Moreover, as an active member of the European Youth Forum, EFIL has been inspired by other youth organisations and developed internal pools of volunteers for training and advocacy.

However, although EFIL has been historically linked to the European youth work sector, which has been at the forefront of the promotion of youth mobility programmes and intercultural dialogue, it has retained a hybrid nature between the youth and school education sector, and identifies itself as arguably less of a youth organisation and more as an educational organisation in the field of intercultural learning. This complex identity makes it hard to fit into the boxes often put in place by European policies. Especially in recent years, therefore, EFIL has been trying

---

10. Definitions of intercultural competence by AFS Intercultural Programs and by EFIL (adapted for the European environment).

11. Intercultura Assessment Protocol: www.fondazioneintercultura.org/en/Studies-and-researches/ Intercultura-Assessment-Protocol/). Fora on intercultural learning and exchange: Assessing intercultural learning in student and pupil exchanges, Exploring evidence of success, Intercultural learning for adolescents: indicators and measurement of competence acquired through non-formal education and informal learning on educational exchanges, The school assessment of the intercultural learning of pupils during and after individual exchanges abroad.

12. https://afs.org/education/education-research/.

to advocate breaking down walls between sectors, and enhancing co-operation between formal and non-formal education, as these have the same target: young people.

Conclusions

Tracing and reflecting on the development of AFS and EFIL over the years, we can clearly see how history has impacted on its evolution, as well as the key role that visionary leaders have had. In particular, the two world wars triggered the creation of the organisation as a peace movement and the vision its leaders had of student exchanges as a tool for intercultural learning and for the promotion of democracy (albeit, at first, the American way). The failure of the latter, however, together with the start of European construction, decolonisation throughout the world and the wave of globalisation challenged the original exchange model and saw the evolution of the AFS and EFIL to the point it has reached today – still looking to the future and how to change again in order to cater for and respond to the changing needs of society.

In the specific European context, it is evident that like many other European youth organisations founded in the 1970s, when the Council of Europe was supporting the early development of European youth work, and that thanks to the opportunities of participation and funding provided by the institutions, EFIL grew and at the same time provided support to the European construction on account of its expertise and the commitment of its value- and mission-driven volunteers.

Throughout the history of AFS young people have been agents of peace and democracy. The ambulance drivers were young when they were helping the wounded in the battlefields, and AFS decided to pursue its mission through exchanges of young people (school students), who would bring back their intercultural experiences to their local communities and make a change. Moreover, AFS can be defined as a transnational movement of citizens willing to promote peace, born at a time when no funding or policy for this was available.

Looking at AFS, we see how the youth work activities offered have been providing a "safe space" for young people, as they have allowed them to experience the challenges of intercultural communication while providing the psychological and risk-management support needed.

Finally, we can also see how youth work in AFS has been serving ideological and cultural interests, as happens continuously in this sector: international exchanges between the US and Europe were seen as a tool for spreading the ideal American democracy, and generally youth work in AFS was a tool to achieve social objectives and promote learning to live together, namely through learning how to behave in society. AFS as a civil society organisation had the "magic intuition" of organising international youth exchanges to promote peace, and this tool has then been taken up by political institutions, the US State Department (German–US exchange programme, YES Programme) and especially by the European institutions which have made learning mobility the key tool to promote European citizenship and have showcased it as their own biggest success, now named the Erasmus+ programme.

References

Chinzari S. and Ruffino R. (2014), *Where the border stands – From war ambulances to intercultural exchanges*, Hoepli, Milan.

Council of Europe (2012), *Intercultural competence for all*, Pestalozzi series No. 2, Council of Europe Publishing, Strasbourg.

EFIL (European Federation for Intercultural Learning) (2011), *40 years of EFIL*, Brussels.

European Parliament and Council (2006), Recommendation of the European Parliament and of the Council of 18 December 2006 on transnational mobility within the Community for education and training purposes: European Quality Charter for Mobility, available at https://eur-lex.europa.eu/legal-content/EN/TXT/PDF/?uri=CELEX:32006H0961&from=EN, accessed 22 July 2019.

Chapter 3

The European Confederation of Youth Clubs

Ioana Şurubaru

A confederation of youth clubs

The European Confederation of Youth Clubs (ECYC) is a European non-governmental and non-profit organisation whose mission is to support youth clubs and other forms of youth work across Europe.[13] It does so mainly in three ways. Firstly, and since the very beginning, ECYC has been promoting co-operation among its member organisations, facilitating the exchange of best practices and offering networking opportunities. At the time of writing (the end of 2018), ECYC's network is composed of 19 member organisations based in 18 Council of Europe countries.[14] This group includes NGOs, foundations, charities, youth-led organisations and youth workers' unions. The one element that these organisations have in common is that they all promote youth work at national or regional level. The heterogeneity in terms of structure and functioning has often made ECYC's work all the more complicated, but it is also a reflection of the diversity that exists in youth work across Europe.

Since its creation, ECYC has also been a prolific provider of international capacity-building opportunities for young people and youth workers. ECYC's vision is to use open youth work and non-formal education to provide young people with the skills and knowledge to make their own informed decisions, encourage them to be actively involved in their communities and promote democratic and civil society.[15] Indeed, getting young people involved is one of the leading principles of open youth work, as delivered by ECYC members. Thanks to funding from Erasmus+ and the European Youth Foundation, ECYC organises activities such as international training courses, webinars and study sessions. The thematic areas ECYC has worked on in the past few years include youth participation, the role of youth work in preventing violent radicalisation of young people, education of youth workers, human rights education, intercultural dialogue and more.[16]

---

13. ECYC constitution and rules of procedure, www.ecyc.org/sites/default/files/ecyc_constitution_and_rules_of_procedure_2.pdf.
14. Full list of ECYC member organisations: www.ecyc.org/members.
15. ECYC constitution and rules of procedure.
16. For information on projects, visit www.ecyc.org/projects.

More recently, and mainly since the relocation of the secretariat to Brussels, Belgium, ECYC has taken on an important advocacy role. With the increase in interest in youth work at European level, ECYC has felt the need to act as advocate for the benefits of youth work and to co-operate with international institutions and organisations on the development of quality youth work policies. This takes the form of developing policy papers, having meetings with the European Commission, participating in various cycles of the EU Structured Dialogue, being active within the European Youth Forum, taking part in meetings organised by the Youth Department of the Council of Europe and more.

During over 40 years of existence, ECYC has gone through considerable change, including location, membership and activities. The red thread in the history of ECYC, however, has been the passion of its people for youth work and their will to improve the level of recognition and support for youth work across Europe. As a vice-president of ECYC since June 2018, I am very proud of being part of a long line of engaged activists fighting on behalf of youth clubs and youth work in general.

First steps in the life of ECYC

In the 1970s, young people from working-class families in Europe were barely represented; neither did they have the same opportunities as other young people. Students and more privileged youth had the chance to get involved in youth exchanges, seminars and camps, or were able to attend a youth club, mostly by being able to manage themselves as organisations or associations. Young people from the working class were the ones whose parents were working or they were working themselves. Who cared for them?

At the start of every movement, of every organisation, there is someone who has a vision, a strategy to implement and a goal to achieve. For ECYC, that person is Niels H. Elberling, who founded ECYC and was its secretary general for the first 20 years. After years of engagement in youth work at national level, Niels thought about sharing the practices from youth work in Denmark with other countries, so he reached out to the UK. The representative from a youth work organisation in the UK, Michael Butterfield, was open to creating a platform and he started to contact other organisations to engage them in the process. Next was Ireland, with an organisation that at the time was deeply rooted in the Catholic Church, where priests acted as youth workers. In 1975, ECYC expanded to Belgium, where a language challenge was faced in relation to the different linguistic communities. In the same year, however, ECYC also sought to expand in France.[17]

Janneth Hunt, the soon-to-be first president of ECYC, had some contacts in Italy and in Cyprus. The latter was a regional organisation from the Greek side of the island, but only national organisations were supposed to be able to join ECYC. Driven by the desire to be part of an international confederation, the Greek Cypriot organisation decided to enlarge in order to fit the requirements.

---

17. From an interview with Niels H. Elberling, former secretary general of ECYC, by Ioana Șurubaru in mid-2018.

The first ever General Assembly of ECYC took place in 1976 in the building of the Danish Parliament in Copenhagen. Some of the applicant organisations became members; Niels H. Elberling was elected as the first secretary general and Janneth Hunt as the first president. During this first General Assembly, there were also debates about the name of the organisation and this is how the "European Confederation of Youth Clubs" came to be.

Over two decades, the Danish Association of Youth Clubs took on a leading role in the organisation, for instance setting up the ECYC offices in Denmark and nominating someone with a background in Danish youth work for the role of secretary general. ECYC's activities at the time focused mainly on networking and capacity building, including a club-to-club international exchange programme, an ECYC international youth camp and seminars for young people and youth workers.

In the 1970s, all of ECYC's member organisations agreed that a person from their national secretariat would work part-time on keeping in contact with ECYC. ECYC's secretariat had calls with them almost every day to check what was new, what were the needs of the organisation and the difficulties they were having to overcome, whether in relation to ECYC or not. The secretary general believed that keeping in contact with member organisations was of paramount importance in order to sustain their engagement with ECYC and keep them open to new projects and partnerships. This communication approach enabled the establishment of a constant and beneficial relationship between ECYC and its member organisations, which shaped the topics and discussion picked for general assemblies and other statutory meetings.

In the late 1980s and beginning of the 1990s, after the fall of the Berlin Wall and the collapse of the communist regimes in eastern Europe, it was one of the European Union's priorities to move towards the east. With this priority came also the responsibility of international youth organisations to engage young people from eastern Europe in their projects. For ECYC that person was John Bateman. He was a successor to Michael Butterfield and the director of UK Youth. He was its delegate to ECYC. John Bateman first made contact with an organisation based in Moscow, Russia, where he then co-organised a seminar. The biggest challenge ECYC had in this process was moving youth work ethics to countries that were still very volatile and unpredictable politically. A fresh start in the youth field for all ex-communist countries meant adopting and developing their own youth work ethics and new approaches, a process which took a while, but which was made easier through international collaboration and partnerships. Young people and youth workers travelled around Europe, exchanging practices and ideas.

Starting from the early 2000s, a few main trends led to some important changes in ECYC's objectives and daily work. Some of ECYC's members grew into strong and powerful organisations that counted dozens of staff members and provided high-quality capacity-building opportunities for their youth workers, including international activities. For several smaller youth work organisations, however, ECYC events had once represented the only opportunity to exchange, brainstorm, plan and work with others. But with the coming of the internet and online communication, one of the key functions of ECYC's meetings lost importance and the organisation had to rethink its role.[18]

---

18. From an interview with Joris De Bleser, former vice-president of ECYC, by Andrea Casamenti in mid-2018.

Challenges and critical moments in the life of ECYC

Over more than 40 years of ECYC's life, changes in society have strongly impacted on the way ECYC works. For instance, regarding international activities, the way young people travel nowadays is very different from the way they did in the 1970s – they travel today much more than in the past, thanks to the increased number of affordable flights. After 9/11, security became stricter. Also, internet privacy regulation was never discussed in the 1990s, but today it affects the everyday lives of young people. Taking pictures and videos of young people was easier and had a common understanding in the past, but now it requires young people's consent. All this has led to a safer and low-risk engagement in projects. The challenge before was to make young people go abroad, open their eyes and their minds, and create a European spirit through exchange programmes and different activities. The multitude of opportunities available for young people at European level and the fact that young people travel abroad much more than they did just 30 years ago has led ECYC to adapt to these changes.

When ECYC was born, the Danish National Organisation of Youth Clubs received funds from the national lottery via the Danish Youth Council. Those funds were divided between national member organisations according to certain criteria. One of the first criteria was international collaboration, because Denmark saw the necessity of young people having international contact in order to promote peace, understanding and cultural exchange. In addition, Denmark at that time was a new member of the European Union, so the need for international partnerships and participation was present. The salaries of the ECYC secretariat at the time came from this fund, Denmark being the only country that could afford it. There were around three people and the secretary general in the secretariat, working from Copenhagen in a building with another Danish organisation. Following that, to be able to afford development and improvement of the ongoing projects, the secretariat approached the EU funding opportunities and received regional structural funds for young people's education and culture. Thanks to that funding, ECYC started organising seminars, one of the most important achievements of that time for the organisation. With time, a membership fee from the member organisations was requested.

When the Danish organisation decided they could no longer host the secretariat, because of some changes in national policies, members were asked to offer proposals to take the lead. After moving to Finland and then to the Netherlands, ECYC finally moved to Belgium, where Formaat, a Flemish organisation based in Antwerp, responded positively to the challenge. After a few years, in 2013, the office then moved again, to Brussels, hosted by the French-speaking Belgian organisation, FCJMP. Over those few years, there were a lot of changes prompted by the need to change how the organisation operated – from financial-related aspects, to changing the secretary general role from an elected to an appointed position.

Joris De Bleser, a former vice-president of ECYC, pointed out that in the 1970s and 1980s everything seemed possible in terms of funding. EU grants were more stable, an aspect which had given ECYC some stability. Then, in the early 2000s, the funding system changed and, consequently, there was a change of culture in the Bureau of ECYC towards trying to be more strict, modifying the statutes, and trying to anticipate the audit.

Alice Taylor, a former president, said that policy changes at a national level impacted on the activity of member organisations, sometimes to the extent of them existing or not. The Dutch member organisation ceased to exist, so ECYC lost a strong member. SAMFES from Iceland was going through a difficult time during the financial crisis and Settlementi in Finland merged with their "parent" organisation, making youth work only a small part of their work rather than the focus.

It can be argued that national and large-scale political events have also affected the history of ECYC. While "there was a clear social democratic majority among the leaders of the national youth club organisations at the time", according to Niels H. Elberling, current member organisations of ECYC are much more politically diverse. However, political influences on ECYC are difficult to prove, as very few testimonies from ECYC "personalities" have been collected so far.[19]

According to Alice Taylor, another challenge has been whether ECYC can be a middle ground between different positions and respond to what different members need from the organisation. For instance, there was a "conflict" among the members of ECYC in terms of youth work as a profession, with some members feeling ECYC should do more to promote the recognition of the profession of youth workers and the establishment of university level education for youth workers. This perspective did not, however, sit well with other member organisations, where youth work was mostly done by volunteers.

Joris De Bleser added that a critical aspect for the internal work of the organisation was, sometimes, the lack of long-term planning and engagement. At each statutory meeting, new representatives were in attendance who were not familiar with ECYC and its work. He noted, "Sometimes people were excluded because it was very troubling. They were not informed about the organisation and kept coming up with ideas that were not doable for ECYC."[20]

Contribution to thinking about youth work

Profound changes in youth work in Europe, such as the professionalisation of youth work, the increasing focus on the quality service that municipal youth work offers and the establishment of university curricula for youth workers, have affected ECYC and its work.

During its 42 years of existence, ECYC has constantly faced the difficulty of agreeing on a European definition of youth work and its methods, one that could cover all its member organisations' approaches and views from the field. The vagueness of youth work practice, apparent at the European level, is due firstly to the national and regional variations in youth work provision, in the reach of youth work as set

---

19. From an interview with Alice Taylor, former president of ECYC, by Rares Craiut in mid-2018.
20. From an interview with Joris De Bleser, former vice-president of ECYC, by Andrea Casamenti in mid-2018.

out from country to country and region to region, on whether it is supported by paid employees or volunteer youth workers, the differences in youth work policies, as well as the differentiation of focus and means when it comes to international co-operation in youth programmes.

Some level of common understanding of the concept of youth work has gradually been brought into being, thanks to the fact that youth workers started to travel more, to exchange experiences and take part in various professional development training. Also, an added value comes from young people who, by being involved at more than local or national level, give extra input to the practices with their knowledge and experience from other cultures. For example, one of the first significant projects carried out by ECYC consisted of seminars organised as exchanges of both young people and youth workers. This should be understood as creating the contexts for youth workers to exchange practices and grow as professionals by meeting youth workers from various cultures, as well as hosting young people coming from different backgrounds. Besides this, young people, through their involvement in youth clubs, had the opportunity to connect with other European youth.

Approaching half a century later, ECYC is well aware of the fact that practices in youth work have changed, but the vision and principles, aims and projects it was established with are still fresh and respected. The organisation understands the constant need for sharing and learning among young people and youth workers, and therefore it develops and delivers training, seminars and other educational events, based on the needs of its member organisations. For all that, ECYC is also innovative and up to date in terms of what the current needs are and ways to fulfil them.

For ECYC, the common understanding of youth work is offering young people, on the basis of their voluntary involvement, developmental and educational experiences which will equip them to play an active part in democratic society as well as meet their own developmental needs. Youth work takes place in youth clubs, youth projects, youth centres, youth houses and on the street through detached youth work. Youth work offers to those who participate important lifelong learning experiences within the transitional period between childhood and adulthood. The lifelong learning cycle may continue if young people attain leadership and volunteering roles within their organisations or in their community.

Furthermore, among the features of youth work in ECYC is the fact that youth work is a partnership between youth workers and young people, involving adults working with young people in a manner that prioritises the active participation of young people as partners in the process. Also, youth work involves young people, irrespective of their race, culture, religion or belief, gender, sexual orientation, socio-economic status or disability, on a voluntary basis and begins with the issues and areas that are of interest and concern to them. The environments where youth work materialises can differ, from community to community, from region to region, from country to country, but it is a planned systematic educational experience implemented outside the formal school curriculum, usually by voluntary groups and organisations as well as by professional youth work providers.

Connection to wider youth work debates

Today, ECYC is much more of a lobby organisation than it was in its early years. In the 1980s and 1990s, ECYC co-operated actively with the Youth Directorate of the Council of Europe. For a long time, ECYC had a seat on the Advisory Council and participated in several activities of the Council of Europe on youth work. Those were the years following the creation of the European Youth Foundation and the European Youth Centre. The Council of Europe had created a network of youth workers and was providing invaluable training opportunities for youth workers from all over Europe. ECYC could not afford not to co-operate with the Council of Europe.

ECYC was one of the founding members of the European Youth Forum (YFJ), the platform of youth organisations in Europe. The YFJ was born in 1996 from the need for international co-operation between youth organisations and national youth councils around Europe. Since the beginning, ECYC has been an active member of the platform, bringing expertise on the topic of youth work and representing unorganised young people. For the first time in the history of ECYC, it has had a candidate on the board of the European Youth Forum. Elected in Varna, Bulgaria, in 2016, Andrea Casamenti has led the advocacy work of the European Youth Forum on youth work, volunteering and non-formal education during the mandate 2017-18.

ECYC has also been influenced by the historical evolution of the European Union. The evolution from an economic union to a wider co-operation has influenced all aspects of young people's lives. The 2001 White Paper on Youth[21] was an invitation for ECYC to think again about undertaking projects linked to problems or issues in relation to various aspects of youth work. Soon after the White Paper on Youth, ECYC started taking its first steps in policy making and lobbying work.

The work on policy advocacy took off in 2014, when the members of ECYC adopted the policy position paper "Support for open youth work". Since then, ECYC's members have developed and adopted joint positions on topics such as European Youth Work, the role of youth work in preventing the violent radicalisation of young people and the education of youth workers.

Today, ECYC is involved in policy processes such as the EU's Structured Dialogue with Young People, the new EU Youth Strategy and more. Today more than ever, ECYC is present on the international scene. ECYC's Secretary General, Rares Craiut, is a member of the Bureau of the Conference of INGOs of the Council of Europe. In terms of funding, ECYC relies nowadays mostly on support from the European Commission and the European Youth Foundation.

Throughout the years, ECYC has also fostered collaborations with other European youth and youth work organisations such as MIJARC,[22] Rural Youth Europe, EEE-YFU[23] and more. This co-operation is vital for the life of the organisation and for promoting the recognition and support of youth work in Europe.

---

21. https://eur-lex.europa.eu/legal-content/EN/TXT/?uri=LEGISSUM%3Ac11055.
22. International Movement of Catholic Agricultural and Rural Youth.
23. European Educational Exchanges – Youth for Understanding.

To conclude, although the values, objectives and vision of ECYC have not changed, its activities, daily work, location and staff have changed considerably. As one of the biggest youth work organisations in Europe, ECYC's contribution to the youth work field is undeniable, although it is impossible to provide quantitative data that would answer questions on the confederation's impact on youth work across Europe. Critical moments for the organisation have helped it shape the work and approach towards projects and policies.

Chapter 4

Don Bosco Youth-Net – Developing a European youth work organisation through youth participation and historical research, 1841-2000

Rein Meus

Introduction

Founded in 2004, Don Bosco Youth-Net ivzw (DBYN) is the international network for non-formal youth work inside the global Don Bosco Movement. The roots of the network go back to a founding father of non-formal education in youth work: Don Giovanni Bosco (1815-88). Don Bosco developed an educational system based on a dialogue between the Catholic Christian tradition and the needs of young people in the society he was living in.

Don Bosco started his first oratorio in 1841. Over the years, through working in the oratories he had set up, he developed a pedagogical approach to working with boys which he called the "preventive system". The system Don Bosco advocated was to prevent dysfunctional behaviour through the proactive encouragement of young people, so that there was no need to enforce authority. The key element in the system was the constant presence of the educators among the boys. The preventive system was based, as Don Bosco called it, on the triad: reason – religion – loving kindness.

The ultimate aim of the preventive system was not just to render young people profitable for the economy, but as a method for them to find autonomy in life, becoming "good Christians and honest citizens". Therefore, Don Bosco also engaged himself in actively building society through the development of solidarity mechanisms (for example 1850 – mutual aid societies), social negotiations (for example 1851 – apprenticeship contracts) and entrepreneurship (for example 1861 – workshops). It is this educational system which still connects all people active in the Don Bosco Movement today; Don Bosco's working style is the common denominator.

The Don Bosco Movement sees educating young people to become active citizens as its main mission. Currently, the Don Bosco Movement has a global impact in over 130 countries, reaching over 16 million people directly through its work. It consists of the religious congregation of the Salesians of Don Bosco and a large diversity of lay organisations including schools (kindergarten to universities), youth clubs, youth centres, sports organisations, development co-operation, social youth care, parishes, spiritual youth movements (Salesian Youth Movement), past-pupil networks and advocacy agencies. These organisations operate at local, regional, national and international levels. There exist several international networks and advocacy agencies which operate within a specific field of expertise: non-formal youth work, formal education, vocational training, special youth care, development co-operation, sports education, human rights advocacy, youth spirituality, and so on.

Don Bosco Youth-Net is the European network of non-formal youth work within the Don Bosco Movement. Unique throughout the development of the network is that it has applied a historical method as the motor for its organisational development. This chapter will focus on how the dialogue between the current reality of young Europeans and the historical model of Don Bosco determined the evolution of a European non-governmental youth work organisation.

Building a European network from grass roots

In order to understand the place of Don Bosco Youth-Net within the Don Bosco Movement, it is necessary to understand how the Salesian congregation is structured throughout the world. The members of the Salesian congregation are called Salesians of Don Bosco (SDB) or Salesians. The congregation has a central General Directorate based in Rome, which is responsible for the overall governance of the congregation. The world is divided into regions (or conferences) co-ordinated by a regional councillor. Each region is divided into a number of provinces. A province can be a state, regions within a state or a combination of (regions of) states. Youth work is part of the Salesian Youth Ministry department. The youth work itself is done at grass-roots level, and co-managed by young volunteers, which has been the case since Don Bosco's days. This results in a huge variety of formats, depending on the culture and needs of young people within the local communities in which the youth work is based.

The origin of the network lies in the 1990s, when most member organisations formalised their structures as non-governmental organisations, becoming autonomous from the provincial youth ministry departments. The reasons for this course of action range from gaining access to public funding to the new opportunities for establishing NGOs in former "Eastern bloc" countries. Salesian provinces which did not create an independent youth NGO can become a member of DBYN with this youth ministry department, with an eye on developing an independent youth NGO.

The gradual expansion of the Schengen travel area allowed travelling more easily through much of the European Union. The Salesian Youth Ministry department encouraged the participation in youth exchanges by Don Bosco youth through different initiatives: European events for the Salesian Youth Movement (SYM), combining leisure activities with spiritual and pastoral encounters, a publication of all Salesian houses in Europe equipped for receiving youth groups, and regular meetings of Salesians responsible for youth work at congregation level. This led to the first bilateral exchanges between member organisations of DBYN.

In March 2000, the Salesian congregation invited a speaker of the EU's programme YOUTH to present this to Salesians responsible for youth work organisations in Europe. Within the YOUTH programme attention was drawn to the funding line to start up international non-governmental youth organisations (INGYOs). Inspired by these new opportunities, three Salesians active in youth work, Guido Stoop SDB from Belgium, Stefan Stöhr SDB from Germany and James Robert Gardner SDB from Great Britain, decided to take the step of creating an INGYO for the Don Bosco Movement. In December 2000, the Belgian organisation, Jeugddienst Don Bosco invited six other organisations to consider whether there was the readiness to create a new network. In October 2001, Jeugddienst Don Bosco received a one-year grant to set up the network's structure. At this time the international secretariat was established, contracting a general secretary to co-ordinate the network. Don Bosco Youth-Net was officially recognised as an INGYO by the Belgian legislature in August 2004. In 2005, the network joined the European Youth Forum as a member with observer status. DBYN remains an observer member on this platform in order to assure its political neutrality. In the following years the membership expanded throughout the European Union. In 2016, the first non-EU members joined the network (Ukraine, Montenegro).

Don Bosco Youth-Net started to develop its educational projects in partnership with the European Union from 2000 onwards, and with the Council of Europe from 2003 onwards, combining the institutional priorities for the youth sector with its own unique educational methodology. The EU's enlargement in 2004 brought a focus on exchange programmes and training in European project management. To counter the effect of the credit crunch in 2008 DBYN started to explore how to tackle youth unemployment and social entrepreneurship. Once the organisational structure was fully developed in 2012, DBYN started to focus strongly on its identity as a value-based organisation. The refugee crisis in 2015 sparked an engagement in refugee projects. Throughout the years DBYN developed educational publications to use its own expertise: I (am) like you! (2003 – on conflict management), Jabbertalk (2005 – a method for youth work), Hujambo (2009 – on value-based education), Dignity (2011 – on safeguarding), Games APP (2016 – games for animators). All publications were developed with the support of the European Youth Foundation, allowing them to be available as open educational resources. This fits with the network's vision that resources for the qualitative improvement of youth work should be available to all youth workers free of charge.

From the inception of the network, young people have been active at all levels of the organisation: young people govern its statutory bodies, ensuring a participatory involvement in the strategic planning of the network. Young people (paid staff or volunteers) are trained as project managers to develop international projects within the framework of DBYN. Three pools of young volunteers support the implementation of the actions: trainers (educational support), Salesian chaplains (interreligious dialogue) and youth representatives (advocacy). As a result, young people are involved in all steps of project management. Through DBYN's educational methodology, all activities implement a learner-centred approach, giving young learners responsibility in steering their own learning process. Interns in the international secretariat co-develop new strategies for the network, helping to integrate recent developments in youth culture into the work of DBYN. This participatory approach stems from the grass-roots tradition of Don Bosco youth work. It not only creates the opportunity for young people to develop leadership competences, but it also ensures the network remains close to societal changes in youth culture.

Dialogue between tradition and progress

The creation of DBYN was the first challenge. At an institutional level the network had to convince the Salesian congregation of the necessity of creating a new European body, which did not fit into their traditional structure. Through mediation of the vicar, Mgr Luc Van Looy SDB, and general councillor for the youth ministry, Antonio Domenech SDB, DBYN managed to receive the mandate of the Salesian congregation to develop as an INGYO. This institutional support from the Salesian congregation remains important for maintaining recognition of DBYN as an official part of the global Don Bosco Movement.

A second hurdle was developing an organisational structure which could accommodate the large diversity in grass-roots youth organisations. It became clear early on that the hierarchal system of an umbrella organisation, like most INGYOs developed in the 20th century, would not fit. The broad diversity in youth work practices between DBYN's member organisations would render such a model inefficient. Alternatively, DBYN decided to construct an adaptive network organisation, which is an organisational model that surfaced in the early 21st century. For this, DBYN put forward some fundamental principles: each member organisation needs to actively participate and carry the ownership of the network's actions. In order to respect cultural diversity each country has an equal vote in the statutory bodies, not taking into account either the size of the member organisation or the number of member organisations per country. Each member organisation has equal access to all information of the network. The strategic work plan needs to be co-managed by the member organisations. The role of international secretariat is restricted to a supportive role towards policy development and actions. The educational methodology of Don Bosco in non-formal education is the common denominator of the network.

Through the experience of running the first international activities of the network it became clear, however, that using Don Bosco's educational methodology as a common denominator was not self-evident. Since Don Bosco's time the methodology has been adapted to different educational and cultural contexts, creating linguistic relativity. To solve this challenge DBYN took inspiration from the Salesian congregation. Since the late 1970s, each Salesian province has been expected to develop its own "Salesian Educative and Pastoral Project", describing the educational methodology within the context of the province. DBYN brings together member organisations active in more than 20 provinces. Between member organisations there is diversity in Salesian Educative and Pastoral Projects which, in the past, has led to confusion. As a result, DBYN decided to develop the publication, *Few words and a lot of action*, which is DBYN's particular Salesian Educative and Pastoral Project.

Developing such a Salesian Educative and Pastoral Project on an international level is fundamentally different from developing one at a provincial or local level. DBYN needed to create a common language that brings together the diversity in cultural interpretations, caters for the diversity of Salesian spirituality and welcomes different denominations and non-faith-based worldviews. Therefore, the Salesian Educative and Pastoral Project shaped by DBYN is a complementary offering to its member organisations, volunteers and young people, to be used as a reference framework for co-operation.

DBYN works together with other INGYOs, civil society organisations and international institutions. The language used within the Don Bosco Movement is often jargon-based, making it difficult for external partners to understand its working style. Inspired by Don Bosco's letter from 21 February 1878 to the Italian Minister for Internal Affairs, Francesco Crispi (1818-1901), in which Don Bosco uses a secularised language to present the preventive system, DBYN chose a similar approach in preparing this document. The text avoids jargon and uses standard educational concepts current in the European field of youth work and human rights education.

In order to support the implementation of the educational methodology, DBYN created a training strategy. Initially this strategy consisted of a fixed path of three consecutive training courses aimed at training a selected group of volunteers for creating international projects within DBYN's structure. This structure allowed DBYN to build a pool of trainers with the responsibility for running its training activities. DBYN also trained volunteers to become project managers and these volunteers often became active as European project managers in its member organisations.

Since the early 2010s, DBYN has recognised that its training strategy needed to be adapted to new trends in education: entrepreneurial learning, peer learning, digitalisation and the European Credit Transfer and Accumulation System (ECTS). ECTS is a method originating in the Bologna Process, which has had a cultural impact on young learners. It allows them to plan their own learning curriculum, acquiring credits that certify their competences. The generation of youth born in the 21st century expects similar learning possibilities in non-formal settings. As a consequence, DBYN had to change its strategy. The educational strategy from 2018 onwards steps away from training young volunteers to support the internationalisation of DBYN's member organisations, in favour of a new structure which aims at the development of different profiles of active citizens: Educator, Advocate, Social Entrepreneur and Salesian Chaplain. Each profile focuses on a different way of shaping local communities through active citizenship. DBYN offers different levels of training for each profile, allowing young people to develop their own learning curriculum according to their personal needs and interests. Each individual training curriculum should lead towards autonomous engagement as an active citizen, achieving the vision laid out in DBYN's educational methodology.

Few words and a lot of action

DBYN brings together a rich diversity of youth work contexts. The target groups for its youth work include mainstream youth, young people facing fewer opportunities, young people who are NEET (not in education, employment or training), young refugees, unaccompanied minors, internally displaced people, and Roma[24] youth. The age ranges from toddlers aged two and a half to young adults up to the age of 30. Youth work is carried out in any setting where young people are, including youth centres, youth clubs, retreat houses, summer playgrounds, parishes, schools, community centres, special youth care facilities, Scout groups, street children projects and shelters, or just on the street and in parks. The actions include games and leisure activities, sports, outdoor education, homework assistance, development co-operation, training and education, the development of publications and festivals. Crucial in the approach is that all actions are carried out not only for young people, but always by young people as well. All the actions are led by young volunteers between 16 and 30 years old. As the educational methodology of Don Bosco is implemented by these young volunteers, they are all considered as educators.

This tradition of giving responsibility to young people as educators originates in a pragmatic need identified by Don Bosco. Don Bosco started up a Sunday school which evolved into an evening school, aiming to battle illiteracy among poor boys and young apprentices. While the number of boys coming to his evening school for education was growing, there were not enough financial resources to attract teachers. He took inspiration from the school system developed by the English educator Joseph Lancaster (1778-1838), in which older students instructed young students as "teaching monitors". Don Bosco approached talented older boys attending classes to become teaching monitors. In return he gave extra private lessons in Italian, Latin, French, arithmetic and other subjects which could support them in obtaining more advantageous employment. This approach evolved into a system where teaching monitors would not be teaching, but aiding and assisting the overall learning process. The evening school was part of Don Bosco's "Oratory". This was a form of youth centre, combining a boarding house, a school, a playground and a parish. It would give young people a safe environment to live, a place where they could learn basic competences, a place where they could play and a place where they could worship. A vital part of this fourfold pattern was balance. Over the years, through working in the oratories he had set up, Don Bosco developed a pedagogical approach to working with the boys which he called the "preventive system". The key element in the system was the constant presence of the educators among the boys.

This systematic approach is the main contribution of the Don Bosco Movement to youth work and education. Rather than being integrated into a specific style of youth work (for example, Scouting, club work or activist youth organisations), it is an educational methodology which can be applied in any educational context for youth. This ensures adaptability to new emerging needs of young people and trends in youth culture. As such, the educational methodology can cater for the large diversity of children and young people of DBYN's member organisations.

---

24. The term "Roma and Travellers" is used at the Council of Europe to encompass the wide diversity of the groups covered by the work of the Council of Europe in this field: on the one hand a) Roma, Sinti/Manush, Calé, Kaale, Romanichals, Boyash/Rudari; b) Balkan Egyptians (Egyptians and Ashkali); c) Eastern groups (Dom, Lom and Abdal); and, on the other hand, groups such as Travellers, Yenish, and the populations designated under the administrative term "Gens du voyage", as well as persons who identify themselves as Gypsies.

Central to the educational methodology is the creation of a strong learning environment through the "Oratory criterion". This criterion translates four places of the Oratory into four educational settings, each promoting a value:

▶ **Home**. Young people need a place "of their own", where they feel at home and where they get the necessary space to be themselves, to express their feelings and to shape their own personality. Through this they develop the value of "Freedom".

▶ **School**. Young people need a place "to learn", where they get the space or opportunity to enhance their skills and knowledge, where they learn to assume the responsibility for the surrounding reality, where they become capable of playing their part in society in a constructive way. Through this they develop the value of "Responsibility".

▶ **Playground**. Young people need a place "to play", where they can meet their peers, can talk and discuss openly, build and maintain relations with others, where they can accept solidarity and can organise and experience things together. Through this they develop the value of "Solidarity".

▶ **Parish**. Young people need a place "of sense", where they are able to search for their *raison d'être*, for meaning in their lives. Through this they develop the value of "Meaning".

The idea of this model is that the four places of the Oratory always need to be present and balanced in Don Bosco youth work, but they can be translated to the needs of the situation. In practice this means that any activity within DBYN and its member organisations will have the Oratory criterion as its underlying structure. Within this system, the approach of the educator is of the uppermost importance. The educational methodology stands or falls by the manner in which it is delivered by the educator. The Don Bosco educator guides the learning process of young people at their own pace. Therefore, the concept of "assistance" can be defined as the working style of a Don Bosco educator. Within assistance the educator should have an eye for the group as well as for the individual, focusing on those young people who need the most attention, without forgetting about the group. Attendance, Reason and Values are the three key elements in assistance:

▶ **Attendance**. In the first place attendance means to be actively present; the educator is among young people and takes part in their daily life, during moments of education and reflection and during games. However, active attendance is not sufficient; attitude is also important in this. Often small things matter, such as remembering someone's name, approaching people and showing interest.

▶ **Reason**. Don Bosco educators associate with young people in a reasonable way. This means, for instance, that they do not behave in an authoritative manner and do not decide on any overly harsh rules or sanctions. It also means that they do not impose false expectations but indicate what they think is acceptable and why. They should approach young people with reason, explain clearly their motives and plans, be confident that young people can be reasonable and are able to bear responsibility themselves, respect a young person and his or her opinion, even when it is a different one from their own.

▶ **Values.** As education by definition has to be developed within different cultural contexts and their prevailing values, educating within intercultural settings provides certain challenges. The educator needs to create common ground on which a dialogue on values can be started. For Don Bosco educators, this common ground is using education as an instrument promoting and protecting the human dignity of all young people. Through such education, DBYN activities strive to create openness towards the diversity in society, by educating young people to become good Christians and honest citizens. In order to offer this value-based education, a Don Bosco educator should be a role model in this.

The Oratory criterion and assistance are present in all youth work settings of Don Bosco Youth-Net. However, when designing specific non-formal training programmes, attention is given to creating an educational flow. Acquiring or improving competences is a complex learning process which goes further than offering a set of chronological workshops. Therefore, it is important to plan educational pathways throughout the full length of a learning programme. In this way, the learning content offered can be built up in a constructive and logical way, nurturing the growth of the targeted competences. The educational flow can also continue over a series of learning activities as part of a larger curriculum.

The educational methodology creates a solid basis for DBYN educational work. Because it is a systematic approach, it also serves as a bridge to other sectors like formal education or social work. It provides concepts which are also applied in these sectors. Often DBYN member organisations work together with local Don Bosco schools or social work organisations, which increases the learning experience of the participants. At the same time, links with such organisations also allow young people to have continued engagement as a volunteer or paid worker in the wider Don Bosco Movement.

Educators, not activists

Don Bosco used the aphorism: "We are educators, not activists" to underline his theory of change, maintaining that by providing quality education to young people they would grow into "good Christians and honest citizens". In order to achieve his mission, it was important to work together with all stakeholders who could play a role in this: politicians, nobility, clergy, industrialists – without whose political and financial support, it would have been impossible to have expanded so rapidly. This aphorism is still a motto for the advocacy strategy within the Don Bosco Movement. It pursues a model of soft advocacy to policy makers, always starting from the promotion of good practices and its impact on youth. Since the credit crunch in 2008, which had a strong impact on youth unemployment, DBYN started looking more closely at how it needed to complement its educational work with advocacy in order to support young people's growth to autonomy. The historical research supporting the development of DBYN's advocacy strategy brought forward an interesting example of this soft advocacy.

On 15 May 1891, Pope Leo XIII issued the encyclical "Rerum novarum", addressing the social question for the working classes. The principles and rights included in the encyclical is a quintessential policy document which influenced policy making in Europe through the Catholic parties. What is lesser known is that Don Bosco's work (mutual aid societies, apprenticeship contracts, social entrepreneurship, vocational training) was one of the inspirations for the development of the Catholic Social Doctrine. It is also interesting to see how the Don Bosco Movement integrated these principles and rights into its work. Just one year after "Rerum novarum", the "Co-operators of Don Bosco" (a movement of lay people who commit to dedicating their life to the mission of Don Bosco) discussed how they would incorporate the principles and rights into their own companies. The 1890s also marked the years Don Bosco's vocational training started to formalise into technical schools. Don Guiseppe Bertello (1848-1910) was appointed to lead this process. When planning the curricula for technical students he developed a three-year course of social economy, focusing on the principles of the Catholic Social Doctrine. This curriculum was disseminated to the technical schools, both at home and abroad. Don Francesco Scaloni (1861-1926), who was responsible for building the Don Bosco Movement in Belgium, brought the school curricula with him and developed a handbook for social economy entitled "Capital et travail". This handbook became very popular in Belgian Catholic technical schools, and was promoted by Cardinal Désiré-Joseph Mercier (1851-1926) along with the other writings of Don Scaloni to the theology students at the University of Louvain. At this time, the young Joseph Cardijn (1882-1967), founder of the Young Christian (Catholic) Workers, was studying at the University of Louvain. These were formative years for Cardinal Cardijn's vision on youth work, where he took inspiration from the work of Don Bosco. However, while Cardijn's youth movement developed a strong activist tradition, implementing its "See–Judge–Act" method, the Don Bosco Movement continued to focus on quality education.

This continued focus on education puts limits on the claim Don Bosco organisations can make over the responsibility of the young people it educates. The educational methodology stipulates that young people are assisted in their growth to youth autonomy and becoming active citizens in their local communities. This puts the responsibility for development on the young people themselves. Once they have finished their education, they are individually responsible for taking social initiatives. The only policy claims the Don Bosco Movement can make relate to the specific circumstances hindering young people's growth to youth autonomy and active citizenship. Moreover, this needs to be done with respect for political neutrality. As Don Bosco organisations are part of a global movement, too strong a political approach in one country can create a backlash in others, directly affecting the children and young people who are being provided for. For this reason, as noted, DBYN's membership of the European Youth Forum remains one of observer status. Under this status, DBYN can contribute to the fields of youth policy relevant for achieving its mission, but can refrain from any input which goes beyond that.

Don Bosco Youth-Net as an INGYO only operates within Europe, even if its members have bilateral projects in other continents. This restricts its focus on youth policy to the European Union and the Council of Europe. Much of DBYN's work is related to human rights, hence DBYN sees the Council of Europe's youth sector as an important partner. The Council of Europe's human rights education methodology has a strong developmental approach. From its own expertise, DBYN aims to adopt a preventive approach through developing educational tools and promoting preventive educational policies. The European Union's youth policy focuses on competence development through civic participation, learning mobility and solidarity action, and quality, innovation and recognition of youth work. Starting from its own educational methodology, DBYN mainly advocates the qualitative improvement of learner mobility and increased access for young people with fewer opportunities to non-formal education. Finally, DBYN works together with other international networks and advocacy agencies of the Don Bosco Movement. In this way, it is possible to target a specific need of children and youth from different sectors (youth work, formal education, vocational training, special youth care, development co-operation, and so on).

Continuing a youth work legacy

Don Bosco did not start his work from a grand theoretical master plan, but from a true belief that young people can be agents of change if they are educated to become moral and upright citizens. This stems from the understanding that real differences in society are created through the engagement of its citizens. Citizenship is a competence people acquire through life itself. Education is a strong driver in this. Giving young people the opportunity to develop citizenship through active participation in youth work is an ideal method of acquiring this competence. If youth work is especially targeted at young people facing exclusion, there will be a strong drive towards building a more equal society. It was through this clear vision and the day-to-day work at the Oratory that Don Bosco developed the preventive system. Due to this pragmatic approach he was open to innovation and support from any direction, as long as it served the young people he was working with. Apart from its solid educational basis, this adaptability remains a key attribute of the Don Bosco Movement's history today.

When DBYN emerged from the movement, choosing a network organisation as its organisational structure guaranteed that it would remain adaptable to change. The legacy of Don Bosco is present in the participatory approach and the educational methodology. Working within such a legacy requires accountability. Even though DBYN is legally independent, it is a subsidiary at a spiritual level of the Salesian congregation. In order to be recognised as part of the Don Bosco Movement, it is essential to remain close to Don Bosco's roots. For this reason, DBYN applies a historical method in its development. The historical method is not only used as inspiration for innovation, but also as the justification for DBYN's orientation towards the Don Bosco Movement.

DBYN's work directly impacts on young volunteers who develop their personal and professional competences through its educational programme. The impact on DBYN's member organisations is mainly the assimilation of innovative approaches through developing and exchanging good practices in non-formal education, European themes relevant for reaching young volunteers at grass-roots level, raising the quality and impact of their youth work, and increasing identification with being part of a global movement. The main contribution outside the global Don Bosco Movement is DBYN's unique educational methodology, which offers a qualitative model for youth work, resulting in innovative training programmes and publications offering new insights to the European youth work sector.

References

Ainsworth W. R. (1988), *Saint John Bosco: the priest, the man, the times*, Salesian publications, Bolton.

Biesmans R. (2000), "Assistentie, de essentie van het preventief systeem", in *Don Bosco. Passie voor jongeren gisteren en vandaag*, Publicatiereeks van het Don Boscovormingscentrum No. 2, ["Assistance, the essence of the preventive system", in *Don Bosco. Passion for youth yesterday and today, Publication series of the Don Bosco Education Centre No. 2*], Don Bosco centrale vzw, Brussels.

Bosco G. (2000), "Het preventief systeem in de opvoeding van de jeugd", in *Don Bosco. Passie voor jongeren gisteren en vandaag*, Publicatiereeks van het Don Boscovormingscentrum No. 2, ["The preventive system in the education of youth", in *Don Bosco. Passion for youth yesterday and today, Publication series of the Don Bosco Education Centre No. 2*], Don Bosco centrale vzw, Brussels.

— (2001), "De 'Algemene artikelen' van het 'Reglement voor de huizen'", in *Een opvoedingsproject in dialoog met Don Bosco. Achtergronden*, Publicatiereeks van het Don Boscovormingscentrum No. 3, ["The 'General articles' in the 'Regulations for the houses'", in *An educational project in dialogue with Don Bosco. Backgrounds*, Publication series of the Don Bosco Education Centre No. 3], Don Bosco centrale vzw, Brussels.

— (2002), "Preventief systeem in de opvoeding van de jeugd", in *Don Bosco uitgedaagd. In gesprek met hedendaagse opvattingen over opvoeding en hulpverlening*, Publicatiereeks van het Don Boscovormingscentrum No. 4, ["Preventive system in the education of youth", *in Don Bosco challenged. In dialogue with contemporary perspectives on education and youth care*, Publication series of the Don Bosco Education Centre No. 4], Don Bosco centrale vzw, Brussels.

— (2003), "Twee brieven uit Rome – mei 1884", in *Begeesterd door Don Bosco. Opvoeding & Spiritualiteit*, Publicatiereeks van het Don Boscovormingscentrum No. 5, ["Two letters from Rome – may 1884", in *Animated by Don Bosco. Education & Spirituality*, Publication series of the Don Bosco Education Centre No.5], Don Bosco centrale vzw, Brussels.

— (2008), *Herinneringen aan het Oratorio van de H. Franciscus van Sales van 1815 tot 1855*, [*Memoirs of the Oratory of St. Francis de Sales from 1815 to 1855*], (ed.) A. Giraudo, Publicatiereeks van het Don Boscovormingscentrum No. 10, [Publication series of the Don Bosco Education Centre No. 10], Don Bosco centrale vzw, Brussels.

Bosco T. (1993), *Don Bosco. Een nieuwe levensbeschrijving*, [*Don Bosco. A new biography*], Don Bosco centrale vzw, Brussels [*Don Bosco. Una biografia nuova*, Elledici, Turin, 1979].

Briado P. (ed.) (1988) *Don Bosco for poor and abandoned young people in two previously unedited documents of 1854 & 1862*, unedited translation of *Don Bosco per I giovani: I' "Oratorio" una "Congregazione degli Oratori". Documenti*, Piccola Biblioteca dell'Instituto Storico Salesiano, 9, LAS, Rome.

Coussée F. (2010), "The saint, the poet, the lord and the cardinal: learning from youth work's history", *Coyote Extra*, First European Youth Work Convention, EU–Council of Europe Youth Partnership, Strasbourg, pp. 10-15.

Desramaut F. (2009), *Life of Fr. Michael Rua: Don Bosco's first successor (1837-1910)*, Giraudo A. (ed.), LAS, Rome.

Dorr D. (2012), *Options for the poor and for the earth: Catholic social teaching* (3rd edn), Orbis Books, New York.

Jeffs T. (2010), "The relevance of history in youth work", in Coussée F., Verschelden G., Van de Walle T., Mędlińska M. and Williamson H. (eds), *The history of youth work in Europe*, Vol. 2, Council of Europe Publishing, Strasbourg.

Lenti A. J. (1995), "Don Bosco's love affair with 'poor and abandoned' young people and the beginnings of the Oratory", *Journal of Salesian Studies* Vol. 6, No. 1, Institute of Salesian Studies, Berkeley, CA, pp. 1-80.

— (1999), "Politics of the "Our Father" and of the Holy Father: Don Bosco's mediation in church-state affairs", *Journal of Salesian Studies* Vol. 10, No. 2, Institute of Salesian Studies, Berkeley, CA, pp. 180-245.

— (2007), *Don Bosco: history and spirit*, A. Giraudo (ed.), LAS, Rome.

Meus R. (2005), "Don Bosco Youth-Net's identity as an international Don Bosco Youth organisation", *Don Bosco Youth-Net's Newsletter* No. 4.2, Oud-Heverlee, pp. 17-22.

— (ed.) (2011), *Dignity: safeguarding of children and young people*, Heverlee.

— (ed.) (2015) *Few words and a lot of action ...: an introduction to the working style of Don Bosco Youth-Net ivzw* (2nd edn), Heverlee.

Petitclerc J. M. (2002), "Het preventief systeem in een geseculariseerde wereld", in *Don Bosco uitgedaagd. In gesprek met hedendaagse opvattingen over opvoeding en hulpverlening*, Publicatiereeks van het Don Boscovormingscentrum No. 4, ["The preventive system in a secularised world", in *Don Bosco challenged. In dialogue with contemporary perspectives on education and youth care*, Publication series of the Don Bosco Education Centre No. 4], Don Bosco centrale vzw, Brussels.

Ribotta A. (1990), "Don Bosco's battle against illiteracy", *Journal of Salesian Studies* Vol. 1, No. 1, Institute of Salesian Studies, Berkeley, CA, pp. 1-15.

— (1993), "Training boys to earn a living: the beginnings of vocational education at the Oratory", *Journal of Salesian Studies* Vol. 4, No. 1, Institute of Salesian Studies, Berkeley, CA, pp. 61-86.

Roose H. (2002), *Managen van een netwerkorganisatie*, [*Managing a network organisation*], Garant, Antwerpen, Apeldoorn.

Salesian Youth Ministry Department (eds) (1993), *Salesians in Europe welcome young people*, Rome.

— (eds) (2014), *Salesian Youth Ministry. Framework of reference*, (revised 3rd edn), Rome.

Scaloni F. (1903), *Capital et travail – Manuel populaire d'economie sociale* (2nd edn), [*Capital and Work – Popular manual on social economy*], Liege.

Staelens F. (1996) *Francesco Scaloni SDB – Auteur en propagandist (1891-1926)*, [*Francesco Scaloni SDB – Author and propagandist (1891–1926)*], unedited translation of *I Salesiani di Don Bosco e le lotte sociopolitiche in Belgio in un'epoca di transizione (1891-1918)*, in *Ricerche Storiche Salesiane. Rivista semestrale die storia religiosa e civile No. 15*, pp. 217-271, LAS, Rome.

Chapter 5

World Scouting: a century of work for youth empowerment

Eduard Vallory

Introduction

S couting is a very large movement that many people are vaguely familiar with, relating it mainly to recreational activities that have no social impact other than the fact that it keeps boys and girls busy. It is a consequence of one of the greatest strengths of the Scout Movement, which is also one of its worst weaknesses: the deeply intuitive nature of its educational action. For young people, Scouting is about enjoying, not about learning, and that is why they become Scouts. At the same time, however, this is also a weakness because most scholars and professionals concerned with education only see the recreational aspects of Scouting, and are unable to perceive the strong educational impact of the movement.

One of Scouting's many fascinating attributes is its ability to make deep roots into disparate societies. That is why we, the Catalans, are convinced that Scouting is a product of our way of life, just as the North Americans, Koreans, French or Egyptians are convinced of the same for themselves. Precisely because of this deep identification with Scouting in each of the societies where it is present, there has been no study of the world movement of Scouting as a whole for many years.[25]

However, few people know that Scouting is a movement particularly strong in developing and emerging countries, that it is one of the strongest associations in Arab countries, and that when it was formalised in 1920, World Scouting had national associations in over 50% of the world's independent countries. That percentage has not dropped since and has actually increased to more than 80% today, with the number of independent countries increasing from 63 (in 1922) to 195 (in 2018). It is likewise not known that former Scouts constitute the main parliamentarian subgroup in the British House of Commons and in the Parliament of Korea. It is mostly unknown that Scouting has been forbidden by totalitarian regimes, and it is still forbidden in communist countries. And not only this – even fewer people know that more than two thirds of all current and former NASA astronauts have been involved in boy and girl Scouting, among them 20 of the 24 men who travelled to the moon, including

---

25. This chapter is based on research synthesised in the book *World Scouting: educating for global citizenship* (Vallory 2012).

11 of the 12 moonwalkers. Scouting is a movement known more by its stereotypes than for what it is. But what is it, actually?

1. Scouting: education as youth work

Scouting is today the largest youth educational movement in the world, gathering 60 million children and young people from around 170 countries over the five continents. Its purpose is to contribute to the self-development of young people in achieving their full physical, intellectual, social and spiritual potential as individuals, as responsible citizens and as members of their local, national and international communities.[26] It does so as a movement of volunteers operating through a world-wide network of local groups, belonging to national Scout associations and to the two world organisations: the World Organization of the Scout Movement (WOSM), with around 50 million members; and the World Association of Girl Guides and Girl Scouts (WAGGGS), with around 10 million members. Both are based on the same principles and were founded by the same person, Robert Baden-Powell.[27]

The purpose of Scouting shows that it does not attempt to establish a particular vision for how society should be, but to shape empowered individuals and responsible citizens with inclusive values for each of them to participate in the definition of their model society, and to contribute to making it possible. It is important to notice that, in general, Scouting as an organisation does not clash with the prevailing social values and institutions; on the contrary, it supports them. But as a voluntary movement, Scouting is a source of critical individuals committed to making a change based on the inclusive values they share, and challenging unfairness and oppression: racial segregation, discrimination by origin (migration, refugees), socio-economic inequality, authoritarianism and lack of freedoms, gender inequality, or homophobic discrimination. This is a consequence of the voluntary participation of its members, based on its shared inclusive values of co-existence.

Another important characteristic of Scouting is that it develops the values of citizenship while embracing national-cultural and religious identities. In this way, it shows that legitimised competing identities challenge the exclusionary visions

---

26. "The purpose of the Scout movement is to contribute to the self-development of young people in achieving their full physical, intellectual, social and spiritual potentials as individuals, as responsible citizens and as members of their local, national, and international communities" (WOSM). "The Aim of the Girl Guide / Girl Scout Movement is to provide girls and young women with opportunities for self-training in the development of character, responsible citizenship and service in their own and world communities" (WAGGGS).

27. Whereas Robert Baden-Powell later constituted separate Scouting entities for boys and for girls, with the same principles, purpose and method, and presided over by himself at British and global levels, we know that in practice he attached no importance to this separation, as is voiced in the preface to the 1919 book directed at Scout leaders (educators), *Aids to Scoutmastership*: "The term 'Scouting' has come to mean a system of training in citizenship, through games, for boys and girls ... The training is needed for both sexes, and is imparted through the Boy Scouts and Girl Guides Movements. The principles are the same for both. It is only in the details that they vary." Therefore, although both world organisations, WOSM and WAGGGS, and their members have differences in their traditions and approaches (starting with the names: boy scouts, girl guides, girl scouts, scouts), I use the term "Scouting" to apply to the whole movement embraced by the two world organisations.

within single identities. In the same way the Scout identity and a sense of global identity challenge national and religious identities, balancing and complementing all. Therefore, Scouting's citizenship combines the values of civic republicanism and liberal-democratic nationalism with cosmopolitan frameworks, duties and openness to diversity. That is why local groups need global identification: to mitigate the temptation of exclusionary identities and to fully educate in global citizenship.

Scouting contributes to the empowerment of autonomous individuals and to their holistic development as active global citizens. Scouting does so through providing learning opportunities from which young people can benefit, co-created with them to achieve the purpose of the movement, and experienced through the Scout method. These experiences have young people at its centre, and adults, through dialogue and co-operation, help them in their learning journey. In that journey, adults also grow with the experience, and this enriches the adult–young people dialogue.

Scouting is based on the concept of self-education. This implies that each youth member is considered a unique individual who, from the outset, has the potential to develop in all dimensions and to take responsibility for his or her own development from a young age: this means learning how to learn, and being equipped for lifelong learning. Implicit in self-education is that it is based on the concept of "education from within", as opposed to "instruction from without". The Scout method, while retaining the same basic elements, adapts them to the different stages of young people's development from childhood to the end of adolescence.

The key elements of the Scout method cannot be understood separately, as they interact with each other to create a dynamic educational environment, formed by: the attitude of welcoming, dialogue and support of adult leaders, the inclusive values of the Scout Law that determine how to assess and enrich common life, the challenge of personal goals, the individual commitment generated by the Promise, the framework of teams and councils that allows democratic decision-making processes and promotes the empowerment of all, the sense of purpose and belonging provided by the symbolic framework, the attractiveness of activities in the privileged setting of nature, and the joy to serve others, which allows young people to find a role in the community.

The educational dimension of Scouting has always been central to its development; however, learning happens in different settings. UNESCO (ISCED 2011) has traditionally defined three main areas: formal education, non-formal education and informal education. However, this clear separation of settings is blurred, because, as indicated in the last UNESCO (2015) report, "there is a move from traditional educational institutions towards mixed, diverse and complex learning landscapes in which formal, non-formal and informal learning occur through a variety of educational institutions". This evolution can lead to new, interesting and productive partnerships between formal and non-formal education, and it also demands that Scouting should keep exploring new ways to contribute to the full development of young people, rather than holding on to practices that have become outdated or claiming exclusivity of those that have been successfully adopted within other education settings.

2. A historical journey: precedents of World Scouting

Scouting started in Britain in 1907, when Robert Baden-Powell, a renowned British lieutenant-general began to write the book, *Scouting for boys*. However, Scouting as a world movement did not exist until 1920, with the formalisation of a worldwide organisation led by Baden-Powell himself. For the sake of clarity, it could be useful to divide the period before the formalisation of World Scouting in 1920 into three phases. The first regards the sequence of events and ideas that led Robert Baden-Powell to publish *Scouting for boys: a handbook for instruction in good citizenship* in 1908, and the path that led from the publication of this book to the creation of the two British associations: the Boy Scouts Association (1909) and the Girl Guides Association (1910). The second phase is longer and covers the sporadic international growth process – under the moral authority of Baden-Powell – simultaneously with the creation of the two British associations, as well as developing and maturing the ideological discourse of Scouting and its relationship with progressive educational movements. Finally, the third phase, which forms the ideological and international basis for the Scout Movement, stretches from the First World War to the creation of the Boy Scouts International Bureau (later called WOSM) in 1920 and of WAGGGS in 1928.

Scouting is, above all else, the fruit of a brilliant idea of Robert Baden-Powell: the ensemble of his technical knowledge, resurgent patriotism, and hopes and dreams of a child, which he, like in *Peter Pan*, would never give up. It is unanimously agreed that the catalyst for the birth of Scouting was *Scouting for boys*. The author was a 50-year-old lieutenant-general in the British Army who had risen to popularity in Britain a decade before, when he successfully commanded the defence of the South African border town of Mafeking in 1899 during the Second Boer War. That same year, Baden-Powell had published the book, *Aids to Scouting for NCOs and men*, a manual in which he recalled his experiences training young soldiers in the techniques for exploring, and emphasised the importance of outdoor games and activities in character development. Though intended for a military public, the book contributed to Baden-Powell's rising popularity with both young people and students.

A first foray into what the later book, *Scouting for boys*, would look like in practice took place in August 1907, when Baden-Powell brought together 20 adolescent boys from various social classes to live together for 10 days in an encampment on the small island of Brownsea, in Poole Harbour (southern England), where they cooked their own food, played games, learned skills, and listened to the fanciful and exotic stories that Baden-Powell told. This date is generally considered the beginning of Scouting. In January of the following year, *Scouting for boys* was published.

The editor of *Scouting for boys* was C. Arthur Pearson, magnate of the newspaper the *Daily Express*, who recognised the commercial potential of the book and published it in six fortnightly instalments beginning in January 1908, and, after its success, as a book in May of the same year. The book became an immediate bestseller: after the first four editions were printed in the first year and were received with great enthusiasm, there were more than 60 000 additional copies published in the second year.

Despite the growing informal following, *Scouting for boys* was not therefore intended to spur the creation of an organisation or movement of any sort. In fact, it was "a fragmentary, porous, non-cohesive mishmash of other texts", many of which were his, others of which were not – such as the notes and experiences on Native-American heritage, which were taken from Ernest T. Seton,[28] an early ecologist and educator. The resulting mixture was tremendously suggestive. It was packed with exotic tales (from Africa and India), games, theatrical works, secret signs and symbols, and written in a style to stimulate adolescent minds, the book combines entertainment with moral lessons, as though it were a game – one that did, in fact, offer a convenient outline for character development for adolescents in their leisure time, ready to be adopted by existing British youth organisations, or directly by civic groups.

In fact, the book began with a letter intended for adults, explaining that the Scout system is "applicable to existing organisations such as schools, boy's brigades, cadet corps, etc., or can supply a simple organisation of its own where these do not exist".[29]

Part of the reason for the success of the book is that it was the "right time" for such an idea. Society was just beginning to recognise adolescence as one of the stages of the human life cycle, and there was a greater understanding of the unique needs of boys during this time. In addition, with the industrialisation of the Western world, children of this age group were in school during the day, rather than working, and fewer participated in apprenticeships. Declining birth rates and an increased standard of living also contributed to an increased value placed on children's well-being and character development.

The ideological background to Baden-Powell's idea revolved around the social and political tensions in England following the post-Victorian age, including the belief that industrialisation was undermining traditional notions of good conduct and leading to the moral and physical degeneration of the lower classes in the British Empire and the possible decline of the Empire. Given the underlying threat of German invasion and his conviction that British youth were not prepared to defend the nation, Baden-Powell believed that he could propose a model to complement the education received by adolescents at school from an overtly patriotic point of view; a model that would shape their character and teach them initiative and useful skills by means of open-air activities, games, and observation, in a popular, motivating format.

Thus, the first edition of Scouting for boys is a bit of a hotchpotch of previous works and materials from different sources, with no clear doctrinal strategy. According to Allen Warren, a historian of the Scout Movement, "Baden-Powell, no systematic thinker or critic, picked up and dropped social and political concerns as he went along".[30] Indeed, there are constant contradictions: it seeks the complicity of parents, the school and the Church, while criticising parental laziness, the inconsistency of schools and the biblical teachings of the Church. Furthermore, the model endeavours to shape autonomous individuals, but proposes doing so through obedience and self-discipline. Overall, the book's emphasis is on the development of the individual's character and the moral influence of the small group – quite the opposite of

---

28. Boehmer 2004: xiii, xliv.
29. Baden-Powell [1908] 2004: 5.
30. Warren 1986: 387.

impersonal training for the masses. It would not be until later that the book, and the Scout Movement, would develop an ideological consistency.

In fact, the book offered an imaginary element of self-identification to its adolescent readers: the feeling of being part of a grand game of sorts. Just like a game, *Scouting for boys* explained who the "Scouts" were – fictional explorers, rather than members of an educational movement – and described how they dressed and behaved. One of the various stories, or "campfire yarns", of the book explains that, "Scouts, all the world over, have unwritten laws which bind them just as much as if they had been printed in black and white. They come down to us from old times."[31]

These values allowed readers to bring the rich world of fantasy of the book into real life, and constituted a universal and positive code of conduct (these "laws" are positive injunctions). Boys engaged and identified with the material in the book, applying the novel principles of this new idea called "Scouting" in their daily lives. Moreover, the references to God and the King in the text of the Oath and the Law must be read in the context of Britain at that time: a religious society with no powerful church that, at the end of the 17th century, had established the independence of its parliament from the monarchy – thus creating a democratic structure: "If the service which was required of the boys was for God, it was for the God of a multi-confessional and tolerant society; if loyalty to the King was asked for, it was faithfulness to a monarch who reigned rather than governed."[32]

Therefore, although the original intention of Robert Baden-Powell was not to create a widespread movement, the extraordinary reception of the book resulted in the success of an idea so great that it surprised even its author. Groups of self-identified "Scouts" soon appeared throughout Britain, clamouring for guidance and a more cohesive identity. But what did it mean to be "considered a Scout"? It was simply to follow the conduct and ethics outlined in *Scouting for boys*. And it seemed that this was happening everywhere. One should bear in mind that the clever intervention of Pearson, the publisher, supplied the book with a commercial appeal, where it was advertised – when the Scout Movement did not yet exist! – That "Scout's Badges, Medals, Patrol Flags, and Crests, Tracking Irons, and such articles of Scouts' equipment, can be obtained at low rates on application here"[33] – with a postal address.

In September 1909, 21 months after the book was published, Pearson sponsored a rally at London's Crystal Palace, spotting a burgeoning business opportunity in doing so. To the surprise of its organisers, headed by Baden-Powell, 11 000 self-identified "Scouts" adolescents turned up at the rally. Baden-Powell described this spontaneous following in an interview in 1937:

> Boys were writing to me telling me how they had started Patrols and Troops and had got men to come and act as their Scoutmasters. So we had to start a Headquarters office in a tiny room to deal with correspondence and supply equipment. … In that year, 1909, I arranged to have a meeting of the would-be Scouts at the Crystal Palace on a certain day. And when I got there, my wig, there were a lot of them. Rain was threatening, so

31. Baden-Powell, [1908] 2004: 36.
32. Nagy 1967: 17.
33. Baden-Powell [1908] 2004: 5-6.

we mustered them inside the Palace and arranged a March Past and counted them as they entered at one door and went out at the other. There were 11,000 of them – 11,000, who had taken it up of their own accord! That is why I say that one didn't see the start: Scouting started itself.[34]

There are probably three reasons as to why Scouting took off so quickly. Firstly, its historical opportunity: the idea came about with emerging concepts of "adolescence" and "leisure time", increasing rates of school attendance for boys in that age group, and a preference for "the country life" over life in industrial cities. Secondly, the project was thoroughly supported by institutions with social and political authority in Great Britain, namely the monarchy, the army, school and the Church – a support that would be replicated in many other countries. And lastly, the heterogeneous and relatively ambiguous model of citizenship espoused in *Scouting for boys* easily gained a wide public acceptance as well as paved the way for the later international expansion of the movement.

It was the ambiguity and heterogeneity of the ideals that help to explain the wide social support for early Scouting. That is the reason why, as Laszlo Nagy indicates, we should not be surprised that the movement has been accused of being too pro-military by some and pacifistic by others; that many have regarded Scouting as overly religious, while churches have criticised its lack of religious content (only two of the 300 pages of *Scouting for boys* discuss religion); or that Britain's Labour Party accused it of promoting values that helped to keep the Conservatives in power, while the Tories attacked it for its socialist overtones. The initial adaptability of the early Scout Movement to the purposes of diverse organisations and bodies of thought has been a double-edged sword, simultaneously a boon to its spread and a target of criticism for having largely undefined core values.

3. Scouting in Britain and its spontaneous internationalisation (1908-20)

Just three months after the Crystal Palace rally in December 1909, the Boy Scouts Association was set up with an astonishing 108 000 members and Baden-Powell himself as chairman. A year later, in 1910, the UK Girl Guides Association was created by Robert Baden-Powell, with 6 000 members, chaired by Baden-Powell's sister Agnes.

Many believe – and Baden-Powell himself has said – that he decided to create a parallel organisation for girls when he saw that some girls had come to the Crystal Palace rally who, like the boys, considered themselves Scouts. Nevertheless, earlier documents of Baden-Powell explicitly indicate the contrary: that girls could also be Scouts. In his "Boy Scouts Scheme" of 1907, the first pamphlet outlining the Scouting project, he wrote that it was the basis "for an attractive organisation and valuable training for girls"; and in an article in 1908 he said: "I think girls can get just as much healthy fun out of Scouting as boys can ... and prove themselves good Scouts in a very short time."[35] Tim Jeal, British biographer of Baden-Powell, argues

---

34. Baden-Powell 1937.
35. "Boy Scouts Scheme", a pamphlet published in 1907 by the Boy Scouts Association UK, and the "Can girls be Scouts?" article in *The Scout* magazine, May 1908. Both quoted in Jeal 2001: 469.

that the idea of a separate organisation came later, due to pressures from the social establishment that thought it inappropriate for girls to carry out activities that were supposed "masculine".

It was in August 1909, therefore, when Baden-Powell decided to adapt a version of *Scouting for boys* for girls, a move that would lead to the eventual creation of a separate organisation. That same year, his book *Yarns for Boy Scouts* already suggested that girls, and society in general, could benefit from girls following the principles of Scouting, albeit with a "slightly modified" system of training, and added: "I am forced to this suggestion by the fact that already some thousands of girls have registered themselves as 'Boy Scouts'!".[36] In effect, the girl "Scouts" were in fact provisionally registered in the Boy Scouts' census until 1910, when the female association was established. In November 1909, Baden-Powell published *The Scheme for Girl Guides*, which finally adapted Scouting for girls, and adopted the term "Guiding"[37] for the female version of the movement.

In 1909, Baden-Powell was knighted by King Edward VII, and the following year, encouraged by this, he retired from the military in order to dedicate himself exclusively to Scouting. In its formalisation as a British association, the combination of the Scout Law and Oath outlined in *Scouting for boys* became the main ideological reference for Scouting. Indeed, the methodology of Scouting, developed for adolescents, offered shared values of living together through its "law", and voluntary commitment to these values through its "oath", the key to self-education through which youth purposefully turned into voluntary members of the Scout Movement.

The educational ideology of Scouting was formed after the movement had already begun, during a pre-war time when the influence and presence of the military in UK society was growing and getting further away from these militarising influences. This is why, in parallel to the progressive education movement's development, Scouting presents itself as a movement for citizenship training, essentially educational, which includes patriotic elements and religious references. Hence, the educational feature of Scouting was particularly highlighted by its promoters in the years prior to 1914, in reaction to the accusations of being militaristic. And in fact, the deepening of its own educational method focused on the individual and on the full development of his or her potential set it apart from the military's method of education en masse.

Moreover, it was around this time – between 1911 and 1914 – that England received the influence of the modern ideas of the Italian feminist and educator Maria Montessori and her "learning by doing" educational philosophy – very similar to the method that Scouting was intuitively developing. The ideological link between Scouting and the progressive education movement was noticed by many of Baden-Powell's contemporaries[38] and is what today we call a complementarity between formal

---

36. Baden-Powell 1909.
37. Baden-Powell chose the name "Guides" after the well-known Corps of Guides in India; however, the term was unacceptable in the United States because it had the connotation of "Indian hunter". As a result, when the USA association was created in 1912, it adopted the name "Girl Scouts", which is now a synonym of "Girl Guides" – as shown a decade later by the name of the world association: World Association of Girl Guides and Girl Scouts.
38. Warren 1986: 392-93; Wonesch 2000; and Jeal 2001: 413-14.

and non-formal education on youth empowerment. Back in 1914, Baden-Powell remarked in a text that "Montessori has proved that by encouraging a child in its natural desires, instead of instructing it in what you think it ought to do, you can educate it on a far more solid and far-reaching base."[39]

In 1916, seven years after the creation of the Boy Scouts Association in Britain, Baden-Powell responded to the demand to extend Scouting to the pre-adolescent age range by creating a version of the book with a mood set around Rudyard Kipling's *The jungle book*, calling the boys "Wolf Cubs" or "Cub Scouts", just as the book character Mowgli's friends are called. In 1922, the Scouting concept was extended upwards to the post-adolescent age range, calling them "Senior Scouts" or "Rovers", while "Scouts" remained the term used for those aged 12 to 15. Although they initially had a certain degree of autonomy, these ranges eventually became sections or age groups within the same movement. The Scout Movement as a whole took its name from the original adolescent group.

Regarding the female association, where the same age adaptations as in the male association were made, Baden-Powell designated his 52-year-old sister Agnes to manage it. In 1912, the two published *How girls can help to build up the Empire*, a supposed feminised version of *Scouting for boys* that never really took off. Additionally, there was a constant clash between the ideas of Agnes, who believed that girls should be refined, and her brother's different ideas.[40] In 1912, Robert Baden-Powell married Olave St Clair Soames, who was 23 years old at the time. Olave quickly replaced Baden-Powell's sister Agnes at the head of the Girl Guides: she was much younger, more active and sporty, and her ideas were closer to those of her husband, who wrote at the time that "girls must be partners and comrades rather than dolls".[41] In 1915, Robert Baden-Powell became Chairman of the Girl Guides Association and in 1918, Olave became the new Chief Guide. Later on, she would become the real world leader. Also in 1918, Robert Baden-Powell published *Girl Guiding: the official handbook*, to replace the poorly received book published with his sister in 1912.

If Baden-Powell had not intended to create an organisation in the UK when he first published *Scouting for boys*, much less was he thinking to do so on an international scale. However, just as it had spread across England, Scouting and, to a lesser degree, female Scouting, immediately began quickly expanding to the rest of the British Empire and the entire world. In fact, the many beliefs and characteristics contained in the original concept of Scouting and the various ways in which it could be interpreted also help to explain how a product designed to revitalise the British Empire could have such an immediately successful reception in Chilean, French, Malaysian and Japanese societies, to name a few.

Nonetheless, both in Britain and abroad, the propagation of the Scout Movement was helped by the public institutions committed to serving citizens, given that societies held these civic values in high regard. Scouting first spread throughout the British Empire (Ireland, Canada, Australia, New Zealand, Zimbabwe, South Africa and

---

39. Jeal 2001: 413.
40. Jeal 2001: 471-87.
41. Letter to the *Morning Post*, 9 August 1913; quoted in Jeal 1989: 470.

India, between 1908 and 1909), which, in the 1920s, had a population of 500 million people, close to a quarter of the world population, and stretched across 37 million square kilometres, a quarter of the earth's land surface. Moreover, the movement also spread to many other countries worldwide, like Chile, Denmark, the United States and Russia (1909), Brazil, France, Finland, Greece and Holland (1910), Belgium, Estonia, Norway, Sweden, Malaysia and Singapore (1911). The untrammelled growth of the Scout Movement in both name and number went hand in hand with the spread of the book *Scouting for boys*: by the end of the 1920s, two decades after it was first published in London, it had already been published in 26 countries – not including editions already printed in the British Empire, making it the fourth bestselling book of the 20th century.

Baden-Powell was an iconic figure for the associations that adopted the Scout method worldwide, and even though the prevailing Chairman of British Scouting did not actively seek the expansion of Scouting, he did maintain close contact with promoters of the movement abroad, travelling often to give talks and attend conferences. This is documented in his 1913 book, *Boy Scouts beyond the seas*, in which Baden-Powell describes his trips to visit Scouts in the United States, Japan, Norway, Sweden, Denmark, Holland, Belgium and the British dependencies of India, South Africa, Australia and New Zealand, and that shows how he maintained close contact with the international emergence of the movement.

This inadvertent international expansion was given a cautious welcome in London. According to Laszlo Nagy, Baden-Powell himself proposed that the association not accept applications to join from outside the British jurisdiction. Alternatively, in the October 1911 edition of the *Scout Headquarters Gazette*, he suggested the idea of setting up a foreign affairs department to maintain contact with Scouts throughout the world. It marked the dawn of a movement with international ties, but not yet a world organisation.

Baden-Powell did not regard the international proliferation of Scouting as simple coincidence, as though it were the mere spread of an institution with a social purpose. In fact, he refused to patent the term for the exclusive use of British Scouting and gradually abandoned the idea of producing "citizens of the Empire" in favour of a more international discourse. It also evolved in this direction because Baden-Powell had travelled to many countries – and continued to do so – with a liberal vision that represented a stark contrast to the expansionist nationalism of continental Europe at that time.

When war finally broke out, the process of defining Scouting was in full swing and the movement was still learning how to run itself. The structural and ideological bases of the movement were still too weak to sustain its new unwieldy size. With origins that lay in romantic tales of frontier pioneers, the First World War was a reality check for the Scout Movement that rocked its foundations.

4. Peace and the ideal of the League of Nations

As Nagy explains, in the summer of 1914, millions of young men from all sides went to war believing that they were fighting for a noble cause and a better world. Amid the patriotic and nationalist fervour, there was no room for nuances. In Great Britain, around 150 000 of the young men mobilised for the war were or had been Scouts, and 10 000 of these died. Many were Scout leaders. Many other boys and girls Scouts carried out auxiliary tasks and services.

But this was not the only setback for the new movement – the war would have a profound effect on the emerging links between organisations following *Scouting for boys*. For example in 1911, in Germany, later the enemy of the British, 80 000 Germans considered themselves Scouts. By the time war broke out, *Scouting for boys* had already been translated into German and close contact had been established between the British Scouting and the German associations that were using the Scout method.

It seemed clear that, after such a bloody conflict between countries, it was highly likely that the international aspirations of Scouting would be reduced to ashes. And yet, once the war was over, the movement did not wane; on the contrary, its numbers increased – Great Britain had almost 200 000 Boy Scouts and, just a few years later, almost half a million Girl Guides – and it had a presence in 30 or so countries. Boys in British Scouting were mainly from the middle to lower-middle classes, rather than the working class.

The First World War, together with the international expansion of Scouting and the possibilities that it offered, are two of the main reasons why Baden-Powell changed the register from citizens of the Empire to the ideal of citizens of the world. The war showed him the first-hand effects of a full-scale conflict on young people. The vision of a soldier trying to maintain the stability of the Empire was transformed into that of a civil activist committed to avoiding another armed conflict by firmly distancing Scouting from nationalist tendencies with expansionist ambitions.[42]

In a text on "Scouting as a peace agent" from 1917, he wrote:

> Nations disillusioned by war are seeking something better than pieces of paper produced by unscrupulous statesmen. They are proposing war reparations and indemnities but beyond these material obligations it is surely possible to encourage the feelings and emotions of peoples as the best hope of permanent peace. The Scout Movement on its relatively small scale has taken root among the youth of all civilized countries and is still growing. It is not too much to hope that in the years to come, with increasing numbers joining this fraternity in the coming generations, they will unite in personal friendship and mutual understanding such as never before and thus find a solution to these horrendous international conflicts.[43]

In each and every one of the first 10 editions of *Scouting for boys*, until 1922, the social and cultural references of the text were increasingly open and global, so that Great Britain was no longer the clear centre of the Scouting world, though the book remained the official point of the United Kingdom's Boy Scouts Association.

Baden-Powell had planned to organise an international meeting in 1918, the tenth anniversary of the movement, with a series of clear aims that he explained in 1916: "to make our ideals and methods more widely known abroad; to promote the spirit

---

42. Parsons 2004: 54; Nagy 1985: 82.
43. Quoted in Reynolds 1942: 190-91.

of brotherhood among the rising generation throughout the world, thereby giving the spirit that is necessary to make the League of Nations a living force".[44]

The project of the League of Nations was the first time that an idea of an international organisation of countries had been put forward to replace war as a way of resolving conflicts. In Great Britain, a civic organisation was created, called the League of Nations Union, in support of the ideals espoused by the League of Nations. Various texts and speeches by Baden-Powell from the time when people began to discuss "the League" reveal his awareness that the Scout Movement could help to create a public mind frame that would encourage the existence of a supranational organisation with peace – and governance – as its basic political aim. This is clearly demonstrated in a 1919 letter from Baden-Powell to the Mayor of London, one of the men behind the Union, in which he said:

> I need scarcely say how, in common with most people, I am anxious to do anything to make the League a living force.
> Through the Boy Scout and Girl Guide Movement we have already instituted ... the training of young citizens of the different countries to think in terms of peace and good will towards each other, so that the League of Nations shall, in the next generation, be a bond between peoples rather than a pact between Governments.
> We have now over a million young members in the different civilised countries, all working under the same Scout Law and ideals, looking on each other as brother and sister members, and in a great number of cases interchanging letters and visits.
> Next year will see a great International Conference of these boys and girls in London. So I hope that our aims and doings will commend themselves as all in the direction in which your society is moving.[45]

This was, therefore, the ideal behind the project of the international Scout meeting, the "great international conference" he refers to in the letter, which had to be postponed originally because of the war.

5. World Scouting –
Under the leadership of Robert Baden-Powell

Before 1920, Scouting could not be considered an international movement, but a British initiative with a clear leadership replicated in other countries. Notwithstanding, in the summer of 1920, the organisation of the international encounter wished for by Baden-Powell was the definitive move to transform Scouting into a worldwide movement.

It should be noted that the aims and ideology of Baden-Powell had evolved significantly since 1908. Firstly, there was the link to the progressive education discourse, particularly in relation to the teaching methods of Maria Montessori, and the rejection of the military tradition. Secondly, an increased emphasis on the need to develop critical thinking skills, clarifying the educational role of obedience. Thirdly, a clear international commitment, linked to the ideals embodied by the League of Nations,

---

44. Quoted in Jeal 2001: 511.
45. Archives of the Scout Association UK, Box "Co-operation-League of Nations", Chief Scout to Lord Mayor of London, 23 September 1919. Quoted in Baden-Powell 2006: 23.

which was partly the result of the international Scout network that was materialising. Lastly, and closely related to the previous point, was the Scout Movement's steadfast commitment to peace stemming from the profound impact of the First World War.

Although these elements constituted the foundations for the formalisation of World Scouting, many countries continued to set up associations based on the early British model. This meant that there was an ambiguous tension in many countries between the early British Scouting model of 1909 – connected to the military sector and based more on discipline with various levels of nationalism – and the evolved model that Baden-Powell promoted in 1920 – civic, socially committed with an emphasis on the education of the individual, internationally oriented, and focused on working towards peace. The paradox is that both visions were based on texts written by Baden-Powell!

The international Scout meeting originally planned for 1918 was finally held in London in August 1920, with 8 000 Scouts from 21 independent countries and 12 British territories. It was the first International Jamboree, an event that has since been held regularly and become an icon of the movement.

It was at the first Jamboree that Robert Baden-Powell was appointed Chief Scout of the World by acclamation – an honorific title. Although the Jamboree was essentially an adolescent gathering, the first International Scout Conference was held there in the presence of 33 Scout organisations from diverse countries and it was agreed to create an international organisation, the Boy Scouts International Bureau (BSIB).[46] In that same year, 1920, the permanent secretariat was set up and, two years later, the organisation was legally established in Paris. Scouting then had a million members worldwide.

The new international Scout organisation established a permanent secretariat (the Bureau), along with an International Conference (a governing body formed by the national associations, each of which had six votes) and an International Committee (an executive body formed by individuals elected by the conference). This bears some resemblance to the structure adopted by the League of Nations a year earlier.

Despite this organisational formalisation, Baden-Powell stressed from the outset that the sense of "movement" was to be maintained, which meant that more importance was placed on principles and methods than on the organisation itself. If that was important at national level, even more so internationally, where while a set of standard principles determining Scout recognition was being established, great measures were

---

46. Nagy 1985: 90-91; Jeal 2001: 511-12. There are no documents listing all of the founding associations of World Scouting either in the archives of the Scout Association UK or the World Scout Bureau (WOSM). Figures vary depending on the source, perhaps because it is not certain that all of the countries that attended the Jamboree in 1920 were in the new Boy Scouts International Bureau. Nagy (1985: 90) says that "8 000 scouts from 21 independent countries and 12 British dependences" attended the Jamboree (making a total of 33). However, he also lists the "Founder countries of the World Scout Movement" (Nagy 1985: 212) in an appendix without references: "Argentina; Austria; Belgium; Brazil; Chile; Czechoslovakia; Denmark; Ecuador; Estonia; Finland; France; Great Britain; Greece; Hungary; Italy; Japan; Latvia; Liberia; Luxembourg; Netherlands; Norway; Peru; Poland; Portugal; Rumania; Sweden; Switzerland; Thailand; United States of America". He does not include the British dominions where Scouting was present, such as Canada, India, South Africa, Australia or New Zealand.

also being taken to avoid the tendency of a potential centralising and controlling world organisation. The world organisation was in charge to democratically establish the ideological framework of Scouting but had no capacity whatsoever to decide how an association should be run or which decisions it should take.

Meanwhile, female Scouting was heading in a similar direction. In 1919, an International Council for Guiding was set up on the initiative of Olave Baden-Powell, Chief Guide of British Guiding since 1918 and wife of its founder. Though the Council lacked a legal structure, it held its first conference in England in 1920. At the 4th International Conference in 1926, steps were taken to formalise the organisation, and, in 1927, the International Bureau (the permanent secretariat) was finally established.

The World Association of Girl Guides and Girl Scouts (WAGGGS) was established on the suggestion of Robert Baden-Powell at the 5th International Conference of Girl Guides (Hungary 1928). Delegates from 26 countries were present at the conference and the association was given a similar organisational structure to that of the international Scout organisation: a permanent secretariat (the Bureau), an elected International Committee with nine members (the executive body) and a plenary International Conference of national associations (the governing body). Robert and Olave Baden-Powell were registered as non-voting members of the International Committee. In 1930, Olave Baden-Powell was elected World Chief Guide, the equivalent to her husband's title in male Scouting. By 1931, female Scouting had a million members around the world, though mainly in English-speaking countries.

The ideals of peace and international fraternity have been a constant in Scouting ever since it was internationally formalised. An official document from 1922 explains that the world organisation was affiliated to the International Peace Bureau, the oldest peace organisation in the world. Baden-Powell himself was the keynote speaker of the 3rd International Conference of Moral Education in 1922 in Geneva, with the conference, Education in Love in Place of Fear.

Baden-Powell's enthusiastic commitment to the League of Nations as a way of securing world peace is evidenced by various statements he made. He openly encouraged Scout groups to work together to promote the League of Nations Union: "probably a local branch exists in your town; if so, you should ask the secretary if you can help him in any way, such as distributing handbills for meetings".[47]

During the first few years of World Scouting, Baden-Powell attempted to make the organisation into a sort of League of Nations youth movement but came up against the staunch opposition of the Committee of the Council, the executive body of the Boy Scouts Association UK, which considered the British League of Nations Union to be a "political organisation". In fact, some of the latter had even opposed the organisation of the International Jamboree in 1920. These tensions came as no surprise; dissidence between the ideals of the movement and the interests of its "stakeholders" had been a constant throughout Scouting history.

The creation of the two world organisations led to the establishment of an official "international recognition system" for Scouting, which became all the more necessary

47.   *The Scout*, 14 August 1920, quoted in Baden-Powell 2006: 24.

when, for example, in 1923, the League of Nations assembly encouraged governments to facilitate the mobility of "recognised associations" of Scouts.[48] After the formalisation of the movement, it would be a democratically operated international organisation (the Boy Scouts International Bureau or the World Association of Girl Guides and Girl Scouts) that would officially approve the membership of national associations.

The establishment of an approval system was timely because Scouting had simply grown too big to allow imitations to use its brand for other purposes. In 1924, for example, the Boy Scouts International Bureau rejected the German associations' request for international Scout recognition on the grounds of dispersion of associations – there were too many disorganised groups adhering only partly or not at all to the Scout method. The refusal was also due – at least in part – to the fact that "the German movement was too pro-military, too nationalistic and overly expansionist in the wrong directions since it was attempting to absorb Austrian Scouting".[49] Therefore, no German "Scouting" obtained international recognition until the fall of the Nazi totalitarianism.[50]

With the new world organisations, although the word of Baden-Powell still held authority, it was gradually being replaced by democratic agreements reached in the world conferences. Nonetheless, Baden-Powell held on to his moral authority. His writing, speeches and even the modifications made to subsequent editions of Scouting for boys reflect the evolution of his thought, particularly after the First World War. While in 1908 the book reads: "You belong to the Great British Empire, one of the greatest empires that has ever existed in the world",[51] by 1921 the book warned of the perils of excessive national pride, pointing out that, "the world-wide crash of war has roughly shaken us all and made us awake to the newer order of things. No longer is one nation better than another".[52]

The world conference agreements can be discerned through the "resolutions", which are the official stances adopted by the organisation. At the 2nd International Scout Conference resolutions (Paris 1922) there are clear signs of the move towards establishing common standards: it established that Scouting membership must be voluntary, not obligatory; it emphasises the need for unity within the movement and cautions against the fragmenting of associations within the same country. This last point clearly demonstrates that the world organisation, from very early on, attempted to ensure that each country had just one association, based on the British model. However, the existence of three distinct "Scout" associations in France in 1920: one secular ("laïque"), one Protestant and one Catholic, resulted in the creation of a federation of associations rather than one single national association. This federation model was spread in Catholic countries by the Church and also in French colonies.

---

48. Report to the Secretary General: Report of the League Representatives to the Third International Scout Conference, Copenhagen, August 1924, p. 10. Document No. 38.191, League of Nations archive, Geneva.

49. Nagy 1985: 102.

50. See Jeal 2001: 543-53, on the interaction between Baden-Powell and the Boy Scouts International Bureau with the fascist and Nazi regimes in Italy and Germany, respectively.

51. Baden-Powell [1908] 2004: 26.

52. Published in Jamboree, January 1921, quoted in Baden-Powell 2006: 19-20.

This set of common standards was also useful to ensure that Scout leaders were on the same page. The standards were a foundation of the educational curriculum at the newly established training school for Scoutmasters set up by the Boy Scouts Association (UK) at Gilwell Park, near London. In 1922, with the launch of the Boy Scouts International Bureau, this school became the world reference for approved training of Scoutmasters and trainers of Scoutmasters around the world, which also made it possible to keep the international ideological unity of the movement until the late 1960s.

In the uneasy calm of the interwar period, the dual national/international condition of the Scout Movement was undeniable. At its third meeting, held in Denmark in 1924, the International Scout Conference passed the "Principles of Scouting" 14/24 resolution, which established that Scouting "is a movement of national, international and universal character, the object of which is to endow each separate nation and the whole world with a youth which is physically, morally and spiritually strong". At the same time, in order to silence criticisms – principally from the Catholic Church – that it was lacking in religious content, the resolution reiterated its commitment to promote religious beliefs, although forbidding "any kind of sectarian propaganda at mixed gatherings". The resolution contains the two key elements that Scouting has repeatedly emphasised, as well as their counterweights: national identity balanced out by internationalism, and individual beliefs balanced out by acceptance of religious plurality. Scouting, therefore, did not wish to become a secular movement[53] without national identities; it was a movement committed to the spiritual dimension of the individual and giving a role to religion, where dialogue between religions was possible and where national identities were the way forward – as opposed to the impediment – to building what we now know as a reference of global citizenship.

Therefore, in just over 10 years, Scouting had undergone critical changes – it had transformed from a training idea based on the experiences of a senior military man to a thriving British youth movement, and from this to an organised international movement composed of national Scout associations determined to stamp out exclusionary nationalist tendencies among its members. In this way, the same 1924 International Scout Conference that refused to recognise German associations pointed out in the 17/24 resolution "that there should be no discrimination as to admission to membership of fellow subjects or citizens for any reason of race, creed or politics" as a condition for recognition. Although it wished to increase membership, the world organisation was determined to have as its unalterable foundation the recognition of Scout brotherhood, regardless of race, creed or class. This condition was established with the full knowledge that public institutions in many countries with Scouting discriminated on grounds of race, creed or ideology, including the United States, where racial segregation would not be abolished until 1954.

In the second half of the 1920s and throughout the 1930s, the structural bases to internationally organise Scouting finally came together. A look at the balance

---

53. Nonetheless, France has had a *laïque* Scout association since 1911, recognised as such since 1920 when the Boy Scouts International Bureau was constituted, a *laïque* nature it still retains today along with other Scout associations.

between national identity and global belonging in the Scout Movement, and the tendency of associations to accept the established order, helps explain how this structured internationalisation was possible. For example, many delegates came to the 1926 conference with messages of support and encouragement for their respective governments, signed by the relevant minister or secretary of state. They included Denmark, Finland, France, the United Kingdom, Hungary, Iraq, Japan, Poland, Romania, Siam, Spain and Yugoslavia.

However, the rise of fascism and its accompanying aggressive nationalism was also a threat to the ideological stability of the Scout Movement. The regenerationist discourses of Benito Mussolini and Adolf Hitler, who were initially somewhat admired in many Western countries during the 1920s, spoke out against political corruption and the decline of their respective countries, overlapping with part of the discourse of Scouting: values such as duty, discipline and self-sacrifice, suspicion of industrialisation, rejection of Soviet communism (that banned Scouting), love for one's country and culture, the importance of physical exercise, the romantic invocation of explorers, and so on. Furthermore, at that stage, when World Scouting was only just starting to develop its structure, unrecognised self-called "Scout" associations existed in many countries that in fact interpreted Scouting as they saw fit.[54] As a result, the international organisation ruled that it would have to approve the text of the "Oath" and the "Law" of each country to make the acceptance of shared values more explicit, with the additional obligation of notifying the international organisation of any changes. Associations were also encouraged to legally protect uniforms and identifying signs against fraudulent use.

In countries with totalitarian regimes, though, the situation was more complicated than the straightforward fraudulent copying of the Scout appearance. In 1917, when the Soviet Union was established, there were 50 000 Scouts in Russia. In 1922, the Scout Movement was banned and replaced by the Young Pioneer movement, which was controlled by the Communist Party and where former Scouts with Bolshevik sympathies collaborated. In turn, many Russian Scouts went into exile, setting up a Russian Scout association headquartered in France, internationally recognised by WOSM from 1928 to 1945. In Italy, the fascist youth organisation Balilla absorbed existing Scouting associations in 1927 under the direction of Mussolini. In the early 1930s, the Nazis also outlawed self-called "Scout" associations, none of which were internationally recognised, and gradually incorporated their members into the Hitler-Jugend (Hitler Youth).[55] To summarise, in the Axis countries, the regime banned

54. In 1933, for example, when the Nazi regime outlawed Scouting, there were 40 associations calling themselves "Scout" in Germany, though none were actually members of the international organisation (Kroonenberg 1998: 16).

55. In 1936, it became compulsory to join the Hitler-Jugend. In his novelised memoirs of life as a young German Scout at the time, Hans E. Ihle describes the situation in which he found himself that year: "The moment will come when you'll have to decide whether or not you want to join one of the branches of the Hitler-Youth organization. But that's not the worst point, as we said before. The worst moment comes when you don't even have that choice anymore; you can't borrow time by pretending to become a Nazi, similar to our German-Jewish citizens. You can't join the Hitler-Youth movement; you became unacceptable to them. Your Scout activities might have forced you to run out of choices. Then all that's left is the concentration camp" (Ihle 1993: 32).

Scouting (Italy after 1922, Germany after 1933 and Japan after 1941, together with fascist Spain after 1939) and replaced it with indoctrinating official youth movements controlled by the regime which imitated the Scouts' aesthetics. The same occurred in the Soviet Union after 1922 and in the occupied Baltic States and Soviet republics as they were formed, with the single exception of Poland.[56]

The brazen imitation of the Scout image and activities by fascist and communist regimes took place at a time when awareness of the Scouting brand was still emerging in many countries, and this led to a confusion that still exists today regarding the Scout Movement's alleged proto-fascist past,[57] while in reality it was the opposite: the Nazis even copied the uniforms and neckerchiefs of Scouting and made unsuccessful arrangements for the Hitler-Jugend to be internationally recognised as German Scouting.[58]

The comparison between World Scouting and official youth movements that pushed the discourse of national loyalty and acceptance of the status quo to their very limits forced Baden-Powell to further clarify the ambiguities that had come about around the time of the establishment of the international organisation. Nagy explains that, in his meeting with Mussolini in 1933, Baden-Powell rejected the idea that the Balilla was a better version of Scouting, arguing that "the Balilla was an official instead of a voluntary organisation; that it aimed at partisan nationalism instead of wider international good feeling; that it was purely physical, without any spiritual balance; and that it developed mass discipline instead of individual character".[59]

In order to dispel doubts about the internationalist commitment of Scouting, in contrast to the nationalist hyperfocus of fascist regimes, the 1937 International Scout Conference, held at the Hague in the Netherlands, officially modified one of the points of the Scout Law, adding references to brotherhood between countries: "A Scout is a friend to all, and a brother to every other Scout, no matter to what country, class, or creed the other may belong." It also approved a very explicit resolution on "Patriotism" (15/37), declaring that the International Committee

> be requested to do all that it can to ensure that Scouting and Rovering in all countries, while fostering true patriotism, are genuinely kept within the limits of international cooperation and friendship, irrespective of creed and race, as has always been outlined by the Chief Scout. Thus, any steps to the militarisation of Scouting or the introduction of political

---

56. Jeal 2001: 543-53; Nagy 1985: 101-03. For an ideological contrast between the aims of the Hitler Youth and the ones of USA Scouting in the 1940s, see Lewin 1947.

57. See the debate between Rosenthal 1986 and Jeal 2001 on Robert Baden-Powell's interaction with the Balilla and Hitler-Jugend. For Rosenthal, Baden-Powell's relationship with these movements indicates that he had a positive attitude towards some fascist and Nazi ideals. Jeal, however, argues that Baden-Powell, like many of his contemporaries, was sympathetic towards some of the ideas of Hitler and Mussolini before they began to use violence, particularly in reaction to the communists, who had dissolved Scouting in Russia. He also maintains that Baden-Powell kept in contact with the German and Italian youth organisations so that they were not isolated and that a recognised form of Scouting could be set up there in the future. In all events, this contact was abruptly terminated following the Night of Broken Glass in October 1938 in Germany (Jeal 2001: 544-47).

58. Nagy 1967: 30.

59. Nagy 1985: 102.

aims, which might cause misunderstanding and thus handicap our work for peace and goodwill among nations and individuals, should be entirely avoided in our programs.

In that same year, 28 000 Scouts had congregated for the 5th International Jamboree, which took place in Holland. It was preceded by Hungary in 1933, with 25 000 participants, England in 1929, with 50 000 participants and Denmark, with 4 500 participants. Seventeen years had passed since the first International Jamboree, when the Boy Scouts International Bureau was set up. To all intents and purposes, the International Jamboree had become the practical representation of the international nature of the movement: adolescents from all over the world coming together to share the principles of Scouting.

In July 1939, the 10th International Scout Conference was held in Edinburgh. Shortly afterwards, war broke out and international activity was paralysed. In most of the countries that took part in the Second World War, whether actively or passively, Scouting played a role in the organised resistance to state oppression, both in the countries that were occupied and in those of the attackers. Only three of the 17 European countries with recognised Scouting had remained neutral. Neutrality took on a new dimension – and not only in Scouting: there were humanity limits to refusing to take a stance that could never again be accepted.

Scouting was banned not only by fascist regimes, but also by the countries they occupied. In spite of this, many of these countries experienced organised resistance at a local level. Hilary St. George Saunders found various examples of Scout resistance in occupied countries such as Czechoslovakia, Poland, Denmark, Norway, Luxembourg, Holland, Belgium, France, Greece, Yugoslavia, Hungary, Philippines and Burma. He also highlights Scouting's contribution to resistance from outside aggressors in China, Formosa and Thailand, and to the internal resistance against regimes in Germany, Italy and Japan. In contrast, while the Catalan Scouting association rebelled against its illegalisation by taking the movement underground, Spanish Scouting accepted the suspension of activities under Franco.[60]

Meanwhile, Robert Baden-Powell retired from Scouting in 1937 and lived the last years of his life in Nyeri, Kenya, where he died peacefully and was buried in 1941. In the six years of international conflict during the Second World War, while Scouting was being persecuted in the occupied countries, the Boy Scouts International Bureau was paralysed and there was no external co-ordination for associations. The death of the founder and inspiration of the Scout Movement occurred at the height of the war, in the midst of a social crisis, mass population movements and the imposed paralysis of the international Scout structure. Everything suggested that Scouting was caught in a downward spiral, with most associations prohibited, shut down or severely weakened.

But this tumultuous time did not extinguish the Scout Movement, on the contrary. The International Committee met in London in November 1945, where two important agreements were reached. First, the foreseen International Jamboree and Conference,

---

60. Balcells and Samper 1993; Orozco C. and Ignacio J. (2003), "Entre la clandestinidad y la legalidad. El escultismo español en el primer franquismo (1939-1953)" ["Between clandestinity and legality. Spanish Scouting in the First Francoism (1939-1953)"], in Cholvy (ed.) (2003), pp. 249-63.

which were supposed to be held in 1941, were planned: they would take place in 1947 in France. Second, the organisational decision was made to separate the Boy Scouts International Bureau from the headquarters of the Boy Scouts Association UK and this was carried out that same month. This decision signals a continued awareness that the Scout Movement needed to continue its international focus and global expansion in order to survive.

As the work began on the reconstruction of the international movement, it was clear that it had gained newfound strength despite the destruction wrought by the Second World War: at the start of the war, male Scouting had just over 3.3 million members while the 1947 census revealed that it had 4.4 million members in 43 countries, despite the demise of 11 associations. Comparing the censuses of 1939 and 1947 (in thousands) reveals that male Scouting doubled in Argentina (from 5 to 10), Denmark (18 to 36), France (94 to 211) and Sweden (23 to 51), and tripled in Belgium (17 to 53), Greece (12 to 41), Holland (36 to 116) and Czechoslovakia (20 to 67). In India, membership increased from 285 000 to 414 000, in China from 315 000 to 570 000 (in 1941) and Britain's membership of 600 000 was maintained. However, almost half of the total 4.4 million members were from the male Scouting organisation of the USA, which had grown from 1.2 million members in 1939 to 2 million in 1948.[61]

The international stage following the Second World War starkly contrasted to the one that had followed the 1914-18 war: though the defeated were not humiliated, the world was divided into two camps. An international organisation, the United Nations, was set up with similar political principles to the League of Nations, but with a stronger moral message following the defeat of fascism.

The United Nations' framework of common principles was reinforced three years later when the United Nations General Assembly proclaimed the Universal Declaration of Human Rights, "as a common standard of achievement for all peoples and all nations, to the end that every individual and every organ of society, keeping this Declaration constantly in mind, shall strive by teaching and education to promote respect for these rights and freedoms".

In this new state of the world, Scouting was outlawed in the countries annexed to the Soviet Union, together with others in the socialist sphere of influence: Poland, Romania, Hungary and Bulgaria, and later on, North Korea, Czechoslovakia, China and Cuba. But the International Scout Movement continued to grow with new recognised associations, not only Federal Germany (recognised in 1950), but with many countries outside Europe, largely as a result of decolonisation. While in 1922, just nine of the 31 Scout associations were non-European, by 1955 only 18 of the 56 recognised associations were European.

6. The globalisation of Scouting

The founding of the United Nations organisation and subsequent Universal Declaration of Human Rights ushered in a new era for Scouting. The renewed strength of World Scouting after the Second World War coincided with these two international initiatives,

---

61. St George Saunders 1949: 246-47.

both of which were in line with the ideology that the Scout Movement had adopted when it was set up in 1920. The principle of equality between countries and their right to sovereignty as a prerequisite for peace, so important in the founding of World Scouting, had now reached new heights and paved the way for decolonisation. In 1949, the International Scout Conference passed the 27/49 resolution affirming: "We rededicate ourselves to the principles of liberty and the freedom of peoples and nations. We believe that the cause of peace and understanding can effectively be served by encouraging the spirit of world brotherhood amongst the youth of the world through Scouting."

This concept of World Scouting as a tool for constructing peace came to the forefront once again alongside the new world institutions, as indicated in another resolution (18/55) of 1955: "The Conference as the central world body of our Movement expresses the conviction that World Scouting in the existing general international atmosphere can play a most important part by preparing good citizens for tomorrow with all the right ideas of a constructive mutual understanding among all nations and towards lasting peace."

It was during the 1950s that the International Scout Conferences were held outside Europe for the first time (Canada, 1955; India, 1959; Mexico, 1967; and in girl Scouting/Guiding: Brazil, 1957; Japan, 1966), together with the jamborees held in Canada, in 1955, and the Philippines, in 1959. The headquarters of the Boy Scouts International Bureau were also moved from London to Ottawa, Canada, in 1958, and then finally to Geneva, Switzerland, in 1968. The International Bureau and Committee also became increasingly multicultural and multiracial during this period: the first Asian member of the International Scout Committee was elected in 1931, followed by the first Arabic member in 1951 and the first African in 1961.

Scouting also played a vital role in the processes of decolonising and nation building. The in-depth study of Timothy H. Parsons on the role of the Scout Movement in British colonial Africa reveals the two faces of the movement outside Europe: its early days (1910s) as a means of social control of the colony, introduced and managed by the colonial authorities, and its subsequent use by the colonised societies, first as a way to achieve greater equality, then as a form of social protest, and finally, as an instrument for national construction during decolonisation.[62] At the 1959 International Scout Conference in New Delhi, Pandit Nehru, the Indian Prime Minister and leader of the non-aligned countries, recognised the importance of Scouting and its excellent potential for Third World countries in his welcome address.

In the 1960s Scouting's mixed co-educational model began to take off in many countries that had until then separated boys and girls. In France, however, that was just one of the most important changes that were carried out. The social-democrat criticism that schools, instead of reproducing social systems, should work to transform society provoked radical changes to the education system and gave a boost to French Scouting, particularly to the laïque association. In this way, they began to incorporate a non-authoritarian educational approach, placing more importance on the group – the so-called social dynamic – instead of on the individual.

---

62. Parsons 2004: especially pp. 4-29, 61-71; also Nagy 1967: 29-30.

At the same time, the Catholic Scouts de France substituted a new "enterprise" approach to Scouting, in which the members of the troop work together towards a goal, instead of the previous patrol approach, in which a group of Scouts have individually assigned duties and roles. This allowed more informal and variable groups of Scouts to form. All of these changes influenced many other associations as well.

Although the Scout Movement spread across the world very early on, its operations and planning capacities were far from those needed by a world organisation. In 1965, the Ford Foundation commissioned the Graduate Institute of International Studies in Geneva to study the situation of the then male Scouting worldwide. The head of research at the Institute, Dr Laszlo Nagy, a Hungarian former Scout exiled in Switzerland, was chosen to prepare the report, which was published two years later as the "Report on World Scouting", presented in 1967. One of its conclusions was the suggestion that the "director" figure of the World Bureau be replaced by a "secretary general" with more executive powers. It was this position that the Boy Scouts International Bureau offered to the principal researcher of the study, Laszlo Nagy, making him its first secretary general in 1968.

The International Scout Conference held in Japan in 1971 approved the incorporation of community development into the Scout programme: in 1972, the first world seminar was held on this issue in Cotonou (now Benin) and 1973 saw the first world seminar on the environment, held in Sweden.

Around this time, new forms of Scouting that could be adapted to contexts such as that of rural Africa were also being explored. The term "international" was replaced with "world", and at the World Scout Conference of 1973 (Kenya), in the framework of wider constitutional reforms, the name "Boy Scouts International Bureau" was changed to the World Organization of the Scout Movement (WOSM). At the 1977 conference, the fundamental principles of the constitutional text were reworked. This was also the year of the death of Olave Baden-Powell, Chief Guide of the World and also keeper of Robert Baden-Powell's Scouting flame for the whole movement.

One of the most important changes in the Scout Movement as a whole in the 1960s was the tendency in several countries, particularly European, to the rapprochement of male and female Scout associations to practise co-education. As a result, some WOSM and WAGGGS member associations were gradually merged or joined to create new associations with dual membership – though associations continued to pay boy's and girl's fees to WOSM and WAGGGS, respectively. Notable changes to the WOSM constitution in 1977 included a new definition that did away with the words "boy" and "adolescent" and kept only "young people", on the pretext that the latter term included the other two, though it was a move that clearly opened the door to the progressive entry of girls in many countries.

Despite the vitality of the movement, membership in industrialised countries began to slump. However, the decline in membership in Europe and the United States was offset by a spectacular increase in membership in developing countries. In 1968, industrialised countries accounted for three quarters of the world membership, and over half of all members hailed from English-speaking countries. But by the mid-1970s, industrialised countries had become the minority and Asia alone accounted for half of the world Scout population. This naturally had repercussions for the content of educational programmes.

It was in this context of a steady growth in international prestige that UNESCO awarded WOSM the first Prize for Peace Education in 1981. The prize came after years of collaboration between World Scouting and United Nations agencies. World Scouting has been active in this since the UN was established, and both WOSM and WAGGGS have been members of the United Nations Economic and Social Council since it was created in 1947. The growing influence of these non-governmental organisations on issues on the international agenda such as civil rights, the environment, and peace and development co-operation, also afforded them greater political involvement in supra-state decisions on matters that nonetheless affected state policies. This meant that individuals who did not represent state governments – such as representatives of WOSM and WAGGGS – could take part in international debates. In 1972 (13 June), the *New York Times* reported that during the United Nations Conference on the Human Environment in Stockholm, a representative of WOSM, on behalf also of WAGGGS and nine other organisations, made an appeal to end "the deliberate destruction of the environment by warfare", and added that "the United States Government's disgraceful war of ecocide in Indochina and similar wars in other parts of the world should have been dealt with by this conference". The traditional non-political stance of the Scout Movement was being replaced by non-partisan political activism.

In 1989, the Berlin Wall fell and the Soviet Union and the communist regimes of its countries of influence quickly began to fall apart. The division of the world into two sides had suddenly disappeared. Scouting had been seen by communist countries as a capitalist tool "for deceiving, oppressing and exploiting young people", and had been outlawed and persecuted as a result.[63] The new situation in these countries after the prohibition was lifted led to an astonishing resurgence of Scouting, especially considering that it had been banned for 40 years; Scout associations were quickly set up in Russia, Czechoslovakia, Poland, Hungary, Yugoslavia (and the countries it was later divided into), Ukraine, Armenia, Albania, Estonia and Lithuania, all of which were swiftly given international recognition.[64] The resurgence of Scouting in eastern Europe came as a surprise and was the first time since WOSM had extended membership to girls that new possibilities for rapid territorial growth had been discovered. In just a few years, 23 new countries[65] joined World Scouting: either WOSM, WAGGGS, or both at the same time.

This process raised a certain rivalry between the two world organisations for the recognition and membership of the new associations. In this context, the gender issue lost importance and the pressure of the two world organisations – WOSM

---

63. Kroonenberg 1998: 65, 99-100.
64. The two detailed studies by the Dutch writer Piet Kroonenberg include countless details about the processes in all of these countries: See Kroonenberg 1998: 72, 101, 161-62, 236-38, 306-07, 354-58, 385-87, 389-414; Kroonenberg 2004: 25-28; 46-50; 72-77.
65. They were Albania, Armenia, Azerbaijan, Belarus, Bosnia and Herzegovina, Bulgaria, Croatia, Slovakia, Slovenia, Estonia, Georgia, Hungary, Latvia, Lithuania, North Macedonia, Moldova, Poland, Romania, Russia, Serbia and Montenegro, Republic of Tajikistan, the Czech Republic, and Ukraine.

and WAGGGS – to increase membership became a more pressing concern. In fact, the 1990s were marked by the strategic update of the two world organisations, as well as by the attempt to merge them by many European associations, mainly members of both organisations. As part of this process, it was agreed to have a joint Scout and Guide region in Europe, which was set up in 1995, with just one committee and one bureau. However, the initiative did not work and it broke down three years later.

In 1997, the cautious international public stance of the two world organisations gave way to a new formula more akin to advocacy: the alliance of the CEOs of four large youth organisations (WOSM, WAGGGS, YMCA and the YWCA) with the Red Cross (as a major humanitarian movement that focused on young people) and The Duke of Edinburgh's International Award Foundation (a worldwide youth programme). In 2000, the alliance was joined by the CEO of the International Youth Foundation, the largest international foundation aimed at young people. World Scouting used this alliance as a platform for articulating its position on long-term policies affecting the world. These stances were communicated as "declarations" by the top executives of the organisations that championed its causes, rather than through agreements reached at world conferences or by committees.

The first declaration made by this alliance (1997) was to raise awareness of non-formal education, a concept that had already been defined by UNESCO, and to ask governments to extend their educational policies beyond school; the second (1999), to request long-term national youth policies; the third (2001), to promote empowerment for girls in the 21st century; the fourth (2003), to promote an initiative for all of Africa to unite against HIV/AIDS, which has since been put into practice; and the fifth (2005), to encourage the participation of young people in decision-making processes.[66]

These declarations show the increasing awareness of the two organisations of World Scouting of social problems that affect all children and young people, one more step in the long process of updating and adaptation to the new realities of the movement. The commitment of World Scouting with the global citizenship challenges have led to several actions linked to either the Millennium Development Goals or, more recently, to the United Nations' 2030 Agenda and its Sustainable Development Goals (SDGs).

Adopted in 2015, the SDGs offer, for the first time, a universal framework that integrates sustainable development and global citizenship. This framework illustrates that at all levels, from local to global, development and sustainability are closely linked and require active global citizens with more complex competences to face the major challenges to come. Education becomes fundamental to making this paradigm shift possible; but as UNESCO states, this also requires "a shift from teaching to learning. It asks for an action-oriented, transformative pedagogy, which supports self-directed learning, participation and collaboration, problem-orientation, and the linking of formal, non-formal and informal learning". Which is precisely the educational approach of Scouting throughout all its history.

---

66. Alliance of Youth CEOs, 1997, 1999, 2001, 2003, 2005.

References

Alliance of Youth CEOs (1997), "The education of young people: a statement at the dawn of the 21st century", IAA, IFRCS, WAGGGS, WOSM, YMCA, YWCA.

— (1999), "National youth policies: towards an autonomous, supportive, responsible and committed youth", IAA, IFRCS, WAGGGS, WOSM, YMCA, YWCA.

— (2001), "Girls and young women in the 21st century: recommendations for action", IAA, IFRCS, IYF, WAGGGS, WOSM, YMCA, YWCA.

— (2003), "The empowering Africa's young people initiative: a holistic approach to countering the HICV/AIDS pandemic", IAA, IFRCS, IYF, WAGGGS, WOSM, YMCA, YWCA.

— (2005), "Children and young people: participating in decision-making. A call for action", IAA, IFRCS, IYF, WAGGGS, WOSM, YMCA, YWCA and UNICEF.

Baden-Powell, A. (1912), *How girls can help to build up the Empire*, Thomas Nelson, London.

Baden-Powell, R. S. S. ([1908] 2004), *Scouting for boys*, (ed.) Boehmer E., Oxford University Press, Oxford .

— (1909), *Yarns for Boy Scouts*, C. Arthur Pearson Ltd, London.

— (1912), *Girl Guiding: the official handbook*, C.Arthur Pearson Ltd, London.

— (1913), *Boy Scouts beyond the seas*, C. Arthur Pearson Ltd, London.

— ([1919] 1949), *Aids to Scoutmastership* (World Brotherhood edn), Herbert Jenkins Ltd, London.

— (1937), "Be prepared" (interview), *The Listener*, British Broadcasting Corporation (January 1937).

— (2006), *Citizens of the world: selected writings on international peace* (comp. and ed.) Sica M., Fiordaliso, Rome.

Balcells A. and Samper G. (1993), *L'escoltisme català (1911-1978)*, Barcanova, Barcelona.

Block N. and Proctor T. (eds) (2009), *Scouting frontiers: youth and Scout Movement's first century*, Cambridge Scholars Publishing, Cambridge.

Boehmer E. (2004), "Introduction", in Baden-Powell ([1908] 2004), pp. xi-xxxix.

Bulman-Lever L. (2010), *One billion girls: the lives of girls around the world*, Marylebone Publishing Ltd, London.

Cholvy G. (ed.) (2003), *Le Scoutisme: un mouvement d'éducation au xxe siècle. Dimensions internationals* [Scouting: an education movement in the 20th century. International dimensions]. Proceedings of the International Colloquium held at Paul-Valéry University, Montpellier III (21-23 September 2000), Paul-Valéry University, Montpellier.

Fauvel-Rouif Denise (ed.) (1992), *La jeunesse et ses mouvements: influence sur l'évolution des sociétés aux xixe et xxe siècles* [Youth and its movements: influence on the evolution of societies in the 19th and 20th centuries], Commission Internationale d'Histoire des Mouvements Sociaux et des Structures Sociaux, Éditions du CNRS, Paris.

Ihle H. E. (1993), *Hitler's Boy Scouts dictator-fighters (along the razor's edge)*, University Press of America, Lanham MD and London.

ISCED (2011), OECD, European Union, UNESCO Institute for Statistics (2015), ISCED 2011 *Operational Manual: Guidelines for Classifying National Education Programmes and Related Qualifications*, OECD Publishing. http://dx.doi.org/10.1787/9789264228368-en. Creative Commons Attribution CC BY-NC-ND 3.0 IGO.

Jeal T. (1989), *Baden-Powell, founder of the Boy Scouts*, Hutchinson, London.

— (2001), *Baden-Powell, founder of the Boy Scouts*, Yale University Press, New Haven CT.

Kerr R. (1932), *The story of the Girl Guides 1908-1932*, Girl Guides Association, London.

Kroonenberg P. J. (1998), *The undaunted: keeping the Scouting spirit alive: the survival and revival of Scouting in central and eastern Europe*, Oriole International Publications, Ginebra.

— (2004), "The undaunted II: keeping the Scouting spirit alive. the survival and revival of Scouting in eastern Europe and Southeast Asia", Las Vegas International Scouting Museum, Las Vegas NV.

Lewin H. S. (1947), "Hitler Youth and the Boy Scouts of America: a comparison of aims", *Human Relations* Vol. 1, No. 2, pp. 202-27.

MacDonald, R. H. (1993), *Sons of the Empire: The frontier and the Boy Scout Movement 1890-1918*, University of Toronto Press, Toronto.

Mills S. (2011), "Scouting for girls? Gender and the Scout Movement in Britain", *Gender, Place and Culture: A Journal of Feminist Geography* Vol. 18, No. 4, pp. 537-56.

Nagy L. (1967), "Report on World Scouting/Etude sur le Scoutisme Mondial" (cyclo-styled), Graduate Institute of International Studies/Institut Universitaire de Hautes Études Internationales, Geneva.

— (1985), *250 million Scouts*, Dartnell, London.

Nielsen H. B. (2003), *One of the boys? Doing gender in Scouting*, WOSM, Geneva, available at www.scout.org/sites/default/files/library_files/Doing%20Gender.pdf, accessed 1 August 2019.

Parsons T. H. (2004), *Race, resistance and the Boy Scout Movement in British colonial Africa*, Ohio University Press, Athens OH.

Reimers F. (2007), "Developing global citizenship: contemporary challenges and opportunities for the World Scout Movement", *World Scientific Congress: Education and Scout Movement*, World Scout Bureau, Geneva.

Reynolds E. E. (1942), *Baden-Powell: A biography of Lord Baden-Powell of Gilwell*, Oxford University Press, London.

— (1950), *The Scout Movement*, Oxford University Press, London.

Rosenthal M. (1986), *The character factory: Baden-Powell's Boy Scouts and the imperatives of Empire*, Pantheon Books, New York.

St George Saunders H. (1948), *The left handshake: the Boy Scout Movement during the War 1939-1945*, Collins, London.

UNESCO (2015), *Rethinking education: towards a global common good?* UNESCO, Paris.

Vallory E. (2009), "Status quo keeper or social change promoter? The double side of World Scouting's citizenship education", in Block N. and Proctor T. (eds) (2009), *Scouting frontiers: youth and Scout Movement's first century*, Cambridge Scholars Publishing, Cambridge.

— (2012), *World Scouting: educating for global citizenship*, Palgrave McMillan, New York NY.

Warren A. (1986), "Sir Robert Baden-Powell, the Scout Movement and citizen training in Great Britain, 1900-1920", *The English Historical Review* Vol. 101, No. 399 (April), pp. 376-98.

Wonesch M. (2000), "Montessori-Pädagogik und Pfadfindererziehung: Gemeinsame Aspekte zweier reformpädagogischer Erziehungsmodelle" ["Montessori Pedagogy and Scout Education: Common Aspects of Two Educational Models for Reformed Education"], *Montessori – Zeitschrift für Montessori-Pädagogik* Vol. 3, pp. 108-132.

Chapter 6

History of the Red Cross and Red Crescent Youth

Vesselina Valcheva Dimitrova

Introduction

From a dream of a young Swiss man, aged 31, who had witnessed the tragic results of a battle near the little Italian town of Solferino back in 1859, the International Red Cross and Red Crescent Movement has grown into the world's biggest humanitarian organisation, consisting of nearly 200 national societies. Sixty years after its foundation, in 1922, the League of the National Societies of the Red Cross and Red Crescent adopted a decision to create a youth structure that would involve children and young people in the activities of the movement. Currently, almost a century later, about a half of the 80 million IRCRC volunteers around the world are young people.

Considering these facts, it is worth saying that this particular international youth movement plays a significant role in the historical formation and current development of youth work both at local and international/European levels. On the one hand, each national community has its own specificities, operating in its unique (social/cultural/legal/economic) environment and addressing local issues to be solved, thereby determining its own mechanisms and tools to work with young people. On the other hand, through different international forums, projects and activities, an extensive exchange of ideas takes place, so methods and approaches for youth work between local communities "migrate" from one place to another and get adjusted to new environments.

This chapter explores briefly the history of the International Red Cross and Red Crescent Youth Movement, as well as examples and tools for the realisation of the youth policy of the International Federation of Red Cross and Red Crescent Societies (IFRC). Special attention is paid to the process of development of the main ideas included in the documents adopted as well as the ways for engaging youth in the IFRC youth policy-making process.

Chronology – An evolutionary narrative or a narrative evolution; the (hi)story of the organisation

Founding and a brief history of the International Red Cross and Red Crescent Movement

The Battle of Solferino on 24 June 1859 is of a great importance not only for Italian history, but also because it is referred to as the event which triggered the birth of the idea for the creation of the International Red Cross and Red Crescent Movement. Jean-Henry Dunant, a young Swiss man aged 31, on a business trip, just happened to be there and, on the days following the battle, he stayed to help the wounded soldiers. He was deeply touched by the consequences of the war – thousands of young men were suffering and dying without getting sufficient help, even for basic things, such as getting their bandages changed and being given drinking water. The local people in the towns around the battlefield had transformed every possible building into a hospital, even taking casualties into their homes. Many young girls and women spent their days and nights tending and nursing the wounded and the dying. However, the number of these voluntary aiders was far less than was needed, and their lack of skills and organisation impeded their effectiveness still further.

Such memories and thoughts stayed with Dunant for years later. Eventually he decided to take action and create an organisation that would stay neutral during war and provide care to wounded soldiers. In 1862, Dunant published his book, *A memory of Solferino*, at his own expense, in which he describes the devastating scenes he witnessed in Solferino, Castiliogne, Brescia and other towns in the region of Lombardy after the battle. At the end of the book, he introduces the idea that

> in time of peace and quiet, to form relief societies for the purpose of having care given to the wounded in wartime by zealous, devoted and thoroughly qualified volunteers. (Dunant 1862)

Dunant is then very active in circulating the book among many influential (political and military) figures throughout Europe. This led soon afterwards, on 17 February 1863, to the formation of the International Committee for Relief to the Wounded, currently known as the International Committee of the Red Cross (ICRC). The founding organisation convened a conference in October 1863 that adopted 10 resolutions which served as a basis for the creation of national committees (societies) for relief to wounded soldiers. Shortly afterwards, the first national societies were established, in Württemburg, the Grand Duchy of Oldenburg, Belgium and Prussia, followed by Denmark, France, Italy, Mecklenburg-Schwerin, Spain, Hamburg and Hesse (ICRC 2004).

In 1864, there was another official diplomatic conference resulting in the adoption of the First Geneva Convention "for the Amelioration of the Condition of the Wounded in Armies in the Field", signed by representatives of 12 countries. This is how modern international humanitarian law was born. Following a series of armed conflicts – the Austro-Prussian War of 1866, Franco-Prussian War in 1870, the Eastern crisis (1875-78), the Serbo-Bulgarian War (1885-86) and the Balkan Wars (1912-13) – the leading role of the ICRC in the promotion and development of international humanitarian law was strengthened (ICRC 2004). At the outbreak of the First World War, the committee already had a rich experience in intervention in war zones and expanded its work. Many national societies had their "finest hour" during this period undertaking "an unprecedented mobilisation that saw volunteers running ambulance services on the battlefield and caring for the wounded in hospitals" (ICRC 2016).

The period following the First World War was a time for taking stock and reflections – on the one hand the national societies had attracted millions of volunteers and built a large body of expertise (ICRC 2005), while on the other hand, many national societies felt that with the coming of peace and hopes for a new world order, the role of the Red Cross had to change (ICRC 2016). Henry Davison, the President of the American Red Cross War Committee, proposed the creation of a federation of the national societies, which would enable closer co-operation between them and would also focus more on activities during peacetime, specifically to "improve the health of people in countries that had suffered greatly during the four years of war" (ICRC 2005). As a result, in 1919 in Paris, the League of Red Cross Societies was founded by Britain, France, Italy, Japan and the United States. In 1991, it became the International Federation of Red Cross and Red Crescent Societies and through the years it has grown into a network of national societies around the globe.

Currently, the International Red Cross and Red Crescent Movement consists of three main components:

▶ **The International Committee of the Red Cross (ICRC)** – An independent, neutral organisation that provides humanitarian assistance and protection to victims of war and armed violence (IFRC 2007). Some of its main field of activity include visiting those deprived of their freedom in detention centres; the distribution of food and relief items in the areas affected by war or armed conflicts; supporting hospitals and health-care facilities; water, sanitation and construction projects; and enabling war-affected families to keep in touch and reunite.

▶ **The International Federation of Red Cross and Red Crescent Societies** – The world's largest humanitarian network that today reaches 150 million people through the work of over 17 million volunteers. Its main purpose is to co-ordinate and direct international assistance following natural and man-made disasters in non-conflict situations. Its relief operations are combined with development work, including disaster-preparedness programmes, health care and prevention activities, and the promotion of humanitarian values (IFRC 2007).

▶ **The National Red Cross and Red Crescent Societies** – Currently, there are 190 national societies. They support the public authorities in their own countries as independent auxiliaries to the government in the humanitarian field. Their local knowledge and expertise, access to communities and infrastructure enable the movement to get the right kind of help where it is needed, fast (IFRC 2007).

The role of youth in the movement

The idea of involving children and young people in the activities of the Red Cross had already been introduced twice in the early days of the movement, but without further realisation. The first time was in 1887, during the 4th International Conference of the Red Cross Societies. The Surgeon General of the Bavarian army, Dr Karl von Lotzbeck, suggested teaching the principles of the Geneva Convention in schools and propagating the values of the Red Cross among children and youth (Plourde 2017). Later on, at the 5th International Conference of the Red Cross Societies in 1892, the Ladies Committee in Moravia proposed the idea to educate children and youth about the principles of the organisation and in this way to awaken interest among them to become involved in its activities at a later age.

It was probably mainly due to the nature of the initial activities of the ICRC – intervention in times of war – that the idea of directly involving young people did not progress. Furthermore, the number of armed conflicts that took place at that time (the second half of the 19th century) did not leave much space and energy available for developing programmes for children and youth. There are, however, many examples of how school students at that time still supported, one way or another, the activities of the "adult" Red Cross. The very first documented case is from as early as 1870, in the Netherlands, when the inspectors of two districts in the Province of Zuid-Holland, together with members of the Red Cross, sent an appeal to school pupils to collect funds that would be directed to providing relief for the victims of the Franco-Prussian War. As a result, 1 200 florins was collected – a very great sum of money at the time (Ruiz 1964). Later, in 1885-86, during the Serbo-Bulgarian and the Balkan Wars (1912-13), many school students left their classes in order to go and help the wounded soldiers on the front (Bulgarian Red Cross Youth n.d.).

In the decades that followed, other temporary attempts to involve young people in Red Cross activities at local level took place, mainly by collecting funds (for example, the youth group "Samson Parlor" in California in 1898 and "The Maple Leaves" in Ontario, Canada in 1890 – see Plourde 2017) but also by performing other types of activities (for instance, in Sweden, about 300 schools co-operated with the Red Cross from 1909 to 1922 by making garments and bedclothes for the charitable activities of the national society – see Ruiz 1964). During the First World War, the number of prepared volunteers was far too small to meet the need for help caused by the war. For this reason, groups of children and students began joining the relief activities of the national societies in several European countries, Australia, Canada and the USA.

It was the founding of the League of the Red Cross Societies and the new focus of work actions to be undertaken during a time of peace that was the catalyst for the creation of the Junior Red Cross. Recognising the successful engagement of young people in activities of the organisation over previous decades, the General Council of the League passed Resolution XVIII in 1922. This resolution recommended:

> That every National Red Cross society should endeavour to organise the enrolment of schoolchildren as Junior Members, the conditions of Junior Members being adapted in each case to the school system of the country. (Ruiz 1964)

This was the formal birth of the Junior Red Cross, although by this time children and youth sections already existed in 21 countries (Ruiz 1964).

Several years after the official establishment of the Junior Red Cross, in 1930, its representatives attended for the first time the 14th International Conference of the Red Cross held in Brussels. At that time, the junior delegates presented school correspondence albums to the "adult" delegates asking them to pass them to the members of the Junior Red Cross sections back in their countries. Since then, the important role of the youth members of the movement was increasingly recognised. In 1946, the IFRC Youth Advisory Committee was established, its main purpose being to give guidance and expertise about decisions concerning RCRC youth programmes.

In terms of formalisation of the organisation's youth policy, the first document appeared in 1991, when the IFRC Youth Policy and Strategy was adopted by the

General Assembly. Eight years later, in 1999, this was revised and confirmed at the 12th session of the General Assembly. In 2011, the new IFRC Youth Policy was adopted by the General Assembly and revised in 2017.

Another important step in the history of the Red Cross Youth was in 2007, when the Youth Commission became a constitutional body. This set the age limit of its members up to 31 and its chair became a full member of the IFRC Governing Board.

In 2009, during the 3rd Red Cross Red Crescent World Youth Meeting in Solferino, Italy, the Youth Declaration was endorsed. This defined the new goals of youth development within the IFRC. Later on, in 2013, the IFRC General Assembly adopted another important document, the Youth Engagement Strategy (YES), which built further on the statements of the Solferino Youth Declaration 2009, IFRC Youth Policy 2011 and IFRC Strategy 2020.

Currently, all of the national societies have young people as members and volunteers and most of them develop youth activities. As stated on the official website of the IFRC, about half of the volunteers of the International Red Cross and Red Crescent Movement are now young people. However, the ways of including those young people in the work of the organisation (both concrete actions and governance structures) varies considerably. According to the Red Cross and Red Crescent Youth Engagement Study Report, from 2015 only 74 of the national societies have a formal youth policy, in contrast to the 97 national societies that do not have a strategic plan for engaging youth.

Critical moments in the evolution of the movement and their effects

A critical moment and a big challenge for the youth organisation happened during the state socialist period in some eastern European countries. At that time, due to the political situation in countries such as Bulgaria, the Youth section of the Red Cross was included in the only legally existing youth organisation in the country. Due to the efforts of the "adult" Red Cross organisation, however, in the early 1990s, the Bulgarian Red Cross Youth once more gained its independence and full control over the functions it wished to promote.

Following this way of working, however, there are still some national societies (such as Russia and Belarus), which develop youth activities, without specifically defining a distinct youth structure within the national society.

Contribution to thinking about youth work – Where it is done, who with and how

As an international organisation, the IFRC developed a youth policy aiming to match the various contexts, needs and specificities of all regions of the world. For this reason, youth activities and youth policy often included a wider scope than some national and regional youth policies. In the context of the IFRC Youth Policy, the definition of youth covers individuals aged from 5 to 30 years old. The age range here is more extended when compared with the official definition of the United Nations (15-24 years old) and that of the European institutions where youth is defined as between 13 and 30 years old – an age definition used both by the European Commission and the Council of Europe (Glossary on Youth). The IFRC does, however, define three subcategories within this wide range: children (5 to 11 years old), adolescents (12 to 17 years old) and young adults (18 to 30 years old) (IFRC 2011). Nonetheless, the IFRC also emphasises that national societies that adopt this strategy may develop their own definition, guided by the strategy but also taking into consideration local laws, social and cultural norms and contexts.

The IFRC in its Youth Strategy identifies three main roles for young people: as leaders, volunteers and beneficiaries. An interesting fact to consider is that in the very first text of the Youth Strategy (dating back to 1991) youth is first mentioned in terms of volunteering, then as a target group or "clients" of Red Cross activities, and only in third place is the leadership role of youth mentioned. In the newest text (the version reviewed in 2017), in contrast, the order is reversed: in first place is the role of youth as leaders, then as volunteers, and third as members of the affected communities needing Red Cross intervention. This change is a sign of the growing recognition of young people as initiators, leaders and actors, rather than beneficiaries and "clients" of IFRC programmes.

Another major change in the latest version of the Youth Strategy from 2017 is the introduction of the term "youth engagement", which refers to:

> youth-led action and youth development. It speaks to active and meaningful participation of youth and inclusion of their voice in the humanitarian work across governance, management, programmes, and service delivery. It also recognises three interconnecting and fluid pathways of engagement: youth as leaders, youth as volunteers, and youth as members of affected communities. As an approach, it goes beyond a symbolic inclusion and is practiced through equal partnership in both the intergenerational cooperation and peer contexts. (IFRC 2017)

So, following the ideas and definitions suggested by the strategy, the IFRC understanding of youth work lies mainly along the lines of youth leadership, which means youth work delivered by young people who are members of the organisation. Of course, many of the national societies do have paid youth workers, too, who in some cases are older than the "youth" threshold of 30 years old. These paid youth workers, at some point, might be beneficiaries of professional development, too: in the example of the Bulgarian Red Cross, there are usually one or two annual meetings of youth workers per year, which are mainly dedicated to discussions of current issues and an exchange of ideas and good practices between the local branches of the organisation all around the country. However, adult youth workers are seen more as supporters, rather than as resources to be developed, so following the ideas of the strategy, most of the training programmes and materials are aimed mainly at developing the potential of the youth leaders.

Besides the definitions of the roles of young people, the IFRC has also a vision of how to involve them in the organisation's activities. The IFRC has developed the so-called 3E Framework for engaging young people through activities, organised in the three main areas: Education, Empowerment and Enabling environment for young people. In that framework, education refers to universal access of individuals to knowledge, resources and training opportunities with and for youth, enabling them to acquire knowledge, skills and competences, and values for a healthy, safe and fulfilling life (IFRC 2013). Empowerment complements education by encouraging positive changes in personal behaviour and in supporting young people to be well informed and make healthier and safer choices that affect themselves and others. The third area – Enabling environment – mostly focuses on internal matters (such as organisational culture, policies, structures and mechanisms) that promote and support youth engagement, but also foster intergenerational dialogue and co-operation within the organisation. As a result, those three components should make smoother and easier the transition of young people between the roles of beneficiaries, through volunteers to leaders. The key components of the YES strategy (IFRC 2013) can be visualised as follows:

Figure 6.1

IFRC YOUTH ENGAG			
	Strategic directions and recommendations for:		
Youth as Leaders	Youth	Youth	Creating Enabling
Youth as Volunteers	Education	Empowerment	Environment
Youth as Beneficiaries			for Youth

Source: www.rcrc-resilience-southeastasia.org/wp-content/uploads/2016/08/IFRC-YESFramework.pdf

And last but not least, the newest text of the Youth Strategy from 2017 defines the different actors sharing the roles and responsibilities for the realisation of the activities of the strategy – the national societies, the IFRC secretariat, the IFRC Youth Commission, the Regional RCRC Youth Networks and young people themselves. It is interesting that the international youth networks, which have existed for quite some time (the European Youth Red Cross and Red Crescent network for instance has existed since 1975) and have only recently finally been recognised for their important role in the realisation of the organisation's youth policy. Initially, those networks were created to foster co-operation between young people from different national societies. The networks are usually based on geographical regions (for example, the European Youth Network, Asia and Pacific Youth Network, Southern European Youth Network) or on a specific topic (such as first aid, international humanitarian law promotion or HIV/AIDS prevention). Besides their specific purpose, however, they can be a very powerful tool for empowering young people, involving them in the activities of the organisation and providing platforms for mutual support and co-operation between the youth leaders from different national societies.

One more tool for the realisation of the IFRC Youth Policy is the "Youth on the move" award. It was launched in 2005 and since then, every two years, the IFRC awards those national societies' youth sectors that are developing projects and activities responding to the needs of those who need the Red Cross and Red Crescent most. There are usually four categories of the award, defined in line with the strategic documents (IFRC Youth Policy and IFRC Strategy) and with specifically defined topics that are set every year.

Connection or disconnection to wider youth work structures and debates

Before exploring the extent to which the Red Cross organisation gets involved in wider structures and debates on youth work, it is useful to step back and be reminded of the inner rules of the movement. After almost a century of experience, debates and analysis, participants at the 20th International Conference of the Red Cross, which took place in Vienna in 1965, voted for and proclaimed its seven Fundamental Principles: Humanity, Impartiality, Neutrality, Independence, Voluntary Service, Unity and Universality. These principles bind together the National Red Cross and Red Crescent Societies, the International Committee of the Red Cross and the International Federation of Red Cross and Red Crescent Societies, and guarantee the continuity of the movement and its humanitarian work (ICRC 1979). According to the principle of Neutrality, the movement may not engage at any time in controversies of a political, racial, religious or ideological nature (ICRC 1979). Furthermore,

> If a National Society branch expresses sympathy for a movement, a cause or a political figure, for example by permitting the latter to take advantage of Red Cross or Red Crescent membership for electoral purposes, many volunteers may cancel their membership. (ICRC 1996)

The second principle to be considered here is Independence:

> The Red Cross is independent. The National Societies, while auxiliaries in the humanitarian services of their Governments and subject to the laws of their respective countries, must always maintain their autonomy so that they may be able at all times to act in accordance with Red Cross principles. (ICRC 1979)

Guided by this principle, the organisation at all levels (local, national and international) has to be very careful when getting involved in the activities of other organisations, or when expressing opinion on a policy or statement. Its position generally is to abstain from taking any explicit side in controversial debates. As a large organisation with a long history, deep experience in different fields and a strong network throughout the world, it is still possible to provide expertise on some questions, and thus influence decision makers and opinion leaders to act in the interests of vulnerable people. For instance, the IFRC has a Delegation to the United Nations, having the status of permanent observer, while the EU Red Cross office is an observer member of the European Youth Forum. At a national level, in Bulgaria for example, the National Youth Law defines a special structure – the National Committee on Youth Matters – which has seats for representatives from all the nationally represented youth organisations, including the Bulgarian Red Cross Youth. Considering these examples, one can conclude that the international movement is included in bigger structures on youth policy and other youth-related discussions in ways that its inner principles allow – having observer status and providing expertise.

When it comes to youth work practice, however, the activities within the movement are much more vivid and intensive. Being the world's biggest humanitarian organisation, and having over 50% of its volunteers classified as young people – indeed, in some national societies the share of young volunteers is up to 80% (IFRC 2015a)

– there is a huge resource and experience of youth work practice, a vast array of tools and examples of ways of delivering youth work.

For the purpose of this research, two examples will be explored, illustrating the connection between the activities of the IFRC and current trends in youth work development in Europe. The first example concerns the very successful use of digital technologies for reaching young people. In 2017, the IFRC's Global Innovation Team launched a massive multiplayer online game called WhatFutures, which was entirely WhatsApp based. The game consists of a series of challenges which participants should solve working in small teams. There is also a competition between those teams for the best solution suggested. The main idea of the team behind the game was to gather the visions and ideas of young people about the new IFRC 2030 Strategy. For the two rounds in 2017, about 3 000 youth volunteers from 120 countries signed up for the game. This project is a great example of using digital technologies for delivering youth work and a very creative way to involve young people in the strategy-creation processes. WhatFutures even got nominated for the Digital Communications Awards 2017 as an innovative internal communications model (WhatFutures official website).

The second example is connected with addressing current "hot" topics in youth work, such as the prevention of violent youth radicalisation. Since the very beginning of the organisation's existence, one of the key topics addressed has been the promotion of the principles and values of the Red Cross. This includes educational activities on international humanitarian law, explaining and promoting the Fundamental Principles and advocating the rights of and respect for vulnerable people. There are many resources developed at national, regional and international levels that can be used in different settings, not only within the organisation. The IFRC vision on humanitarian education is that

> by 2020 all youth will have access to Humanitarian Education through formal education systems by including it in school curricula, and/or non-formal educational settings focusing on the age group from 5-11 years. (IFRC 2019)

Combining forces and developing common projects with other organisations and structures that are also working in this field might be of value for all sides involved.

Conclusion

The International Red Cross and Red Crescent Movement has come a long way in its development as an organisation in itself, but also in terms of creating its own vision in relation to young people. As stated on the official website of the Federation, young people have multiple roles including being

> innovators, early adopters of communication, social media, and other technologies, inter-cultural ambassadors, peer-to-peer facilitators, community mobilisers, agents of behaviour change, and advocates for vulnerable people. (IFRC 2011)

Based on these principles the movement, on all of its levels (national, regional and international) is taking action to educate, empower and motivate young people to have their say in the strategic decisions of the organisation and get actively involved in creating our common future, in line with the IFRC Strategy 2020 motto: Saving lives, changing minds

References

Bulgarian Red Cross Youth (n.d.), "Mission/Vision/Structure", available at https://en.redcross.bg/activities/activities10, accessed 26 November 2019.

Dunant H. (1862), *A memory of Solferino*, English version, American Red Cross (1939, 1959), reprinted by the International Committee of the Red Cross by courtesy of the American Red Cross, Geneva.

ICRC (1864), Convention for the Amelioration of the Condition of the Wounded in Armies in the Field, Geneva, 22 August 1864, available at https://ihl-databases.icrc.org/ihl/INTRO/120, accessed 26 November 2019.

ICRC (1979), "The Fundamental Principles of the Red Cross: commentary", available at www.icrc.org/en/doc/resources/documents/misc/fundamental-principles-commentary-010179.htm, accessed 2 August 2019.

ICRC (1996), "The Fundamental Principles of the Red Cross and Red Crescent", ref. 0513, available at www.icrc.org/en/doc/assets/files/other/icrc_002_0513.pdf, accessed 2 August 2019.

ICRC (1998), "Henry Dunant (1828-1910)", available at: www.icrc.org/fr/doc/resources/documents/misc/5fzf29.htm, accessed 2 August 2019.

ICRC (2004), "From the battle of Solferino to the eve of the First World War", available at www.icrc.org/eng/resources/, accessed 26 November 2019.

ICRC (2005), "Founding of the International Federation of Red Cross & Red Crescent Societies", available at www.icrc.org/en/doc/resources/documents/misc/68ujd6.htm, accessed 26 November 2019.

ICRC (2016), "History of the ICRC", available at www.icrc.org/en/document/history-icrc, accessed 2 August 2019.

IFRC (1991), "Youth Policy and Strategy", available at www.cruzroja.es/pls/portal30/url/ITEM/1FAEFF6FC0BD32A3E0440003BA5D2517

IFRC (2007), "The International Red Cross and Red Crescent Movement at a glance", available at www.ifrc.org/Global/Publications/general/at_a_glance-en.pdf, accessed 2 August 2019.

IFRC (2009), Solferino Youth Declaration, available at www.ifrc.org/Global/Publications/youth/170700-Youth_declaration-EN.pdf, accessed 2 August 2019.

IFRC (2011), Youth Policy, available at www.ifrc.org/Global/Governance/Policies/youth-policy-en.pdf, accessed 2 August 2019.

IFRC (2013), "Y.E.S. Youth Engagement Strategy", International Federation of Red Cross and Red Crescent Societies, Geneva.

IFRC (2015a), "Global review on volunteering report", available at www.ifrc.org/Global/Publications/volunteers/1301100-Global-Review-on-Volunteering-Report_EN.pdf, accessed 2 August 2019.

IFRC (2015b), "Red Cross and Red Crescent Youth Engagement Study Report", available at https://ifrcgo.org/africa/docs/YOUTH/2015%20Youth%20Engagement%20Study%20Report_Infographics_FIN.pdf, accessed 26 November 2019.

IFRC (2017), "Youth Policy", International Federation of Red Cross and Red Crescent Societies, Geneva.

IFRC (2019), "What is humanitarian education?", available at www.ifrc.org/en/get-involved/learning-education-training/humanitarian-education/what-is-humanitarian-education/, accessed 2 August 2019.

Plourde A.-A., (2017), "Rome, 1892: The beginnings of the Red Cross Youth Movement", in Klose F., Palen M., Paulmann J. and Thompson A. (eds), *Online atlas on the history of humanitarianism and human rights*, available at http://wiki.ieg-mainz.de/ghra/articles/plourde-rome, accessed 2 August 2019.

Ruiz J. Gomez (1964), "How the Junior Red Cross was born", *International Review of the Red Cross* Vol. 46, No. 543, Geneva, pp. 147-51.

Chapter 7

International Young Naturefriends

Petre Mrkev

Introduction

When the first Naturefriends founded their organisation in Vienna in 1895, they described their aims as follows: to stand beside the bourgeois alpine clubs and by asking low membership fees, give the opportunity to working-people to practice mountaineering. (Renner 1946)

The language of Karl Renner shows that the "Naturfreunde" already understood themselves as part of the emerging working-class movement. The founders of the "Touristenverrein der Naturfreunde" wanted to give working-class people the opportunity to enjoy the outdoor life as a way to escape from their unhealthy living and working conditions. Gaining access to untransformed nature was crucial to this undertaking. As a result, the rallying call of Naturefriends, still used today, became "Berg Frei" (Mountains free). It represents the first claim of the Naturefriends: equal access to nature for everyone, not only for the wealthy and privileged.

> We want to pull the working-class-people out of the places of alcohol, gambling and playing cards. We want to get them out of their small houses, the smoke of the factories and the pubs, to lead them into the wonderful nature, to let them discover beauty and happiness. (K. Volkert, General Assembly of Friends of Nature Austria, Vienna, 1925)

The organisation's activities were aimed not only at getting their members to beautiful natural settings, but also at awakening their love for nature and offering them opportunities for educating themselves. From the beginning, "outdoor sports" were a core business of the Naturefriends. Even more, outdoor sports for them were tools of education, in addition to being fun and a healthy means of spending leisure time. From the beginning, Naturefriends wanted to spend time in nature in a specific way, their way.

At a time when working-class people had to work up to 10 hours a day, six days a week and without paid holidays, gathering people together in local groups and offering them "sports and culture" in their leisure time was something new. From the beginning, they also started building shelters, the "Naturfreunde Häuser" (Naturefriends houses), as an alternative to the inaccessible, elitist and expensive mountain huts run by the alpine clubs. Building their own huts was a social activity, promoting and putting into practice solidarity (all the work was done by volunteers), and at the same time a political statement.

The shelters were a concrete expression of their slogan: "Berg Frei!", often being used as an alternative to "Berg Heil!" (Mountains be greeted!) – common within the bourgeois clubs.

1970s and beyond: a difficult road towards independent youth work

The activities involving young people seemed to be an integral part of the work of Naturefriends' adult organisations in the period after the Second World War. But besides a few examples of national member organisations, there was still no official and – more importantly – independent organisation of young Naturefriends on an international scale. This was because of the different interests and understanding of Naturefriends' work. However, the efforts and attempts to secure clear independence for youth became more and more explicit and visible, not only in particular national groups, but also on an international level. For example, the adult sections were more concerned with the work and management of the Naturefriends' houses, while different youth groups focused more on cultural and political work instead. Therefore, as a natural consequence, in 1974, the national youth segments agreed on the necessity for an international youth organisation (NFJI or in English Internatonal Youth Nature Friends (IYNF)).

As an initial decision for the creation of an independent, international youth segment of the Naturefriends, a landmark moment was the establishment of a working group in March 1974, led by Jochen Zimmer, who was already active as the first International Youth Secretary of Naturfreunde Internationale. Within a few months, this working group had proposed the structure of the NFJI and the majority of Naturfreunde Internationale (NFI) member organisations had agreed to it. But, the executive board of the NFI opposed the draft directive for the establishment of the Naturfreundejugend Internationale (NFJI), due to disputes over the independence of the NFJI and over the acknowledgement of "democratic socialism" in the directive's preamble. These disputes continued for more than a year, between the strong position of the NFI board and growing support for the idea of an "independent" youth organisation. Supporters of the idea included Werner Schneider (the President of NFI) and Hans Welti (the Secretary General of NFI).

Finally, a consensus proposal was approved by the congress and NFJI became an independent part of the NFI, though subject to its statutes. NFI provided a financing guarantee but in turn also had the authority to revise NFJI finances. The seat of the NFJI was supposed to be the same as the seat of NFI, which at that point was Stuttgart, for a variety of reasons. Common internal regulations were supposed to deal with the relations between the NFJI presidium and secretariat on the one side and the executive board of NFI on the other. The first official presidium of NFJI was composed of Wim Bergans, Walter Gscheider and Rudi Bergmann and they met for their first session in the interim office in Stuttgart, Germany, in late July 1975.

During its first years of existence, NFJI was still part of IUSY (International Union of Socialist Youth) and IFM-SEI (International Falcon Movement-Socialist Educational International), organising its main activities within these umbrella organisations.

In addition, NFJI was a member of the Kinder Internationale – the only pan-European youth co-operation with the Soviet Union, mainly organising international children's camps. As was noted at the time:

> Being a Naturefriend means being a fighter for a better humanity, means to break with the traditions, means to give life new significance. Being a Naturefriend means to be a pioneer for the socialist society. For this, the old are mostly not capable, and the young generation has to be educated in this spirit. That is why the youth has to wander with us. (Heinz Hoffman, Jochen Zimmer, 1986)

At the beginning, the basic principles of the NFJI were driven by the political standpoint and the pedagogic concepts of Naturefriends' youth work in Austria. The central question was: "The NFJI is a socialist, cultural and sports organisation – What does socialist mean in this context?"

"Social hiking" was a term used to describe the Naturefriends' interrelated understanding of body and mind:

> Hiking and hiking are two different terms. It depends whether it is an end in itself, as is the case with most bourgeoisie clubs, or a means to an end. The latter is the case with the Naturefriends: via hiking, they not only want to raise thinking youths, but also give content to the monotonous life of the proletariat. Brisk hiking in the spirit of the NF creates free people, thinking proletarians, a bodily healthy and spiritually active proletariat. (Heinz Hoffman, Jochen Zimmer, 1986)

For Naturefriends hiking meant all of the following:

▶ to experience homeland, nature, and people in their social context;

▶ to see people work, see their sorrows and distress, and their striving for a better life;

▶ to realise the unfair distribution of wealth, realise how a handful of parasites sit in the world's most beautiful places while millions have to live in their shadows.

In that sense, social hiking was considered to be very different from group hiking. It rather meant hiking in a spirit of discovery, critically observing society, economy and nature, always focusing on the human as the centre of these observations.

The NFJI activities were clearly "red" (deriving from the socialist roots of the organisation). Over the years, they slowly moved to become more "pink" (with its primary focus and value-added activities not operating on a political level). As an example of this evolution, in 1989, in Western Berlin, IYNF had a seminar on songs of protest as a tool for political work, while the other activities were related to anti-racism, peace and political education, with a clear political positioning in the socialist field. The 1990s, in contrast, were marked by an end of the old left–right paradigm. The "grave" topics of workers' education, political emancipation and the ideological roots of the NF movement made way for an organisation focused more on recreational activities. Learning from international exchanges and discussing topics like racism, poverty and environmental catastrophes remained, however, a key element of NF work. Yet, a more loose and fun working approach pushed more fierce ideological discussions into the background.

Travelling journeymen were the best propagandists as well as organisers in the early years of the organisation. Skilled and trained craftsmen, as well as apprentices, founded and dominated the early NF youth groups. The spirit of self-help and its fruits (such as the NF houses), the idea of soft tourism and an alternative approach to sports attracted more and more politically motivated and nature-romantic young people to the organisation.

Conflict between generations

Controversies and discussions about the relationship between adults and youth were always present in the history of the NF movement. The strong positions held in the early years of the 20th century meant that some older members argued from their Marxist perspective that the youth should line up at the front with the workers and fight together with the adults for the liberation of the working class. By the end of the century such strong positions were radically reformulated to the point that the main goal for youth structures was perceived to be the maintenance of existing and the establishment of new NF houses, as the crucial point for regular gatherings of old and young Naturefriends. On the other side, however, most young NFs argued more and more forcefully for their need for independence in order to win more supporters among young people by addressing specific "youth" topics and cultural issues. In that sense, IYNF saw itself being engaged more with the emotional issues of youth, in contrast to the adults who were more focused on the practical contribution young people could make.

This fault line in the relationship between NFI and IYNF has remained complicated, particularly during the transition from a youth member to an adult member – from IYNF to NFI. It has been an issue not only because of the different focus, but also especially because of the different work ethic and different issues addressed. Over the years, it happened that the young NF turning into adults increasingly took over the role of youth leaders, still demanding the prioritising of youth issues globally and taking these on board in the work of adults.

Mutual respect and co-operation has been enabled more formally, and also in practice, with the provision that NFI representatives attend the IYNF general assemblies, but especially through the provision that there is an IYNF representative on the board of NFI. Furthermore, over time, the IYNF delegation attending the general assemblies of NFI (with the right to vote) has grown from three to 10 youth delegates.

Emancipatory theory of youth work

According to the NF ideology, the tasks of youth work are:

▶ To show, analyse and explain the everyday environment to young people so that relationships and the backgrounds of industrial society become more visible. The proposed methods for doing this are: alienation,[67] learning with contradictions, working with models.

---

67. As a youth work method, this is best thought of in terms of isolation in nature, in order to re-establish the ability to think about what determines life, think about how to define relationships with other people, and regain a sense of being directors of their own actions.

- ▶ Young people have to be taken out of a self-destructive world controlled by adults and be enabled to experience their own existence. The proposed methods for achieving this are: seminars, plays, lectures, theatre, role play, songs and dance.
- ▶ To help young people to get along in industrial living conditions and enhance their tools and knowledge to live a life worth living, and make them realise that the world they live in can be changed. The proposed methodology is teaching them about manipulation techniques of the mainstream media.

One example of such activities, at the beginning of the 1960s, concerned the anti-nuclear energy and nuclear weapon movement. It aimed to make clear that both Western and Eastern nuclear weapons are a threat to the whole world population. Another example is related to environmental protection and natural education, which arises out of social hiking. The protection argument stems from the fact that most lands were privately owned, and hence private persons could decide what happens with that piece of nature. Therefore, not only is the protection of leisure and recreational areas (like lake beaches, for example) important, but it is also important to understand the economic and political reasons for private land use and land destruction. Furthermore, the issue also raises a debate about the relationship between natural exploitation and destruction and capitalist profit interests.

Enlargement of the network

The first enlargement of IYNF soon after its establishment as a separate entity was towards the Nordic countries. The pure socialist policy, merged with nature-linked activities, proved to be readily attractive for the youth structures in this region, which were often dealing with similar issues and working in a similar environment. However, arguably the most important development in terms of the enlargement of the network was with affiliated organisations from central and eastern Europe during the early 1990s. IYNF declared itself as one of the first international youth NGOs that opened itself transparently to this region. Banners declaring "East meets West" were carried around the streets of Gödöllö (Hungary) during an international camp, the first real activity held behind the former Iron Curtain. Although traditionally associated with the socialist movement, IYNF did not promote a political ideology, despite being committed to social and ecological issues. Having such an approach made it easier to get in touch with the newly emerging organisations in central and eastern Europe which were hesitant about being associated with socialist, liberal or Christian democratic organisations. IYNF was open, and therefore a suitable partner for new-born organisations, as well as for all those young people who could finally travel across borders and meet their peers in "the West". A new category of member organisations was created (affiliate members) and more stable relationships with Hungary, Czechoslovakia and Poland were soon developed.

No less important was enlargement towards Russia. Once again, IYNF was among the first international youth NGOs to expand its network in that direction. The Union of Young Naturefriends emerged in 1991 on the basis of the Nature Protection Group of the Geographical Department in the State University of Moscow. It was named after its founder Mikhail Lomonosov and its students and young faculty members became permanent members of seminars, workshops and other international activities within IYNF. Furthermore, in the spring of 1993 the Union of Young Naturefriends became officially registered as the Russian national branch of the IYNF. It was successfully followed by the first IYNF activity in Russia named "Bloody foreigners, Friendly visitors", organised in Krasnovidevo, Russia in May 1994. Its main topic was tackling the issue of soft tourism – how can regions (such as the Russian countryside, which is still not affected by mass tourism) develop ecologically and implement socially sustainable tourism?

Challenging moments

Only several years after its official birth, one of the most profound changes in the history of IYNF took place, leading to a *de facto* rebirth of the organisation. A seminar about soft tourism in the European Youth Centre in Strasbourg (December 1984), attended by 25 international participants, constituted the tip of the iceberg: no member of the presidium showed up to lead the event. As a consequence, the participants created and organised the seminar on their own and, critically, they brainstormed ideas for a new and better IYNF. In 1986 in Valkenburg in the Netherlands, a new presidium was elected entirely by the participants of the famous seminar in 1984, with Geert Ates as its president.

The newly elected IYNF presidium was immediately faced with several difficult situations:

▶ contacts were broken;

▶ no enthusiastic participation in the IYNF activities, and also in its partners' activities;

▶ public relations work near zero;

▶ almost no co-operation/co-ordination with member organisations;

▶ financial problems;

▶ former presidium/secretariat did not hand over the work in an acceptable form.

The need for radical reforms was urgent. One of the most crucial was that, as well as German, English became an official language. Furthermore, new posters, pamphlets, reports and IYNF self-portraits were produced not only in English and German but also in French, Italian, Spanish, Dutch, Russian, Turkish, Maltese and even Korean. This helped in moving from a German-speaking dominated organisation to a truly international one, as it seemed to be the only way to co-operate with the new affiliated countries like Malta, Portugal, Poland, Hungary, Czechoslovakia and Russia.

In the spirit of the holistic concept of sustainability, the presidium held the new position that IYNF was neither a purely environmental, nor a purely social organisation, but instead deals with the whole. In line with this, the different orientations of member organisations and different working realities were a valuable asset instead of a problem and prevented the network from going in one or other direction. Still, the new diversity had to be defined better in order to cope properly with the general themes and character as well as the purpose of the activities. In addition, this forthcoming diversity needed to be better analysed and accepted, in order to plan adequately the new themes and character of the future activities.

Showing IYNF's work to a wider audience was one of the new goals. As the new board members all agreed, a bit more pride would maybe help in that matter. While on the one hand IYNF should make efforts to lobby better at EU level, on the other hand the grass-roots work of activities for learning and working with young people in Europe has remained the fundamental, educational basis of the organisation. Therefore, an appropriate balance has had to be achieved, as too much focus on the political representation could take energy away from the main work.

In such a working environment, the main challenge for IYNF at the end of 20th century was how best to combine environmental and social issues. Such a combined approach distinguishes IYNF from the other purely environmental or purely social youth organisations. Yet it can also make presenting the organisation problematic. Furthermore, it was important to avoid spreading its priorities so thinly that it might be unable to make a significant impact in any field. For that particular reason, it was felt that IYNF activities needed to be put in the context of longer-term campaigns, the topics of which could be given a special emphasis during that period but without excluding the opportunity to work on and organise activities relating to other themes as well.

Such trends were maintained into the new millennium, which started with new challenges and opportunities for IYNF's development. One of the important decisions was to move its office from Brussels to Prague. Besides the financial pressures, the IYNF leadership also wanted to move closer to its new member organisations from central Europe. Slowly leaving its socialist roots and placing itself in a more neutral political position, the organisation has created advantages in attracting new organisations, but at the same time it created an empty space for some of its members, because a clear ideology was somehow lost. The way out was found in the famous campaign, Gotcha! – Attractive Youth Work, developed by the new Czech leadership and organised from 2003 to 2005. It had a tremendous effect on the future of IYNF, giving it the necessary environment and atmosphere to bring its member organisations and its leadership together. The major outcome was a new profile of the organisation which selected the best of the IYNF history and applied it in order to transform the organisation into a powerful new movement.

In 2010, IYNF started with the implementation of the model of Topic of the Year. The initial topic was linked to the Get Green Campaigning, later moving to the Year of Volunteering, Sustainability, Action for Change and Outdoors, respectively, in the following years. The pinnacle of outreach regarding the participation of member organisations in annual activities, co-operation with the adult organisation, organising most of its events in Naturefriends houses and finally producing publicity and promotion of its work was achieved in 2015, which was a year when the network was celebrating 40 years of Connecting and Inspiring.

Conclusions

The existence of IYNF has been threatened several times due to financial problems and accusations that young people would not be active enough and provide no added value. Over the years, its leadership has made a lot of effort to strengthen its membership – besides the fact that some member organisations have become inactive or have disappeared completely, the network has opened up to other countries, introducing the model of partner organisations, as a first step towards future full membership. Such modality brought advantages in attracting new organisations in central Europe, south-east Europe as well as in eastern Europe and the Caucasus, but conveyed a less clear ideology with which members had previously identified. The IYNF office has travelled through many countries, including Germany, the Netherlands (the IYNF archive is still in Amsterdam) and Belgium, and in 2002 it settled in Prague in the Czech Republic, where it is today.

IYNF has slowly moved away from its socialist roots to a more neutral political position, which has translated into certain values such as solidarity, friendship, democracy, learning from nature, training of body and mind, and self-help.

The political involvement of IYNF nowadays is much less than it was in earlier times and the network is no longer interested in starting active campaigns on environmental topics. It seemed to be too hard, despite its roots, to come to a shared agreement among all of its member organisations. They would rather leave such campaigning to other organisations, such as Greenpeace. Nevertheless, they do have an opinion, and when needed or when they feel the need, they always express it.

Naturefriends organisations are not very well known for their innovation and quick adjustments to changing surroundings, which is often needed in order to survive as an organisation. However, IYNF has developed its own models and mechanisms to identify new challenges and opportunities, which has resulted in better visibility of the organisation, increased and diverse financial resources and concrete and sustainable results. One of the major successes is that NFI is showing much greater interest in these positive experiences and is willing t5 adopt them in their work. There has never been such an interest and recognition of IYNF work and achievements as during the last two NFI congresses. Growing from an umbrella organisation to a network structure, IYNF has managed to change and adapt to new times, needs and surroundings. This is reflected in the high interest of participants in the activities on offer, the extremely large number of visits to the new online communication channels, which are now regularly used to engage with their target groups, and, finally, in the priceless efforts of the many volunteers who still believe in the organisation and its values.

References

Menkenhagen M. (2016a), 1895-1933: The origins of the Naturefriends movement, IYNF Archive: www.iynf.org/2016/09/1895-1933-origins-naturefriends-movement/.

Menkenhagen M. (2016b), 1933-1945: The break-up of the Naturefriends in Europe, IYNF Archive.

Menkenhagen M. (2016c), 1950-1975: An era for Naturefriends Internationalism, IYNF Archive.

Rener K. (1946), *An der Werde Zweier Zeiter* [At the turning point of the centuries], Vienna.

Zimmer J. (1993), Small international timeline of the Young Naturefriends movement since 1943, Archive of the Arbeiterjugendbewegung Oer Erkenschwick, Germany.

Chapter 8

The Duke of Edinburgh's International Award

Amy Pearce and Melek De-Wint

Introduction

The Duke of Edinburgh's International Award (the Award) is a framework for young people aged 14 to 24 that encourages learning and self-development outside the classroom. It supports the development of confidence, resilience, determination, creativity and adaptability, intercultural and civic competence, personal and social well-being, the acquisition of leadership skills, and communication and problem-solving skills.

The Award was founded in the UK in 1956 by Prince Philip, The Duke of Edinburgh, along with Kurt Hahn, a German educationalist, and Lord Hunt, leader of the first successful ascent of Mount Everest. It was developed as a response to growing concern in the UK about the development of boys, due to the gap between leaving school at 15 and entering National Service at 18. It became available to girls and in other countries soon afterwards, and today the Award is present in over 130 countries and territories, with over 1.3 million participants taking part annually. The basic principles and the framework of the Award have remained the same, but the modes of delivery continue to evolve and adapt, to ensure quality and consistency in delivery, and to suit the demands of different cultural contexts and the varying needs and interests of young people around the world.

The Award is a non-formal education programme, with the aim to equip young people with skills for life and, in Kurt Hahn's words, show young people that "there is more in you than you think". It can be used as a youth development or enhancement framework by organisations working with young people such as schools, universities, workplaces, uniformed organisations, social clubs, young offenders' institutions, religious organisations and other civic organisations. Each young person taking part participates in activities of their own choice in volunteering, physical exercise and skills development. There is also an outdoor education component (the "Expedition" or "Adventurous Journey") which provides opportunities to develop teamwork skills.

The Award is internationally accredited; when participants complete the requirements of their Award programme they receive an Award certificate which is recognised in many parts of the world. In this way, the Award offers an internationally consistent way to recognise and celebrate young people's learning, development and achievement through their activities outside the classroom.

The Duke of Edinburgh's International Award Foundation (the Foundation), a charity registered in the UK, drives and supports the Award's global delivery and growth through a social franchising business model. Working through a network of licensed Award Operators, the Foundation supports national organisations in delivering the Award in their countries, ensures consistency and quality in delivery globally, and works to increase global awareness of the value of non-formal education.

This chapter outlines the framework of the Award, how it has developed over time, how it is governed and managed by the Foundation and Award Operators, and how the social franchising model and its tools support its growth worldwide. Detail is provided on the digital platforms the Award uses and two case studies are presented to contextualise how the licensing model works for a new National Award Operator, and how National Award Operators use the Award to address and improve local, social issues.

The history of the Award

After the Second World War there was a growing concern in the UK about the development of boys, due to the gap between leaving school at 15 and entering National Service at 18. Seeing that young people's development was lacking in certain key areas, Kurt Hahn, founder and headmaster of Gordonstoun School in Scotland, began developing a scheme for boys of this age. With a solution to this social question in mind, Hahn assembled a select group of individuals with relevant expertise and influence to launch the scheme on a national level. As chairman of the "Originating Committee", formed in 1954, Prince Philip used his personal enthusiasm for the scheme and his significant influence to ensure that the scheme was put into practice, developed and sustained. Meanwhile, John Hunt quit his successful army career to act as the first Secretary of the Award, establishing it as a charitable trust and leading its development in the initial years, until 1967 (Peyton-Jones 1991). Based on Hahn's philosophies, the Award was designed around four sections and launched in 1956.

The Award framework

The foundations of the Award's framework were built on Hahn's "Six Declines of Modern Youth" (Stremba and Bisson 2009). These were:

- **Decline of fitness** due to modern methods of locomotion.
- **Decline of initiative and enterprise** due to the widespread disease of spectatoritis.
- **Decline of memory and imagination** due to the confused restlessness of modern life.
- **Decline of skill and care** due to the weakened tradition of craftsmanship.
- **Decline of self-discipline** due to the ever-present availability of stimulants and tranquillisers.
- **Decline of compassion** due to the unseemly haste with which modern life is conducted.

Hahn, who had established the progressive Salem school in Germany before fleeing the Nazi regime, further developed a programme of "experiential therapy"

(Erlebnistherapie) as an antidote to these declines. This thinking went on to form the basic structure of the Award Framework (Knoll 2011):

- ► **Fitness training**, to train the discipline and determination of the mind through the body.
- ► **Project work,** involving crafts and manual skills.
- ► **Service**, for example surf life-saving or first aid.
- ► **Expeditions**, to engage in long, challenging endurance tasks.

Initially, this framework was only available to boys aged between 14 and 18, but there was a demand for a similar scheme for girls so this was launched two years later, in 1958. The Award continued to evolve until 1980 when the upper age limit for participation in the Award was extended to 24, and the Award took on its current five section format:

- ► Fitness training became **Physical Recreation** of all kinds.
- ► Expeditions became an **Adventurous Journey** – a journey in an unfamiliar environment, planned and undertaken by a team of young people.
- ► Projects became regular **Skills** practice.
- ► Rescue Service became **Voluntary Service** for those in need, the community or the environment.
- ► The **Gold Residential Project** is added.

The rules around length of participation in activities and age requirements for participants went through a number of changes until 2004, when the framework was fixed in its current format (with regular review).

The Award Framework consists of three levels and four sections (five at Gold level):

Figure 8.1: The levels and sections of the Award

There are three levels to the Award...

 **Bronze**
14 years +
6 months minimum

 Silver
15 years +
12 months minimum

 Gold
16 years +
18 months minimum

Each level of the Award has four sections (five at the Gold level):

Voluntary Service	Physical Recreation	Skill	Adventurous Journey	Gold Residential Project
Participants volunteer in their communities, make a positive contribution to society and demonstrate social responsibility.	Encourages young people to improve their fitness, performance and enjoy healthy lifestyles for good mental and physical wellbeing.	Enables participants to develop their talents, broaden their abilities, increase their self-confidence and improve their employability.	Young people discover a spirit of adventure and gain a deeper understanding of the environment and the great outdoors.	Participants broaden their outlook and horizons. They undertake a shared, purposeful experience with people who are not their usual companions, working towards a common goal.

Young people choose activities to do regularly over a defined period of time, in the four Award sections (five at Gold level). The Award is voluntary and participant-led.

The content and target of each section is decided upon by the young person in close co-operation with their Award Leader, who mentors them through their Award Journey. An Award Leader is typically a teacher, youth worker or social worker.

In the Voluntary Service, Physical Recreation and Skills sections, participants can do their activities individually or as a team. They are expected to take part in these activities regularly during their Award Journey at each level (Bronze, Silver or Gold). The Adventurous Journey section requires teamwork, as it is completed in a team of four to seven participants who plan, train for and complete a journey in an unknown environment together. In the Gold Residential Project, participants engage in a shared purposeful activity with other young people who are not their usual colleagues or friends, and in an unfamiliar residential setting, for example away from home or other locations where they have already undertaken their Award activities.

The Award is designed to be inclusive, achievable and enjoyable for any 14 to 24 year old who wishes to take part, regardless of their abilities, interests or background. For each section, Award Leaders help participants create individual targets that are achievable yet challenging. The framework is also non-competitive as participants work to achieve their own personal targets, rather than comparing their achievements to predefined standards, or to others. Since participants can choose any activity that fits within the ethos of the Award section, the Award has maintained its relevance over time and across cultures, with activities, for instance, for the Skills section varying from learning to code to learning Latin.

Participants must show a commitment to their chosen activities over time. This regularity and commitment supports the development of leadership, communication and problem-solving skills and other outcomes such as confidence, resilience, determination, intercultural and civic competence, and personal and social well-being. Research shows that after participating in these activities regularly for the duration of the Award, the majority of participants plan to continue, or actually do continue pursuing these activities, forming positive and purposeful habits for life (Terry 2012; Campbell et al. 2009). In 2010, The Duke of Edinburgh's Award Canada and McKinsey & Company found that participants who have completed the physical recreation component of the Award are 29% more likely to engage in regular physical activity than the average Canadian aged 12-24. Moreover, the Foundation's recent participant satisfaction survey conducted between July 2017 and July 2018 shows that while 48% of the participants reported taking part in a volunteering activity regularly prior to doing their Award, 84% of the participants said they intend to continue regularly with their volunteering activities after completing their Award. In the same survey, 24% of participants reported undertaking regular outdoor activity such as hiking, kayaking, sailing and so on prior to doing their Award, while 59% of them said they intend to continue their outdoor activity regularly, at least once a month (The Foundation 2018).

Adults in the Award

According to the 2017 annual statistical report compiled by the Foundation, in 2016 around 200 000 adults supported the delivery of the Award worldwide. These adults, often volunteers, form the backbone of Award operations. The support provided by adults is of paramount importance in the quality of a young person's Award experience. Hence, from the very beginning, emphasis has been placed not only on developing young people, but also on supporting and developing the adults who give their time to supporting and developing young people.

There are reflections of Kurt Hahn's educational philosophy in the learning and training strategy for the adults. For example, Hahn's seven laws of Salem (the school he founded in pre-War Germany), highlighted a need to "have children meet with triumph and defeat" and "give the children the opportunity of self-effacement in the common cause" (Stremba and Bisson 2009). Today, the adults who support and assess participants' Adventurous Journeys are taught to let the participants lead and make their own mistakes, and to learn lessons about working as a team in order to get through hardship during their journeys. Adventurous Journey supervisors watch Award groups from afar, ensuring the young people's safety but allowing them authentic responsibility and challenge. Award Leaders support and mentor participants through their Award Journey but allow them to take responsibility for their own participation and achievements.

The Award's international expansion and development

Soon after the Award was founded, it was embraced by the Scouts, the Guides, the Armed Forces cadet units and other youth organisations in the UK, and in some cases spread to their subsidiary movements overseas, particularly in the Commonwealth countries (Peyton-Jones 1991). Within a few years, Commonwealth countries like Hong Kong, Malta, Zimbabwe, Australia, Kenya and Canada had become interested in the Award and the Award became international.

These overseas operators were initially supported by a dedicated department within the Duke of Edinburgh's Award office in the UK. This continued for a number of years until in 1988 it was decided to formally constitute The Duke of Edinburgh's International Award Foundation Trust with its own set of trustees, its own appointed staff at the International Secretariat (IS) and with an overarching International Award Association (IAA) with authority over National Award Operators worldwide (The Association 2004). The IAA, through its constitution, linked all operators within an agreed common philosophy, set of principles, operating standards, code of conduct, and an international partnership and responsibility.

Expansion of the Award continued to be fairly reactive, working "on request" from individuals and organisations interested in setting up the Award in their country (De-Wint 2012), and by the first decade of the 2000s, the Award had spread to over 100 countries. However, there were challenges and risks involved in this expansion. The Award's entry into a country or organisation was organic, making it somewhat unco-ordinated, unpredictable and at times unsustainable. Growth was driven by expansion into new territories – not maximising the potential in existing territories. Delivery relied on staff and volunteers' willingness to support the Award, quality assurance was not a consistent process, and growth was not systematic, or a focus for most involved.

As a response to this, in 2012 the Foundation started a major change process, moving from a loose partnership model with Award Operators towards a social franchising model.

Figure 8.2: Diagram of business replication options

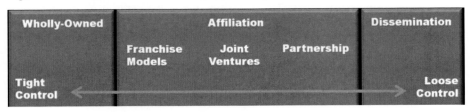

(Adapted by De-Wint 2012, from McNeill Ritchie et al. 2011)

Social franchising is similar to commercial franchising, though driven by a social goal rather than for profit. It can be explained as a "contract-based co-operation of decentralised entrepreneurial units" with central support, uniform quality standards and a common philosophy (Braun and Lotter 2004, cited in Ahlert et al. 2008). The purpose of the social franchising model was to address issues of clarity and complexity within the Award's identity and brand, enhance its capacity for growth and improve its ability to manage the quality of experience for participants (De-Wint 2012). This change process had five strands, all of which evolved to be critical developments in the expansion of Award operations worldwide:

▶ improved licensing agreements and revised services and interaction with the Foundation, supporting licensing and stronger quality assurance;

▶ a new, clear and consistent visual identity for the Award;

▶ new research and performance management framework;

▶ new online "tools" for managing and developing the Award;

▶ a new capacity-building strategy and training approach.

In the next section, we expand more on the development of digital tools, to exemplify how one of the strands of this change process has helped the Award manage some of the complexities of international growth.

Digital innovations

In 2012, the Foundation released the Online Record Book (ORB), a system allowing young people to record their Award progress online rather than in paper books, which enables Award Leaders to better follow their participants' progress and manage the Award in their schools or youth organisations. The system was developed in response to the growth of the Award worldwide and reflects the general increase in usage and popularity of technology within society.

The online system is not intended to replace the face-to-face time that Award Leaders spend with their participants but acts as an accessible record book that will allow Award Leaders to use the time they spend with participants, mentoring them and supporting them, rather than filling in paperwork. Having an online system allows for easier portability where participants and Award Leaders move locations and countries, since accounts can be transferred and maintained in a flexible and secure manner. Furthermore, the system pulls real-time reports on participation, enrolments and payments, which supports Award Operators to manage the quality, growth and performance of their organisational, regional or national Award delivery.

Developing and setting up an online Award management system did not come without its challenges. Translating into local languages is an intensive process, as is designing an online system which contains rules and algorithms, but which does not take away the flexible nature of the Award Framework. Through stakeholder engagement and rigorous testing, the ORB continues to undergo development to meet the needs of the large network of Award Leaders and participants around the world, and it is being iteratively rolled out globally. In 2016, the smartphone application of the ORB was launched, now allowing participants to record their progress on the go, uploading pictures and videos from their journey through the Award (for more information, see Attfield 2018).

In order to maintain a good level of support to the Award's operating network, the Foundation has been developing an intranet, the Award Community (also known as the Online Learning Hub). The site hosts training videos and content for adults supporting Award delivery, and encourages networking, sharing of best practice, and supports general communication within a growing global Award community. Meanwhile, to improve stakeholder relationship management, a customer relationship management system, Salesforce, has been implemented within the Foundation and in some National Award Operators.

The Foundation and the network of Award Operators are always on the lookout for innovations in digitisation and technology which can further support Award Leaders and participants or enable them to reach young people that previously have not had the opportunity to be involved. Recently the National Award Operators in the UK and USA have begun experimenting with "Virtual Award Centres" and recruiting volunteers from non-traditional places (for instance, corporate supporters) to act as online leaders and assessors.

The Award in the field of youth work

Youth work today remains an open, complex and interconnected field. Its practice varies country to country, even youth worker to youth worker, and there is no internationally used definition and understanding of what youth work is (Schild, Vanhee and Williamson 2017). They provide an overarching definition that

> Youth work, as it is largely understood at European level, is based on values and is about the promotion of human rights, diversity, social cohesion, peace and democracy … what youth workers have and indeed should have in common is the fact that they all work directly with and for young people in non-formal education settings and with a defined intention. (Schild, Vanhee and Williamson 2017, p.8)

Youth work may be a fluid, informal process within an open-access youth setting, in which youth workers try to foster a connection with the young person, then work together on set activities or objectives. On the other hand, youth work can also be set programmes and projects that young people opt into. While the Award can be delivered in an open-access setting, it requires persistent engagement over a long period of time and so it is most often delivered in settings where there is guaranteed contact with the young people. Within each section of the Award, there are defined aims which trained Award Leaders support their young people to reach. For example, the Voluntary Service section's aim is "To learn how to give useful service to others and their communities".

There is evidence that taking part in organised activities during after-school hours, rather than other common after-school pursuits like watching television, makes an essential contribution to an individual's capability to thrive in adolescence and adulthood and is positively associated with educational, civic and occupational success in young adulthood (Gardner et al. 2008). The Council of Europe and the European Commission recognise that non-formal and informal education through youth work is an important field that contributes to the preparation of young people for the knowledge-based and civil society in which they live. Looking at the outcomes from all kinds of youth work, young people acquire essential skills and competences often named "soft skills", and they benefit from personal development, social inclusion and engage in active citizenship, thereby improving their employment prospects (European Commission and the Council of Europe 2011).

By drawing on research and recommendations on the Award, non-formal education and within similar youth programmes, The Foundation has identified the following outcomes of the Award for young people. This is published in its Outcomes Framework.

Figure 8.3: The outcomes of the Award for young people, 2015

No	Outcome	Definition
1	Confidence	Self-reliance, self-esteem, self-efficacy, capacity to act in one's own interest and need, self-belief, ability to shape your own life and the world around you
2	Managing feelings	Reviewing, self-awareness, reflecting, self-regulating, self-accepting
3	Resilience and determination	Self-disciplined, self-management, self-motivated, concentrated, having a sense of purpose, persistent, self-controlled
4	Relationships and leadership	Motivating others, valuing and contributing to team working, negotiating, establishing positive relationships, interpreting others, managing conflict, empathising
5	Creativity and adaptability	Imagining alternative ways of doing things, applying learning in new contexts, enterprising, innovating, remaining open to new ideas, reading situations correctly and adapting as relevant
6	Planning and problem solving	Navigating resources; organising, setting and achieving goals; decision-making, researching, analysing, critical thinking, questioning and challenging, evaluating risks, reliability
7	Civic competence	The ability and willingness to engage in active participation, based on an attitude of trust in other people, in all the contexts of social life: school, local community, working place, recreational activities
8	Intercultural competence	Ability to operate in different cultural settings (of different ages, skills, religions, languages, etc.) and adaptability to changing circumstances and ability to sense and respond to new contexts

No	Outcome	Definition
9	Personal and social well-being	A person's state of mind, relationship with the world around them, and the fulfilment they get from life: well-being, life satisfaction
10	Communication	Explaining, expressing, presenting, listening, questioning, using different ways of communicating

When young people experience these beneficial outcomes, longer-term changes in individuals and within communities may occur. All of the ways in which the Award has been found to, and intends to, positively affect individuals and their communities in the long term, are laid out in the Impact Framework.

Figure 8.4: The Impact Framework of the Award, 2017

Title	Definition
1. Improved employability and earning potential	Increase in employability and earning potential due to improved life skills.
2. Improved physical health and fitness	Improved physical health due to increased long-term participation in physical activities.
3. Improved mental health and emotional wellbeing	Improved mental health and emotional wellbeing due to increased social interaction, self-confidence, enhanced life skills and sense of purpose.
4. Increased engagement with charitable and community causes	Increased engagement with charitable and community causes directly, through the Service section of the Award, and indirectly, through increased likelihood of long-term participation in volunteering and other forms of community and local participation.
5. Improved environmental impact	Increase in positive, or reduction in negative, environmental impacts as a result of behaviour change resulting from being more aware of environmental issues and having increased connection with and compassion for nature.
6. Increased social cohesion	Increased social inclusion and community cohesion, not specifically captured by the other impacts in the framework. This encompasses the resources and relationships provided by people and society, including skills, knowledge, wellbeing, relationships, shared values and institutions.
7. Reduced offending	Reduction in first-term offending and reduction in reoffending by young offenders, due to long-term increased levels of physical activity, improved life skills, increased social inclusion and improved social skills resulting from increased levels of social interaction.

These impact areas align well with the values of human rights, diversity, social cohesion, peace and democracy that are mentioned in Schild et al.'s (2017) definition of youth work, as previously cited. Supportive of social cohesion and peace and democracy, the Award fosters social cohesion, reduces offending and increases engagement with charitable and community causes. Supportive of human rights and diversity, the Award is inclusive in design since it is achievable by any young person who wishes to take part.

Youth work may be run by or associated with the public sector, the state or the social economy (or third sector). Looking at the organisations that run the Award nationally, there is a varied approach. The Foundation and the majority of the National Award Operators (NAOs) exist as a charity within their social economy, while some NAOs are set up under a government institution. For example, in Malaysia and Lithuania, the NAOs sit within governmental departments under the Department of Youth and Sports, and the Ministry of Science and Education respectively. In Turkey, the NAO is hosted by the Turkish Human Resources Education and Health Foundation (TIKAV), a national organisation set up to carry out social responsibility projects of Akfen Holding, a for-profit business. On the other hand, in the UK, New Zealand, South Africa and many other countries, the NAO is set up as a non-governmental organisation solely to run the Award.

Often, the Award is sustainably delivered where partnering relationships with other national organisations are formed. For example, in Slovenia, the Slovenian Catholic Girl Guides and Boy Scouts Association have a partnership agreement with the Award. In the UK and Ireland, there is a long history of partnership between the Scouts and the Award, where the educational programmes are directly aligned. In Bermuda, outdoor education training elements are shared between the Award and Outward Bound, which count towards Outward Bound skills development and towards preparation for the Adventurous Journey of the Award. Around the world, the Award works closely with, and is part of, the "Big 6" global youth volunteer and membership organisations – YMCA, YWCA, Red Cross and Red Crescent, Scouts, Guides and The Duke of Edinburgh's International Award. Excellent opportunities have been proven to exist when such organisations partner with the Award, and collaboration in the field can encourage best practice.

Case studies

How the Award works in practice is now illustrated in more depth through two case studies. The first details how the Award was set up as a social franchisee in Slovakia and highlights the value of knowledge sharing and collaborative work between NAOs to ensure a high-quality delivery of the Award. The second focuses on a project that aims to improve access to the Award within marginalised communities in Bangladesh. It sheds light on how the work of the Award not only provides positive outcomes for young people but can go some way to support communities to address social issues.

Slovakia – Setting up the Award for success

This case study gives some insight into the use and benefits of the Award's licensing structure, by detailing how Slovakia successfully introduced the Award nationally in 2016 and became one of the fastest growing NAOs.

Marian Zachar, the first and current National Director in Slovakia, was drawn to the Award when he heard about it and approached people in his network and the Foundation, looking to set up the Award in Slovakia. Zachar and his team wanted to bring about societal change for the benefit of Slovakia's next generation:

> Young people in Slovakia fall behind other OECD countries in educational attainment as well as well-rounded life skills and character development. Over the years, they fall behind in employment, community volunteering and civic engagement. We believe that by increasing motivation and expectations of young people, and offering global recognition through the Award, young people in Slovakia could significantly improve their life prospects. … we hope to shift the culture of education in Slovakia to focus on young people achieving well-rounded growth.

First, Zachar sought advice from fellow NAOs in different countries and from the Foundation on how to set up an NAO team. They founded an executive board, and found partner companies and supporting foundations. The team performed a legal analysis of all the possible types of organisations that could operate the Award in Slovakia and decided to set up the NAO as an association, the most flexible legal entity in Slovakia that can adapt its processes to the level of maturity of the organisation. The Slovak team benefited from learning from the experience of other organisations that have been through the same process. They made close ties with the Czech Republic NAO, which offered vital support in the development of Slovakia's website, holding joint Award Leader training sessions and sharing best practice on Award delivery.

After going through an induction and training programme and piloting the Award in a handful of Award Centres, the Slovak NAO received its first licence in 2016. Zachar explains how the licensing process supported their set up and growth:

> The Foundation provided us with a valuable quality assurance system through its licence review. This helped us set the quality benchmarks of the Award in Slovakia right from the start. The development of Slovak trainers through the "train the trainer" initiative was also crucial for the growth of the organisation. It allowed us to develop a network of qualified trainers that would deliver the Award to consistently high standards.

Slovakia was able to use the strength of the global brand to recruit partner organisations, since organisations can see the impact of the Award on young people around the world and how it might help them reach the goals of their own organisations. Among the young people in Slovakia there was not much awareness of the Award but the Slovak team was able to use this to their advantage, creating all the branding and profile of the Award specific to the local youth culture of Slovakia.

Equipped with a passion for the Award, and using the collective knowledge of the entire Award network built over the last 60 years, Zachar and the NAO team managed to set up and grow the Award within the first year of operations in 2016 to 1 268 participants. Since then, they have continued to grow, with over 1 600 young people enrolled in the Award in 2017. Within three years of setting up, Slovakia has become the 7th largest NAO in the Europe, Mediterranean and Arab States (EMAS) region, out of 19 countries.

Bangladesh – Reaching marginalised young people

Bangladesh has one of the largest youth populations in the world (UN 2014). The country is making huge strides in raising income levels and reducing poverty, however 24.3% of the population lives in poverty, which rises to 26.4% in rural areas (World Bank 2016). Educational access and quality of teaching is low, meaning many young people have a low level of education, and may lack the skills required for higher skilled (and therefore higher paying) jobs (UNICEF 2018). Young people need alternative ways of building their readiness for work, thereby increasing their confidence and level of aspiration. Unemployment among 15-24 year olds stands at 12%, which is more than twice the rate for adults (World Bank 2018). Job creation is not keeping up with population growth, leading to high competition for jobs. Young people need to be able to demonstrate that they have a robust set of transferable skills to distinguish themselves in the job market. They also need to become job creators who enable the economy, and skilled employment, to grow.

Over the last four years the NAO in Bangladesh has been addressing these challenges by running a project to increase access to the Award for young people from marginalised communities. It created a detailed strategic plan and a human resource policy, and brought on more executives and Award Leaders to deliver training, provide IT support and support Award delivery. They were then able to form strategic partnerships with youth development centres, Foundations who work with street children and at-risk and marginalised young people, and remote village schools, improve the access of the Award for young people in rural and marginalised communities.

Award Leader Monira Islam, from the Jaago Foundation School, who works to provide educational advantages to underprivileged children, has described the Award as a great tool they use to improve their children's abilities and to develop their self-confidence, helping them to achieve something which was beyond their reach previously. Islam explains that since starting the Award, their students' educational performances have improved, along with their motivation and confidence:

> After joining this Award their perspective has changed. Now they are working with more effort, more enthusiasm, and are inspired to do their best. Their performance has changed. Their results are better than before.

One of her students commented,

> We never thought that we would be able to participate in such an internationally recognised programme as we come from poor backgrounds. The Award will help me in my future career, because I will get an international certificate and that proves I am capable of meeting the requirements for employment.

As a result of this project in 2012, the number of Award Centres in Bangladesh went up by 80% in the subsequent two years, and the number of new entrants to the Award more than doubled. Additionally, participation by at-risk and marginalised young people increased by almost 5%, and funding was secured from the board to work in slum areas. One of the Foundation's strategic aims is to increase the participation of "at-risk and marginalised"[68] young people. Part of the Foundation's work towards this aim involves providing grants to projects such as this one, which are designed to give young people from such backgrounds the opportunity to take part. The positive effect of the Award on young people has been widely documented over the years and anecdotal evidence such as this case study suggests it can have a profound and transformative effect on young people who face significant challenges within their lives.

Conclusion

This chapter has given an overview of the origins of the Award Framework, how the Award's international operating structure has developed through time, and has delved into some critical moments within this history. As contextualised within the given case studies, in recent years the Foundation and Award Operators around the world have been working together more strategically to bring the Award to young people and communities who could particularly benefit from the Award's presence, and to increase the access of the Award to areas with potential for Award growth.

For the future, there is a shared vision among Award Operators to reach more young people from diverse backgrounds and equip them to succeed in life. The long-term ambition identified in the Association's Global Strategy is that every eligible young person will have the opportunity to participate in the Award. Challenges remain of scaling up Award operations while maintaining international standards and providing enough support to Award Operators, staff and volunteers, and participants around the world. Nonetheless, research is uncovering how the Award is an effective tool for youth workers and organisations which aim to develop young people, and that the Award can have a far-reaching impact not only on those involved, but at a community and even national level.

References

Ahlert D., Ahlert M., Duong Dinh H. V., Fleisch H., Heussler T. and Meuter J. (2008), *Social franchising: a way of systematic replication to increase social impact*, Bundesverband Deutscher Stiftungen, Berlin, Germany.

Attfield P. (2018), "Duke of Edinburgh's Awards takes a leap with smartphone app", *The Globe and Mail*, available at www.theglobeandmail.com/business/article-duke-of-edinburghs-awards-takes-a-leap-with-smartphone-app/, accessed 4 August 2019.

Campbell J., Bell V., Armstrong S. C., Horton J., Mansukhani N., Matthews M. H. and Pilkington A. (2009), *The impact of the Duke of Edinburgh's Award on young people*, available at http://nectar.northampton.ac.uk/2447/1/Final_report_master_document.pdf, accessed 4 August 2019.

---

68. "At-risk" describes young people whose circumstances mean they are vulnerable to negative influences or consequences and who, through the Award, can reduce many if not all the risks and permanently change their circumstances for the better; for example, lack of engagement in school and becoming "at risk" of low education attainment. "Marginalised" describes young people experiencing isolation from society either physically or psychologically and who, through the Award, can feel included and become positive contributors to mainstream society, for example young people with physical and/or learning disabilities, or young offenders.

Council of Europe (2018), European Youth Foundation, *Definitions*, available at www.coe.int/en/web/european-youth-foundation/definitions, accessed 4 August 2019.

De-Wint S. (2012), "Growing a charity internationally – the use of social franchising as a model of replication", a management project presented in part consideration for the degree of Executive Master of Business Administration, University of Nottingham, Nottingham.

European Commission and the Council of Europe (2011), *Pathways 2.0 towards recognition of non-formal learning/education and of youth work in Europe*, available at http://www.alliance-network.eu/wp-content/uploads/2014/05/Pathways_II_towards_recognition_of_non-formal_learning_Jan_2011.pdf, accessed 4 August 2019.

Gardner M., Roth J. and Brooks-Gunn J. (2008), "Adolescents' participation in organized activities and developmental Success 2 and 8 years after high school: do sponsorship, duration, and intensity matter?", *Developmental Psychology* Vol. 44, No. 3, pp. 814-30.

Peyton-Jones L. (1991), *Challenge and opportunity: the story of the Duke of Edinburgh's Award worldwide*. Foreword by HRH The Duke of Edinburgh, The Duke of Edinburgh's International Award Association, Hong Kong.

Knoll M. (2011), *Schulreform through "experiential therapy": Kurt Hahn – An efficacious educator*, Catholic University of Eichstätt-Ingolstadt, Germany.

Le Gouvernement de Grand-Duché de Luxembourg Ministère de la Famille, de l'Intégration (2013), *Non-formal education with children and young people: learning in out-of-school-settings*, Luxembourg.

McNeill Ritchie S., Shine P. and Hawkins A. (2011), *Social franchising: scaling up for success*, The Shaftesbury Partnership, London.

Schild H., Vanhee J. and Williamson H. (2017) "Youth work – An incomprehensible subject? Introductory reflections on youth work", in *Thinking seriously about youth work, and how to prepare people to do it*, Youth Knowledge #20, Council of Europe and European Commission, Strasbourg.

Stremba B. and Bisson C. A. (2009), *Teaching adventure education theory: best practices*, Human Kinetics, Champaign IL.

The Duke of Edinburgh's International Award Association (2004), *The International Award for Young People Handbook*.

The Duke of Edinburgh's International Award Foundation (2013), Guiding principles of The Duke of Edinburgh's International Award, available at www.intaward.org/resource/guiding-principles-0, accessed 4 August 2019.

— (2017), "A summary of research to date into The Duke of Edinburgh's International Award", Version 5.

— (2017), "Presenting the results from our Award participant and Award team satisfaction surveys during the period July 2015 to May 2017".

— (2018), "Presenting the results from our Award participant and Award team satisfaction surveys during the period June 2017 to June 2018", Manuscript in progress.

— (2018), "The Duke of Edinburgh's International Award Association Strategy, 2018-2023", available at www.intaward.org/resource/duke-edinburgh%E2%80%99s-international-award-association-strategy-2018-2023, accessed 4 August 2019.

Terry S. (2012), *The Duke of Edinburgh's Award in Australia – historical and contemporary responses*, Student Directed Study, St Michael's Collegiate School, Hobart, Australia.

UNICEF (2018), "Bangladesh, Overview, Challenges facing the children of Bangladesh", Accessible at: www.unicef.org/bangladesh/en/children-bangladesh

United Nations (2014), "India has world's largest youth population: UN report", The Hindu, available at www.thehindu.com/todays-paper/tp-in-school/india-has-worlds-largest-youth-population-un-report/article6612615.ece, accessed 4 August 2019.

World Bank (2016), "Bangladesh continues to reduce poverty but at slower pace", Feature story, available at www.worldbank.org/en/news/feature/2017/10/24/bangladesh-continues-to-reduce-poverty-but-at-slower-pace, accessed 4 August 2019.

World Bank (2018), "Unemployment, youth total (% of total labor force ages 15-24)", Data pages, available at https://data.worldbank.org/indicator/SL.UEM.1524.ZS?locations=BD, accessed 4 August 2019.

Chapter 9

International Falcon Movement – Socialist Education International (IFM-SEI): a history of the movement in the context of the political and social influences of the 20th century

Sabine Troitzsch

Introduction

This chapter provides a history of an international socialist youth movement that is now active in five regions of the world. Even though the text tells the story chronologically of the last 100 years since the establishment of the International Falcon Movement – Socialist Education International (IFM-SEI), the emphasis will be more on the wider social contexts, circumstances, crises and crossroads rather than on inner structures or on individuals that have shaped the movement. Of course, it must still be acknowledged that social contexts have a direct influence on internal decisions and on educational principles.

The chapter is structured through different stages in the history of IFM-SEI and tries to summarise each era under a different predominant theme. The beginning and the end of every phase is often difficult to determine exactly, because in most cases these transitions between different periods were fluid and, in many respects, merged into one another. However, the division of the organisation's history into different stages seems helpful in order to capture the general developments within IFM-SEI in the context of other youth movements, political parties and institutions, and in relation to other political and social influences in Europe and worldwide.

What is IFM-SEI ... and how did it all start?

IFM-SEI is an international educational movement working to empower children and young people to take an active role in society and to fight for their rights. They are an umbrella organisation for child and youth-led movements all over the world, educating on the basis of socialist values of equality, democracy, peace, solidarity, co-operation, anti-capitalism and friendship.

The complex and long name of the organisation is a result of many restructures and has been changed several times. "Red Falcons" are children and youth organisations in west and central Europe that were established around 100 years ago (in Austria about 10 years earlier than in other countries). Their main idea was to offer meaningful free-time activities and education especially to children and young people from working-class families. Working-class youth usually lived under very poor social and economic conditions during the time of the establishment of the Red Falcon movements. Young people had to leave school early in order to get a job and contribute financially to family resources. Apprentices, who usually started at the age of 14, were often exploited rather than trained, and working-class families usually lived in cramped and often unhealthy conditions. Moreover, even after the official abolition of child labour, young children still often had to help in the fields, in the household and in taking care of younger siblings.

In 1922, representatives of Red Falcon organisations, from a broad spectrum of socialist and social democratic educational organisations from Switzerland, Germany, Great Britain, the Netherlands, Italy, Austria and Czechoslovakia met to form an international association that was the forerunner of what IFM-SEI is today. In their first constitution, the educators defined the need for democratic socialist education and the self-organisation of young people. This, it was argued, should play a key role in enabling children with a working-class background to criticise and overcome inequalities in society today and to be able to build a peaceful society without exploitation tomorrow.

From the very start, the organisation always derived its power from the wish to change society through education and the conviction that many systematic inequalities can only be tackled internationally, not nationally. IFM-SEI thereby combines a political analysis with educational concepts and calls this integrated concept "socialist education". The aim is not to indoctrinate young people with socialist theory but to use education and core principles of socialism (which are, for example, peace, solidarity, democracy, children's rights, equality, anti-capitalism) as the vehicle for creating space for children and young people to develop critical awareness and, as a result, empower them to challenge inequalities in the world.

International partnerships are not understood as a solely theoretical concept, but rather as deriving from the need and attempts to make international solidarity a practical reality. This was to be achieved by IFM-SEI through solidarity campaigns, through financial support and through experiencing internationalism on summer camps, where young people from different parts of the world live and decide about things together.

Roots in the working-class youth movement and the foundation of a socialist children's organisation

Before the international umbrella IFM-SEI organisation was founded, the first socialist youth groups were aged between 14 and 18 years. As minors by law they were not allowed in many countries to join any political party or a trade union. Internationally, they formed Socialist Youth International in 1907 (which is today the International Union of Socialist Youth) and most founding member organisations later transformed into the social democratic party youth in their countries (after the laws changed and they were allowed to become politically active). Their motivation was to fight for better working conditions, to educate themselves in their free time and to have fun together by going on hikes in nature (and out of the dirty polluted cities) or organising other cultural activities together on Sundays. When, in 1914, the First World War broke out many of these youth groups demonstrated against militarism and the war in their countries.

The history of the IFM-SEI itself, which mainly works with younger children, started on an international level – as noted above – with a conference in Austria in 1922 with representatives of socialist educational organisations from seven European countries. In their speeches the socialist educators made it clear that, following the First World War (and with the end of the monarchies in some European countries), they expected quick progress to be made towards a socialist society.

Part of securing such progress was through a socialist education that should play a key role in enabling children to criticise and overcome societal inequality. In the long run, the education provided in socialist children's organisations should serve the class struggle. In their leisure time, children should experience an alternative from the "bourgeois influences of the school system" with the help of socialist educators. They should have the chance to experience a better world with participatory elements, solidarity and international friendships forged during summer camps. At the same time, IFM members participated in reforming the state school system, for example by founding new prototype schools.

The 1922 conference decided to found the Internationale Arbeitsgemeinschaft Sozialistischer Erziehungsorganisationen (IASE, the International Committee of Socialist Educational Organisations) with an executive office at the Austrian Kinderfreunde central office in Vienna. In the beginning it only had German, Austrian and Czech member organisations. By 1931, however, the international umbrella organisation had attracted members from another seven European countries and kept close contact with organisations from several more European as well as non-European countries such as Argentina, the United States and Palestine.

Two years later, the IASE was renamed ISE (Internationale Sozialistische Erziehungsorganisation/International Socialist Educational Organisation) and it not only broadened the basis of its members but also its educational concept. On the one hand, this process was influenced by organisations from European countries where the working-class movement had been less excluded than in the German-speaking states. In those countries the member organisations concentrated more on participation in existing society than on class struggle. On the other hand, the development itself of the German-speaking organisations led to a break with the original idea of conscious class-struggle education for children by trained adults. With the birth of the Red Falcon youth groups, elements of practice from other youth movements, like the outdoor activities and camping by the Scouts, became incorporated into the activities and educational practice carried out by the children's organisations. The opportunities for group activities and identity and of self-organised life in camps brought with them a focus on wider experiences and not merely their educational elements. The larger camps also had a strong international representation that proved attractive in their own right. The international umbrella helped in organising large national children's "republics" (see below) composed of their member organisations, where international guests also took part. Soon the SEI took on the responsibility for organising its own international summer camps as well.

Many member organisations had problems with the Christian Church, not just because they called themselves socialists and did not actively practise any religious rituals with their children but also mainly because boys and girls were gathered together in all educational and free-time activities (because of the belief in co-education). In some organisations boys and girls even shared the same tent, as the educational focus was on group work (one group, one tent). This approach to spending leisure time and collective learning was very much at odds with the perspectives of the Church at the time.

The international camps of the SEI started in the early 1930s and were often the highlight in experiences for working-class children (travelling abroad, seeing the ocean for the first time). One of the core aims of international camps was that children from different nations should experience peaceful co-existence. Children from countries that had been enemies in the First World War celebrated festivals of peace, which had now become integral parts of international camps.

The pedagogical and political basis of the summer camps

The summer camps organised by IFM-SEI derived from and were anchored in principles of self-governance and socialism. The Kinderfreunde movement had, in the 1920s, started organising what were called "children's republics",[69] in which thousands of children and their guides would practise this approach. It was based on the thinking of Kurt Löwenstein (who was chair of the German Kinderfreunde and of the SEI during the 1920s). He argued that a new form of workers' organisation needed to be developed, based on what he saw as a fundamental contradiction in society. He felt that most people's consciousness was lagging behind the "differentiated collective work processes" that were increasingly shaping both factory life in particular and societal life more generally. Individuals no longer acted with the community in mind. The recognition and renewal of mutual and collective responsibility, in order to bridge the increasing divergence between social development on the one hand and individual consciousness on the other, formed the basis of the educational practice of the Kinderfreunde movement:

> And thus the educational problem is created: to prepare the new generation through practical training and influence on the consciousness for the nascent society. Based on this insight, we practice practical self-governance in our groups. We give children roles

---

69. This was the original name for the summer camps. The camps were participatory and structured democratically. Each tent group sent one person to the children's parliament. On the second day of the camp, all children elected a mayor of their tent town. All issues were taken to the children's parliament, where adults also had a voice but no majority. The idea was that working-class children should self-organise and learn to act within democratic structures (which was still very new in some European countries) and, through doing so, they would become the future leaders of the socialist society of tomorrow.

which they can seriously and solidly fulfil and which are subject to the self-governance of their group. (Löwenstein 1929)

This sense of cultivating youth autonomy and self-governance is a theme that persists to the present and, indeed, permeates the philosophy of many youth organisations, both within and beyond wider socialist traditions.

During the Second World War and the dictatorship of Nazi Germany

The establishment of fascist regimes in Germany and Europe in the 1930s weakened the SEI because its member organisations were often outlawed. Many adult educators were persecuted, emigrated abroad, went into "inner emigration" and were murdered. The SEI office in Vienna had to close in 1934. In 1939, the last SEI camp in Belgium took place. A pivotal moment at that camp was the expression of opposition against the war, on 6 August, just a few weeks before Nazi Germany began the Second World War. The international office moved from Vienna to Paris. From 1939 on, however, its international activities were not possible anymore. There are two heart-warming anecdotes of international solidarity during this period when Nazi Germany suppressed all other youth organisations except their own:

1. Near the end of a summer camp in 1933 Kinderfreunde, the Austrian organisation, already had great problems with the fascist dictatorship in Austria. They asked the Flemish, Rode Valken, to keep their flags safe for them until they would be free again to use them in Austria. These flags remained hidden in Belgium during the war and were handed back to the Austrians after the war ended in 1945.
2. An example of life-saving friendships: In 1939, when Nazi Germany were agitating in the Sudetenland in western Czechoslovakia, the "Woodcraft Folk" (the SEI member organisation from Great Britain) organised a "Kindertransport" with children to Britain, rescuing Jewish and non-Jewish children from the socialist partner organisation in Slovakia. Despite its own financial problems, Woodcraft Folk members collected enough money to smuggle hundreds of children via Belgium to England. The Woodcraft Folk had met these children two years before on a summer camp in Brighton.

1945: after the Second World War – re-establishment or re-foundation?

For the duration of the Second World War, then, the SEI was mostly inactive. However, the idea which had formed the basis of the SEI remained alive and, with the re-establishment of Falcon organisations in Europe after the end of the war, the spirit of the international organisation was revived. The former president of the SEI, Jean Nihon, and his secretary, Willi Hocke, had survived the war and established contacts to bring the organisation back to life. In 1946, the Woodcraft Folk from Great Britain, in collaboration with the former SEI secretary, managed to organise an international camp in Brighton with delegations from Belgium, France, Denmark, Sweden and the Netherlands.

This idea of post-war international friendship established its first organisational structure through the Internationales Falken-Sekretariat (IFS, International Falcon Office), which facilitated communication between the different national member organisations. At the 4th conference of the IFS in 1953, and after some preliminary talks, the International Falcon Movement (IFM) was founded. The preliminary talks had shown that the member organisations followed different ideas of socialist education. Generally, there was an atmosphere throughout Europe to be less ideological and militant and to focus instead more on human rights than on class struggle. These differences among the member organisations and the further opening of the IFM for new members meant that there was no way back to the old concepts from the interwar years. The Scandinavian members in particular, but also the British Woodcraft Folk, who joined IFM-SEI in the late 1920s but was never a Red Falcon organisation, made sure that the future key areas would be international co-operation, education for tolerance, for co-operation, for solidarity and for human rights.

Despite many inner debates and conflicts the "Falcon family" agreed to organise international camps under the slogan "Span the world with friendship". In 1952, the re-founded IFM member organisation in Germany hosted a big international summer camp under the theme: Falcon State "Young Europe", formulating the vision to learn from the Second World War and to establish a continent of peace. More than 3 000 children and young people from 12 countries participated. The camp was a commitment to co-operate despite the rising East–West conflict. Many member organisations of IFM in eastern European countries had not been able to re-establish themselves after 1945 or had been merged into the youth movements of the socialist states behind the Iron Curtain. At the same time, young people started to organise educational tours to former concentration camps of the Nazi period. Under the slogan "Never again" they tried to analyse the circumstances of the 1920s and 1930s that paved the way for fascism, inferiority, racial ideology, anti-Semitism and industrial-scale mass murder.

1950s and 1960s: trying out global perspectives

In the aftermath of decolonisation of many other parts of the world during the 1960s, the IFM started to include new non-European members and new fields of action. In particular, it expressed solidarity with non-European liberation movements and the attempts to tackle the problems of the new independent states, which often received the status of "developing countries" within the global system. The new tasks, which extended the former frame of European-centred Falcon work, also resulted in another change in the name of the organisation. The 1970 conference decided on a merger of the two older names IFM and SEI to IFM-SEI (International Falcon Movement – Socialist Education International). With these decisions the organisation signalled that it was willing to co-operate with like-minded organisations which did not necessarily have the same background as that of the classic Falcon groups.

Furthermore, what were new, experimental, educational concepts of international co-operation were tried out. At the Rallye to France in 1954, thousands of young people travelled by bicycle from their homes, though Europe to Paris, instead of living together on the same campsite for weeks. The closer they came to France the bigger the groups became.

IFM-SEI's member organisations continued to have intense debates about the strategies towards achieving an end to the exploitation of human beings by other human beings, about the necessary steps to be taken towards a fair and just society, and about capitalism. They often did not agree on the many theoretical perspectives that were advanced and educational tools that derived from them. Nevertheless, when it came to IFM-SEI camps, such differences were usually easily put aside in the interests of organising these big events and the educators were more willing to compromise in order to ensure a successful experience.

By the end of the 1960s, IFM-SEI had contacts with more than 70 countries worldwide and had the aim to become a global movement. Some of the contacts became members; some did not. Moreover, besides looking at the North–South divide and progressive strategies for this, the East–West divide attracted more and more attention. Most member organisations were rather hesitant to co-operate with youth movements from eastern European countries (which was now the Eastern bloc), as they already had their own international platforms and the social democratic family was sceptical about such exchanges. However, educationally, IFM-SEI became more political due to the Cold War, for example by discussing on a summer camp whether or not education can be neutral (as it is claimed by many institutions), and debating possible forms of resistance and active solidarity with people who live in authoritarian countries.

During the 1960s, IFM camps were established every three years as their peak and profile experience and, in addition, the IFM umbrella organisation developed many educational resources and concepts for educators, with the aim that even young people in local youth clubs would also know what was going on internationally and about their parallel organisations in different parts of the world. All members, it was felt, should feel ownership and a sense of being part of IFM-SEI, even if they had never participated at an international activity.

1970s and 1980s: socialism – a global struggle for equality and peace

From the 1970s on, IFM-SEI politicised even more. One reason was probably the global tensions between East and West and the fascist regimes in Chile and Nicaragua that brutally worked against left-wing groups, socialist political parties and ideas. IFM-SEI strengthened relations with the European Youth Forum, the Socialist International (SI) and the European Youth Foundation of the Council of Europe, organised joint activities with the International Union of Socialist Youth and had several co-operation meetings and joint activities with the Scouts and Guides movements and CIMEA, the international platform of the Pioneer movement organisation from the communist states of central and eastern Europe. During the 1970s, IFM-SEI member organisations from western Europe invited representatives from CIMEA and organised the first international exchanges with youth groups from Poland and Romania.

The groups did not exchange much about socialist concepts (as they knew they would not agree). The aim of the partnerships was more to overcome borders and isolation and not agreeing to a possible new war by meeting each other. In 1981, IYNF (International Young Naturefriends), CIMEA (International Committee of Children's and Adolescents' Movements), WOSM (World Organisation of Scouts), WAGGGS (World Association of Girl Guides and Girl Scouts) and IFM-SEI formed an international co-operation called CAIC, which organised common youth activities between western and eastern Europe in the spirit of peace, friendship and children's rights. In the 1980s, IFM-SEI ran a big anti-war-toy campaign with many European member organisations. In recognition of their contribution to the programme and objectives of the International Year of Peace, proclaimed by the United Nations General Assembly, the UN Secretary-General designated IFM-SEI with the honorary title of Peace Messenger for their anti-war-toy campaign in 1987.

The Latin American work of IFM-SEI reached its climax in 1973 with the murder of Salvador Allende in Chile and in 1974 with the arrest of the IFM-SEI leader Aloides Molina in Paraguay. IFM-SEI member organisations organised large-scale solidarity campaigns and addressed the economic and political oppression in Latin America. These global solidarity campaigns also became part of IFM camps.

The situation in Latin America and the oppression of those countries, and indeed of the entire global South, became more and more clearly a thematic focus of international camps and shaped a culture of political activism and practical solidarity inside IFM-SEI. In 1974, for instance, children from different continents produced musical instruments, together with comrades from Chile, on the IFM-SEI camp in Austria and sold them on the open camp day to guests and to the local community near the campsite. The money was used to help people from Chile go into exile or to help open a kindergarten in Chile. A few years later, during 1984-85, the miners' strike in Great Britain was followed by a massive solidarity wave in western European IFM-SEI organisations. Local groups collected money for the miners' families by organising concerts. They sent Christmas presents to the children in Britain and invited them to their own summer camps on the European continent.

Educationally, the first concepts of IFM-SEI as a feminist movement had been discussed during the 1970s. This did not aim to overthrow the practice of co-education but to find strategies against the discrimination of women in society and within its own structures. Some member organisations established women's conferences and developed the first concepts on how to talk to young people about sexual topics and relationships. Other educational topics were child abuse and the life of young people in conflict areas. The UN Convention on the Rights of the Child was still under discussion and IFM-SEI played a significant role in supporting the advocacy work towards the adoption of this convention.

1990s – Say the dirty word? Socialism

After the Berlin Wall came down in Germany in November 1989 and the Soviet Union broke apart (by 1991), the concept of socialism was not very attractive in many societies. Free market capitalism had apparently "won"; it was the "end of history" according to the political scientist Francis Fukuyama. Even though solidarity campaigns continued to activate co-operation between left-wing youth movements in Latin America, the 1990s in IFM-SEI can be summarised as a decade of de-ideologisation. The first movements from eastern Europe joined the international umbrella of IFM-SEI but were rather hesitant to discuss socialist values and alternatives to the world economic system. IFM-SEI organised a series of training programmes and seminars to strengthen the eastern European region. They focused on different topics (such as campaigning, training for trainers, participation) and were an attempt to establish a network of organisations in eastern Europe.

In 1997, the first IFM-SEI summer camp took place in the former Eastern bloc, in Hungary. By that time, eastern Europe had become a relatively strong European IFM region, following many member organisations from the region joining in the early 1990s and benefiting from training and seminars organised by IFM-SEI. The focus of the summer camp was put on children's rights and children's participation. At a "camp tribunal" children could sue their countries for violations of children's rights. The organisation of the summer camp led to big internal discussions. It took place at a holiday resort in Hungary and not on a campsite with tents. The discussions about how to organise an IFM-SEI summer camp show quite clearly that socialism as a core principle of IFM-SEI was in crisis. Regrettably, by the turn of the millennium, the membership of IFM-SEI in eastern Europe had declined quite dramatically. Today, there are only a small number of active member organisations in central and eastern Europe.

In 1995, the IFM-SEI conference voted the first female leadership of IFM-SEI, with Odette Lambert from the Belgian Faucons Rouges as secretary general and Jessi Sörense from the Danish Dui-Leg og Virke as President.

IFM-SEI has member organisations from Israel and Palestine. In 1992, Rabin was re-elected as Prime Minister of Israel and took the Israeli–Palestinian peace process to a new promising level by signing several historic agreements with the Palestinian leadership as part of the Oslo Accords. During this time, the Middle East region formed itself as its own world region inside IFM-SEI and started a peace process by Israeli and Palestinian youth meeting each other, and by organising peace camps with the support of the IFM-SEI secretariat in Brussels and sister organisations from Europe. The Middle East Youth for Peace co-operation continues until today. The Palestinian and Israeli members work closely together in the regional leading group, a core group of two members from each organisation, which has a big impact on the co-operation between the Israeli and Palestinian member organisations.

From 2001 on, IFM-SEI was also very active in the area of reproductive health education and on corporal punishment. In Latin America, Africa, Asia and Europe a series of seminars took place to tackle this taboo subject and to train peer educators to work on this topic.

Plus ça change, plus c'est la même chose?

In May 2018, the Socialist Youth of Germany (Die Falken), the German member organisation of IFM-SEI held a conference on organisational development. By way of introduction, there was a reflection on the evolution of socialist education, with some level of nostalgia for the past but an equal determination to transform the future. The start of the text is worth reporting in full:

> The history of our working youth movement has been long and rich in tradition. Already more than one hundred years ago young people joined forces to fight the injustices in this society and those forces who deprive them of the good life. Unfortunately, this

fight has been only partly successful. On the one hand, over the many decades the workers' movement has successfully pushed for a lot of improvements. In recent years, however, progress for workers has stagnated and sometimes even regressed as state and society have incorporated modern technology and adopted greater flexibility at the expense of the working population. We still live in a class society in which people have to work for a wage in order to survive while this work is making others rich. At the same time the concrete organisation of this class society has changed: The big industry which once employed tens of thousands in its factories has mostly vanished. In the few places in which large-scale industrial production still exists, the number of employees has been significantly reduced due to modern technology. Many centres of production have long shifted to the Global South.

All of these developments have also impacted on the *Falken*. Particularly the milieu from which our membership traditionally came has changed radically. The old workers' quarters, in which workers from one factory used to live together, where children played in the court yards and where workers would meet one another in shops, pubs and at work, have vanished. Today most of our members work in the offices of small enterprises, their colleagues usually live in different parts of town. As a result, we all live a mostly isolated life – we do not even know our own neighbours, let alone their worries and qualms. As the old social relations among the workers have been dissolved, their consciousness of belonging to the social collective of wage labourers has also been lost. Today almost everyone has to work. But almost no one considers her- or himself as belonging to a class of people who all share the same destiny. For that reason people generally do not identify with socialism anymore.

In the days of the *Kinderfreunde* (the children and youth organisation which preceded the *Falken*), there was such thing as a workers' movement which encompassed all aspects of life, from culture and sports to the upbringing of children. Among the conscious workers' families it was thus a given that their children would join the *Kinderfreunde* and would be educated by older proletarians ("by the working class, for the working class"). In those days the movement was educating children for a socialist future they were sure they would attain: They were convinced that the quasi naturally necessary and progressive development towards socialism was inevitable, that they would step by step build a new society from the capitalist one.

In the Weimar Republic the task of the *Kinderfreunde* was, accordingly, to educate workers' children so as to enable them to shape this new socialist society together. On this path, the community of the *Kinderfreunde* groups represented the first cell of the future society. Here children and youth could experience in practice what it means to live in solidarity and could acquire socialist thinking and feeling. The annual "children's republic", as the *Kinderfreunde* called their summer camps, represented the annual highlight of the movement's work. Here the *Kinderfreunde* could put their socialist and democratic ideas into practice, if only for a short amount of time: Together with their guides, children would build and administer their own "states" and they were having heated discussions and arguments about how to do this, both in their groups and in the camps' parliament. This new society, the future they talked about so much, never came into being and the "utopian consciousness" of those days has how disappeared almost completely. Accordingly, wage labourers no longer send their children to the *Falken* because they believe that the children of the working class should be raised by the movement of the working class. Rather, they appreciate that the *Falken* summer camps are very affordable or perhaps (if less and less so) they know nice *Falken* members from their own membership in the Social Democratic Party (SPD) or the trade unions. In other cases still, families from the alternative, urban bourgeois society send their children to the movement camps because they support the *Falken* approach of giving children a say in their education and their way of life.

Looking into the future, however, if we want to remain relevant as a socialist educational movement, we have to ask ourselves: As a socialist youth movement, how do we want to organise our social critique? And what does socialist education mean under the current conditions?

Undeniably, we do no longer share the endless optimism of our comrades in the 1920s, who believed that capitalism would automatically dissolve into a classless society. In contrast with these old, progress-oriented conceptions of education for a socialist future, we must thus focus on managing the present in a socialist way. The goal of the education in the movement must be to further and sustain critical self-reflection and a critical investigation of the current social order. The forms and methods we employ to attain this goal can take different shapes: From recognising and formulating interests in a group and independently or collectively fighting for them, to developing a debating culture based on solidarity, to classic educational activities. In the best case, we will empower youth to change their immediate environment and then to push for change on a larger scale and in the whole society.

In our groups we must live as a community in solidarity. Unlike in the old days, we do not simply aim to create a collective in which the individuality of each and everyone of us will be dissolved. Rather the goal is to create a community of solidarity of different people, who can live and express their difference and enjoy equality. Groups are the places where youths can study in solidarity and as a community and where each one can enjoy at least partial protection from the unacceptable demands of society. In our camps, even very young people can experience a different world on a small scale. The Falken's pedagogical works is also always a way of creating a concrete, lived utopia: We are not waiting for tomorrow, we want to live differently and treat each other differently here and now.

We can state: Capitalist society is constantly changing. This means that we, too, must constantly reflect and adapt our analysis of society and our pedagogical concepts accordingly. We might still have a long way to go, but giving up is not an option! Things are definitely not going to improve if we don't do anything. Instead, building on a critical reading of our own history, we must develop a modernised theory and practice of socialist education and finally use the power of our movement to its full potential. We must recommit to the challenge of changing this world. In other words: We cannot wait for better times to come, we need to create them ourselves.

(Original in German, translated into English by Frederik Schwieger and Sabine Troitzsch)

Conclusion – Back to the roots!?

Since the 2000s, IFM-SEI's work has become more political again. The Train for Change summer camp, organised by Kinderfreunde Austria, Czech Pionyr and IFM-SEI brought together children and young people from all over the world. The children themselves decided that the camp should be about Action for Social Change with the themes Gender and Sexuality, Discrimination and Prejudices, the World Economic System, Climate Change and Children's Rights. In addition, IFM-SEI increased its number of projects and activities, especially at a global level, on topics such as poverty, equality and inclusion, sustainable development, co-operation and on the Millennium Development Goals (now the Sustainable Development Goals).

The co-operation of IFM-SEI with the social democratic family is still close but it continues to be ambiguous. Some member organisations have close links, others none at all. However, it can doubtlessly be said that the shrinking of social democratic influences in society also creates a difficult situation for IFM-SEI and many of its member organisations. Right-wing parties or groups are increasingly attacking some member organisations and those organisations are currently struggling with the political shift to the right (in Europe, in Brazil, in the Philippines and elsewhere).

Moreover, many funding possibilities do not focus on long-term support for weekly group work anymore but instead on projects, which organisations have to apply for time and time again. For an organisation where young people decide on topics it is sometimes difficult to pin down topics, aims and objectives before the activities take place (hardly an uncommon problem for youth work more generally, but perhaps particularly acute given the methodological principles of IFM-SEI). The pressure to fulfil criteria from applications and funders puts self-organised youth groups into a difficult situation and tends to pressure young educators to fulfil them by any means. This challenge is compounded for a world movement such as IFM-SEI, which always tries to find ways to equally involve all world regions in their activities, when most available funding is primarily for European projects.

IFM-SEI will become 100 years old very soon and will take this centennial anniversary opportunity to focus on what it was originally founded for – first, the fostering of shared socialist values through non-formal education at local, national and international levels; second, promoting the active and meaningful participation and inclusion of children and young people; and third, ensuring that the work of IFM-SEI and its member organisations is led by children and young people, not simply for or with them.

References

Brücher B. (1995), *Die Sozialistische Erziehungsinternationale 1922-1970*. Das politisch-pädagogische Selbstverständnis der Sozialistischen Erziehungsinternationale von ihren Anfängen bis 1970 [The Socialist Educational International 1922-1970. Political-educational self-understanding for the Socialist Educational International from the beginning until 1970], Bonn (Leben und Geschichte, Bd. 5).

Eppe H. and Uellenberg W. (1976), *70 Jahre Sozialistische Jugendinternationale*. Zur Geschichte der internationalen Kinder- und Jugendorganisationen [70 years Socialist Youth International. The history of international children- and youth movements], Bonn (Schriftenreihe der Sozialistischen Jugend Deutschlands – Die Falken, Dokumente 12/13).

Fukuyama F. (1992), *The end of history and the last man*, Free Press, New York.

IFM-SEI (2018), Strategy and work plan 2019-22.

Löwenstein K. (1929), "Die Aufgaben der Kinderfreundebewegung" ["The task of the childfriends movement"], *Sozialistische Monatshefte* Vol. 35, No.12, p. 1118.

Schwitanski A. (2006), *Sozialistische Jugend Deutschland – Die Falken*, We turn the world into a global village: span the world with friendship; a short history of international IFM-SEI camps in pictures.

Chapter 10

Europe in the interwar years: youth organisations of authoritarian regimes

Eli Pilve, Marti Taru, Simona Sglavo

Introduction

The social integration of young people is a challenge that lies ahead of every society. At the individual level, youth may be viewed as a period during which young people acquire the skills and knowledge they need for coping in society. Today, part of the activities assembled under the umbrella term youth work represents a domain that provides an opportunity to guide the integration of young people into society. Throughout the history of youth work, one of the aims of voluntary activities, in which young people are involved outside the school, home or workplace, has been to support the development of personality and acquisition of skills required for coping in society. It also aims to develop young people's identity as citizens.

At the level of society, a significant, but certainly not the only, role of youth work may be viewed as a sphere that helps to increase social coherence. The key to exploiting the potential of influencing youth and society is to use specific educational methods (such as Scouting, or open youth work). However, employing sociopolitically neutral methods may also pose some risks. The instrumentalisation of youth work is seen as a process whereby the attention and objectives have shifted from the development of young people to promoting a specific goal, organisation or ideology and to socialising them into that organisation or worldview. For any government, the support or at least the passiveness of the population is a prerequisite for attaining the rulers' political ambitions, not active resistance. Instrumentalising youth work to absorb young people's periods of free time and influence their worldview, emotions and thoughts is extremely attractive and seizing this opportunity is also understandable.

In the last century, European political systems have varied from democratic to totalitarian forms of government. The time between the two major wars shows that the transition in a country from one regime to another may be fast. Since the activities focused on youth do not develop independently from the rest of society, we start with a brief survey of the past social and political development in Europe between the two world wars.

A brief look at the interwar period in Europe

Three empires collapsed in the First World War: Tsarist Russia, the Austro-Hungarian Empire and Imperial Germany. The Ottoman Empire came to an end in 1924, also because of the First World War. By the end of the war the former dominions of all three empires were replaced by 11 dependent countries that were all, except Russia, trying to build parliamentary democracies. The newly established national states released national sentiments and considerable social change took place.

The influence of the middle classes rose at the expense of the traditional aristocracy, the conditions of peasants improved through agricultural reforms, the working class strengthened and women gained suffrage. At the same time, democracy was unable to solve the protracted economic instability increased by war debts and payable reparations. As a result, autocratic governments managed to sustain a few dictatorships that had developed between the two wars with the support of active crowds and ideology, primarily communism and fascism. Hence, we can say that the First World War obliterated the 19th-century autocracies but due to its failure to create any viable alternative, it made way for the 20th-century dictatorships (Lee 2002: 20-24). The initial euphoria relating to democracy was gradually replaced by disappointment. The inflation of the 1920s in Germany, the world economic crisis of 1929, the hostility of ethnic groups and social classes strongly influenced political parties. The support groups for liberal parties diminished, whereas populist and Catholic parties managed to keep their supporters, becoming consciously more right wing. Conservative parties became more and more anti-democratic and authoritarian, while left-wing parties wavered between socialism and communism. In such unstable circumstances people began to long for firm political leadership that would restore stability. Extraordinarily frequent government crises developed, bringing along the situation where a head of state in the person of a king or a president would take most of the power from the head of government. In the majority of European countries, constitutions permitted heads of state to implement extraordinary powers if "necessity" demanded, grafting dictatorship to the existing democratic basis. Bolshevist Russia was the only country that completely destroyed its former institutions. The others, including Nazi Germany, retained most of their initial constitutional framework. In the context of general discontent, however, it was not hard for Mussolini, Hitler, Piłsudski, Dollfussi, Primo de Rivera and others to enthral crowds with their charisma, big promises and simple solutions (Lee 2002: 28-30). They all possessed their own ideology according to which they began to restructure their societies. They all ruled their sole governing parties to which both legislative and executive power were subordinated. The party would secure massive support, particularly among the younger generation, subordinating the individual to the state dictatorship by coercion and brainwashing. Education, literature, art and music were put into the service of ideological propaganda and free enterprise was replaced by a state-controlled economy (Lee 2002: 416). During this period, voluntary paramilitary organisations as well as military forces emerged in democratic states. The emergence of these organisations was in response to increasingly active protest movements, not a top-down initiative of the state.

Alongside the increasing authoritarianism of the regime, control over young people became more intense. For that, state-regulated youth organisations were founded which aimed at controlling young people and socialising them into the atmosphere and social order of the time. It was most apparent in Italy, Germany and the Soviet Union (Miller 1938: 965). Below, a short overview will be given of how it happened in five states: Italy, Germany, Spain, Portugal and Estonia.

Italy

The first ideas of founding an autonomous fascist organisation for uniting younger generations had emerged in Italy as early as 1919. In January 1920, the organisation Avanguardia Studentesca dei Fasci Italiani di Combattimento (Student Avant-garde of the Italian Fascist of Combat) was founded in Milan. Even though the organisation had some discord with the Italian Nationalist Fascist Party (Partito Nazionale Fascista), the latter would receive its support the following year, which in turn resulted in the enlargement of the organisation itself, involving not only students but also workers aged 15-18. Before the law on the Opera Nazionale Balilla (ONB) was adopted in 1926, other groupings for children aged 8-14 were set up in 1922. The ONB was more popular in northern parts of Italy where economic and organisational opportunities were better than in the southern part of the country. The ONB was faced with competition from Catholic and Methodist youth organisations, and also from the Voluntary Militia for National Security (MVSN, Milizia Volontaria per la Sicurezza Nazionale), which had been founded in 1923. In 1924, after the murder of Giacomo Matteotti, a political opponent of the fascists, the party assumed direct control over all Italian youth organisations (Stellavato 2008).

While founding the authoritarian fascist paramilitary youth organisation ONB, Mussolini received great help from Renato Ricci, Minister of Education, who supported Mussolini's vision of a new Italy (*Italiano nuovo*). In order to achieve the goals, Ricci visited educational institutions in England and the USA and also met with Robert Baden-Powell, the founder of the Boy Scout Movement. The inclusion of sports and physical activity in his educational project was driven by his wish to be admired and followed throughout Europe. In his views on developing strong and physically capable young people, Ricci relied on the example of Eugenio Ferrauto and formed the theory and ideology on which the activity of the ONB was based. The law on the foundation of the ONB was adopted on 3 April 1926. Initially, becoming a member of the organisation was voluntary, but membership was made mandatory in 1935, much to the displeasure of other fascist and Catholic youth organisations. The activity of the latter, however, was not banned (Meakin 2007). From 1937, however, all Italian youth organisations for members aged 6-21, excluding students' organisations, were merged with the ONB and the consolidated organisation was called the Italian Youth of the Lictors (GIL, Gioventù Italiana del Littorio). Ricci, the founder of the Balilla, had by then fallen into disfavour with the authorities and was discharged. The new organisation started under the slogan "Believe! Obey! Fight!". When organising youth, the Italian regime learned from the Soviet Union but adopted an ideology that was extremely militant. At the same time, they also followed the example of the 10 commandments of the Catholic Church, creating for themselves parallel forms which stated, for example, that Mussolini was always right and imprisonment was always deserved (Delzell 1971: 143-45).

By 1939, the organisation had a membership of almost 7 million children and young people. In the early 1930s, the number of voluntary members had been approximately 2 million (Pasqualini 2013).

Despite the fact that formally the ONB was controlled by the Italian Ministry of National Education, it was to some degree independent. The presence of the organisation in the school system was ensured by the mandatory membership of schoolchildren and teachers (Stellavato 2008).

Germany

The Italian organisation ONB is regarded as a model used for the foundation of another authoritarian paramilitary youth organisation, Hitler-Jugend (the Hitler Youth), and the repeating pattern in the history of these two organisations is easily noticed. The origins of the Hitler Youth date back to the year 1922 when the organisation was one of many youth organisations in Germany and also one of the two youth groups of the Nazi Party. In the spring of 1922, the Nazi Party founded two youth organisations, the Jugendbund der Nationalsozialistische Deutsche Arbeiterpartei and the Jungsturm Adolf Hitler, which were both disbanded after the Beer Hall Putsch in 1923 but continued their activity underground. In 1924, the Jugendbund was renamed Grossdeutsche Jugendbewegung (Greater German Youth Movement) and the date when the organisation was renamed again (although not for the last time), 4 July 1926, is considered the foundation day of the Hitler Youth. The official name of the organisation was the Hitler-Jugend, Bund der deutscher Arbeiterjugend (Hitler Youth, League of German Worker Youth). In the same month, the organisation was given its final name, Hitler-Jugend, Bund Deutscher Arbeiterjugend (Hitler Youth, League of German Worker Youth). After a short power-struggle period with a rival Nazi youth organisation, the Jungsturm Adolf Hitler, the Hitler Youth became the Nazi Party's official youth organisation. The organisation was banned in 1932 by Chancellor Heinrich Brüning, but the ban was lifted by Franz von Papen, the successor of Brüning.

Despite the temporary illegal status of the Hitler Youth, the number of its members increased steadily. Before and especially after the First World War, numerous youth movements existed across Germany, but the most important among them were those formed for political reasons, so the Hitler Youth with its political orientation was swiftly integrated into society. The activity of Kurt Gruber, the founder and chairman of the organisation, was held in good esteem in the party. His deteriorating health prevented him from staying in this position and in 1931, he was replaced by a young and enthusiastic man called Baldur von Schirach, who concurred with Hitler's view that youth should be led by youth (*Jugend muss von Jugend geführt werden*) (Sauerwein 2006).

Although the origins of the Hitler Youth date back to 1922, it can be considered authoritarian only after 1933, when, following the coup by the Nazi Party and its takeover of power, the conditions became favourable for imposing Hitler's vision of how youth should be led, through incorporating all existing youth organisations into the Hitler Youth and disbanding Jewish organisations. In 1930, the Hitler Youth had affiliated around 25 000 boys from the age of 14, and two years later, the membership was already about 70 000. After the Nazi Party took over the government in

1933, the membership increased dramatically to over 2 million. Mostly, this increase resulted from the forced takeover of other youth organisations. In 1934, the Hitler Youth became the only legally permitted youth organisation in Germany and the incorporation of all youth organisations under the Hitler Youth was completed by 1938 when the organisation had 7.5 million members, including girls (Miller 1938: 965-66).

The Hitler Youth was structured as a Scout organisation and it drew together boys aged between 10 and 18. The leaders were young people aged 18-19, who were in charge of about 1 000 members, but their responsibility was limited. The activity was mainly physical training, but in many communities, members came together twice a week to listen to ideological lectures. As in the Young Communist League (the Komsomol), the members were encouraged to spy on other young people so as to reveal their views (Miller 1938: 967).

As the girls' wing of the Hitler Youth, the League of German Girls (BDM, Bund Deutscher Mädel) was established in 1930 for girls aged 10-17. The origins of the girls' organisation also date back to the 1920s when the predecessor organisations of the Hitler Youth started. Similar to the Hitler Youth, the BDM became a mass organisation after 1933 when the integration of other girls' organisations into the BDM started. Formally, membership was voluntary until 1936. All members had to be ethnic Germans, German citizens and free of hereditary diseases. In 1938, the BDM section Glaube und Schönheit (Faith and Beauty) was added, which was voluntary and accessible to girls between 17 and 21. The aim was to groom girls for marriage and domestic life, but also for future careers. Sports and physical capability were also considered important (Krentz 2002).

Spain

In Spain, following the civil war during the 1930s, General Franco emulated the regimes described above, namely Fascist Italy and Nazi Germany. The closest ally of Spain at that time was Italy; the Spanish Interior Minister Serrano paid a state visit to Italy and returned with a large collection of fascist books for guidance on the further development of the Spanish regime (Payne 1987: 234).

When Franco took power in 1937, the party immediately started to pay attention to the ideological education of youth, establishing the National Delegation of the Youth Organisation (Delegación Nacional de la Organización Juvenil) (Cruz Orozco 2012), which in reality started its activity after the civil war, of course. The state aspired to have all young people aged 7-21 under its control (Manrique Arribas 2011: 233-72). The law establishing Frente de la Juventudes (Youth Front) was adopted on 6 December 1940 and its membership was made mandatory for all learners of basic and secondary schools, be it a private or public institution (Mauri Medrano 2015). The aim was to facilitate the military and political development of young people and to educate new loyal members of the party. The main division of the organisation, the Falanges Juveniles de Franco (FJF), assumed a central role in organising young people (Cruz Orozco 2012), but it never became a full mass movement, mobilising at its height, according to its own official statistics, only 13% of boys and 8% of girls. Membership of the FJF was voluntary (Payne 1987: 240). The link uniting the organisations was the Falangist mentality, appropriated with theoretical views on educating youth chiefly from José Antonio Primo de Rivera, one of the founders of the Falange Española Tradicionalista (Traditionalist Spanish Phalanx) (former Falange Española) and Juntas de Ofensiva Nacional-Sindicalista (the Councils of the National Syndicalist Offensive) (Manrique Arribas 2011: 233-72).

By a law of 1939, all spare-time organisations that had been set up before the Spanish coup of 17 July 1936 were disbanded. In January 1941, establishing new organisations without the government's approval was prohibited. Some exceptions still remained: those regulated by the Civil or Merchant Code, Catholic associations with religious purposes only, the institutes and corporations approved by a special legislation, co-operatives registered in the Ministry of Labour and those groups under the law of Falange Española Tradicionalista y de las Juntas de Ofensiva Nacional-Sindicalista. Therefore, the only educational bodies had to be part either of the Falange or of the Catholic Church (Sanz Fernández 2000: 333-58). Other non-governmental activities organised for youth, such as those by the Asociación Nacional de los Excursionistas de España or by the "Boy Scouts" were prohibited and almost became clandestine bodies, often protected by the Church (Manrique Arribas 2011: 233-72). Despite the initial limits imposed on the Catholic Church to religious functions only, over time it acquired a stronger influence over education. This translated into the creation of several movements of Catholic Action, which inevitably created some clashes with the central authorities, although in fact, since their creation, every institution with the Falange provided a Catholic consultancy and the same organisation was obliged by law to collaborate with the Church and family (Sanz Fernández 2000: 333-58).

***

The three states – Italy, Germany and Spain – even attempted to establish a European Youth Association. The first session of the international congress was held in Vienna between 14 and 18 September 1942, a meeting that also included participants from other European countries. At the meeting, apparent discrepancies between Germany and Spain occurred in their views on the role of family and religion in society. Even though the Franco regime admired the way the Hitler Youth organised young people, it was hard for them to agree with anticlericalism, which is why Spain was, with regard to educational issues, closer to the Italian ONB. Even though the latter had some clashes with the Church, Catholicism was clearly important in the ideology of the organisation (Cruz Orozco 2012).

Portugal

After the military coup of 28 May 1926, the president was vested with absolute power in Portugal, but in 1932, real power was seized by António de Oliveira Salazar, who had been appointed prime minister. In a short time, educational reforms were pushed through with the aim of provoking ideological reform; intellectual aspects were only of secondary importance. In addition, attempts were made to control young people outside school.

The establishment of the youth organisation Mocidade Portuguesa in 1936 was preceded by several other initiatives aiming to organise young people, all built around school. Junta Escolar do Integralismo Lusitano de Lisboa, formed in 1929, was meant to guide young people willing to contribute to the development of their country. Yet, from 1932, the body ceased to be independent and was gradually incorporated into the new National Syndicalist Movement (MNS). Back in 1930, the Ordem Lusa (OL) had been established, which had a goal to educate young people towards greater discipline, physical activity and moral integrity so that they could easily be integrated into the defence forces. Although the OL was considered independent from state institutions, it was presided over by the President of the Portuguese Republic and its management board was appointed by the Ministry of Education. All children, young people and adults aged 8-35 were automatically registered as voluntary members of the OL; they were also defined as non-active members. The initiator of the OL was Gustavo Cordeiro Ramos, the Minister of Public Education, who later launched Liga da Mocidade Portuguesa (LMP) (the League of Portuguese Youth). Similar to the OL, the League aimed at organising all young people aged 8-21, who were voluntarily recruited in school. More specifically, LMP was created to form adolescents' bodies for the militia service and instil in them love and loyalty for the motherland (Flunser Pimentel 2006-07: 19-43). In January 1934, the Acção Escolar Vanguarda (AEV) was constituted by António d'Eça de Queirós, António Ferro and the law student Ernesto de Oliveira e Silva. The latter soon became the head of this new youth movement. Controlled by the Secretariado de Propaganda Nacional (SPN), it represented an attempt to educate youth and shape the future National Syndicalists after the dissolution of the MNS (National Syndicalist Movement). The new organisation promoted the values of family and church and also nationalist attitudes. It was based mainly on volunteers and was organised around schools. However, accusations of financial misdealing in its management proved fatal for this organisation and led to establishing a new one (Cobbe Dias 2014).

In a propaganda session of the União Nacional (UN) in 1935, Portuguese diplomat Francisco José Nobre Guedes launched the idea of establishing an organisation aiming to educate young men. António Faria Carneiro Pacheco, Minister of Education, envisaged the creation of a new organisation to achieve that. An act was adopted in April 1936 that led to the official establishment of Mocidade Portuguesa soon afterwards, in May 1936. The organisation aimed to activate male youth between 7 and 14 years old. Its goal was to ensure the civic, moral and physical education of young people, for which obligatory membership was established. Discipline was one of the main values because this was seen as useful for paramilitary training, in order to prepare new militants for the Estado Novo (New State) (Cobbe Dias 2014).

In August, 1936, another organisation – the Obra das Mães pela Educação Nacional (OMEN; Mothers' Work for National Education) – was created. Its main objective was supporting the development of girls and young women in their future role as mothers, wives and workers in social services. OMEN was managed mainly by women from the aristocracy or by wives of party members. The following year the Mocidade Portuguesa Feminina (MPF) was created, involving all Portuguese girls and young women aged 7-14. The Mocidade Portuguesa Feminina aimed to strengthen national and religious sentiments among young women, while cherishing traditional feminine ideals. Its activities revolved around three main axes: preparation for traditional female roles, physical education and artistic expression (Flunser Pimentel 2006-07: 19-43).

The state was responsible for the control over youth, which led to the situation where all NGOs depended on and were controlled by the Mocidade Portuguesa. Moreover, their statutes had to be approved by the Alto Comissário para a Mocidade Portuguesa (High Commissioner for Portuguese Youth). The first High Commissioner, Francisco José Nobre Guedes (1936-40) used Hitler's Germany as a model. His successor, Marcello Caetano (1940-44) focused instead on building links with the Catholic Church and Scouts, and on overcoming previous clashes between state and Church (Orlando Queirós 2014). Mocidade Portuguesa and Mocidade Portuguesa Feminina had close connections with youth organisations in Italy, Germany and Spain.

To some extent, Portuguese authorities and state institutions were influenced by Italian Fascism and German National Socialism in their approach to the organisation of youth. Nevertheless, there are also some differences in the role and position of the Mocidade Portuguesa and the Mocidade Portuguesa Feminina. Unlike in Italy and Germany, in Portugal, state and Church managed to collaborate in the education of youth, and the school system successfully defended itself against totalitarian attacks (Flunser Pimentel 2006-07: 19-43). As a result, the control over youth did not develop to the same degree as in Germany and Italy.

Estonia

In 1918, after Estonia regained its independence, a paramilitary organisation Kaitseliit (Estonian Defence League) was founded that united adult men on a voluntary basis. An affiliate organisation of the Defence League for adult women was set up in 1927 under the name Naiskodukaitse (Women`s Voluntary Defence Organisation). Both of them had a significant role not only in the broader development of youth organisations in Estonia, but also in the 1930s, after the idea to unite different youth organisations had been proposed. But already in 1925, when the Defence League did not yet have its own youth organisation, integration of the existing Scout movements with the Defence League was thought of as a way ahead rather than establishing a new youth organisation (Hünerson 1926: 487-90; Petrov 1925: 17-19). However, an idea of a completely new organisation was soon launched and in 1928 the intention of establishing youth groups was approved by the leaders of the Defence League. The key idea was to involve young people who had not yet joined any organisation and to collaborate with the existing organisations (Kaitse Kodu 1928: 371-72; Neggo 1930: 32-34). On 24 March 1928, the newly established youth organisation was given a name: Noored Kotkad (Young Eagles) (Neggo 1928: 379-81). The organisation for girls was to be named Kodutütred (Home Daughters). While laying the foundation for these organisations, the existing patriotic Scouting organisation Noorsepad (Young Black Smiths) was believed to be of use. Since at that time the state did not support the activities of youth organisations, including the Young Black Smiths, the initiators of the latter might have found it reasonable to be under the wing of a strong organisation, that is, the Estonian Defence League. Besides, they had been somewhat separated from the Scouts because they felt the Scout Movement was not patriotic enough, which is also why integration with the Defence League seemed appropriate ideologically. For the Estonian Defence League, it was sensible to incorporate an organisation whose annual average membership was around 2 000 (Kaitse Kodu 1933: 493; Tilk 1991: 28). For a number of reasons, the Young Black Smiths became the first Young Eagles.

After the coup of 1934, attempts by the state to organise youth and to join together existing youth organisations became more deliberate. One of the aims still was to also involve those who had not joined any of the organisations (Kaitse Kodu 1934: 737-38). After establishing the authoritarian regime in 1934 (Vaan 2005: 35-36; Vahtre 2005: 92-106), the State Elder Konstantin Päts took a clearer course of integrating youth associations into one (Kaitse Kodu 1935: 14). In 1935, the *Kaitse Kodu* journal of the Estonian Defence League published an article on the idea of organising youth groups by force or subjecting all the organisations to unitary leadership. In the activity of this united organisation, adopting appropriate methods was considered important (Kadak 1935: 743) – but the choice over what was appropriate was left to adults. In 1936, Päts[70] issued a decree – the Youth Organisation Act – aimed at involving young people in organisations, and unifying and controlling the targeted activities of these organisations in line with national interests and educational principles. Also, the meaning of the term youth was defined as including persons under 20 years old (Riigi Teataja 1936).

In the spring of 1938, a law amending the Youth Organisation Act was adopted, under which the president of the republic, who after the amendment of the constitution of 1938 was the then Prime Minister Konstantin Päts, became the patron of all Estonian youth organisations who led their activity through the Ministry of Education. The president of the republic was also granted the right to form associations and unions of the existing youth organisations and determine the principles and foundation of their activity. At the same time, the commander of the Defence Forces became the representative and the leader of all youth organisations. All organisations that involved members under the age of 18 had to be registered and approved by the minister of education (Riigi Teataja 1938). At the beginning of 1939, the president of the republic issued Guidelines No. 2 on youth work, according to which the united youth organisation called the Estonian Youth (Eesti Noored) included the organisations Noored Kotkad, Kodutütred, Eesti Skautide Malev, Eesti Gaidide Malev, Tallinna Noorseppade Malev, all the youth divisions of ethnic minority associations or other Scouts' friends, namely all Scouting organisations or divisions for youth existing in Estonia so far (ERA 1939a, 1939b). Merging existing organisations into the Estonian Youth was to be started from the Scouting-based organisations but the president had the right to integrate all other youth organisations when he deemed this necessary. The united organisation was also made accessible, upon request, to non-Scouting youth organisations, that is to all existing youth organisations. The new centralised youth organisation was to start its activity on 1 January 1940 (ERA 1939a). In reality, it never took place since, due to the changed international situation and national politics, the state was confronted with more pressing problems. In 1939, the Soviet Union forced the Republic of Estonia to sign the Soviet–Estonian Mutual Assistance Treaty, also known as the Bases Treaty, and Estonia had to allow Soviet troops to be stationed on its territory. In 1940, Estonia was occupied by the

---

70. The official title of Konstantin Päts was *Riigivanem* (State Elder) in the years 1934-37, 1937-38 *Riigihoidja* (President-Regent), 1938-40 *Vabariigi President* (President of the Republic).

Soviet Union. Because of these events, the establishment of the Estonian Youth Organisation never in fact took place. An organisation bearing the same name, but following a different ideology, was founded in Estonia in 1942 when Estonia was occupied by Germany.

Conclusion

This chapter has looked into youth organisations within European authoritarian regimes between the two great wars of the 20th century. One of the important characteristics of authoritarian and totalitarian regimes was the establishment of centrally guided youth organisations. Dictatorships and democratic forms of government take a different approach to the issue of educating youth. Both democratic and authoritarian societies have their own values and principles that are considered right (or wrong) and these are passed on to young members of society. However, democracies tolerate different opinions and discussions on values and principles while authoritarian regimes do not accept independent thought of citizens in public and the principles pronounced by the authorities cannot be challenged or discussed. Questioning the truth announced by the authority may, depending on the brutality of the regime, result in repression of the dissenter. Under such regimes, the views and needs of young people are secondary; priority is given to the ideals defined by organisations and/or ideologies. Over time, youth work has been greatly influenced by the nature of the regime in power, not by its internal development in appreciating young people and meeting their needs.

This history illustrates that authoritarian regimes try to set up youth organisations that enable them to control the minds of young citizens and provide the means for ensuring the obedience of youth to the regime. Youth work is instrumentalised for shaping the politically correct worldview of young people. Alternative youth associations or activities are not tolerated (Coussée et al. 2013). Drawing on some vivid examples, this chapter describes the ways in which, during the 1920s and mainly in the 1930s, European authoritarian regimes established youth organisations in support of the regimes.

After the First World War, European nations were extremely enthusiastic about democracy and national independence. Over time, it became apparent that independence and democratic government did not necessarily ensure political stability and economic prosperity. The governments changed frequently, the states suffered from the global economic crisis, and all this fuelled discontent and sentiments that allowed for the imposition of a strict order. In some countries, this resulted in the establishment of an authoritarian regime by the head of state or government. This happened not only in the larger European states but also in new small states that had only recently freed themselves from foreign dictatorships and gained independence. Naturally, these tendencies had direct consequences for society, including youth organisations. As illustrated by the above examples, authoritarian regimes also imposed more or less authoritarian rules on the spare-time activities of youth. The main aim of the state-controlled youth organisations was to socialise and mobilise young people so that they would support and realise the objectives of the political regime, and to develop loyal citizens who can be controlled.

All the states discussed above followed the same pattern. First, those in power found that a state-controlled youth organisation was needed. This would provide an opportunity to develop loyal supporters of the regime whose energy could be employed for promoting ideological objectives. The establishment of organisations did not have to start from empty space; instead, they were built on existing associations. By using the command-and-forbid mechanisms that were available only to the state, like legislative power, administrative power (control over the registration and disbanding of associations) and state resources, an organisation was founded that had or was intended to have a central role in organising youth. In all countries, the highest representatives of the state authority played a part in the process – ministers and heads of the state – and they were often also the instigators of the organisational reforms. Other powerful organisations allied with the state, such as political parties or paramilitary organisations of adults, were also involved in the processes. One significant aspect that can be pointed out in the case of Estonia, and also Germany and Italy, is the fact that the interference and support of the state also meant considerable material and financial assistance, which in turn provided an opportunity to offer activities and facilities to young participants that the weaker organisations operating only or mainly on a voluntary basis could not afford. Better opportunities and conditions made the organisations more attractive to young people, so that they became very popular and increased their membership remarkably. The main goal, however, was to promote support of the regime. Obviously, these developments had little to do with the needs and preferences of most of the young members and their leaders.

As the examples show, some international exchanges were also going on at the same time with the intra-national developments of establishing state-supported youth organisations. Clearly, there was some exchange of information, perhaps also exchange of best practices. Such exchanges took place, however, between the political leaders and institutions, not between members and leaders of the youth organisations; in other words, this too happened over the heads of youth.

References

Cobbe Dias R. (2014), "O regime salazarista português nas escolas elementares" [The Portuguese Salazar regime in elementary schools], *Intersaberes* Vol. 9, No. 17, available at www.uninter.com/intersaberes/index.php/revista/article/view/574, accessed 6 August 2019.

Coussée F., Taru M. and Williamson H. (2013), "Youth work in connection to policies and politics", in Coussée F., Taru M. and Williamson H. (eds), *The history of youth work in Europe*, Vol. 4, Council of Europe Publishing, Strasbourg.

Cruz Orozco J. I. (2012), *Falange, Frente de Juventudes y el nuevo orden europeo. Discrepancias y coincidencias en la política de juventud durante el primer franquismo* [Falange, Frente de Juventudes and the new European order: agreements and discrepancies in youth politics during the early Franco years], available at http://www.educacionyfp.gob.es/dam/jcr:a20cc371-8971-440a-b778-6b23b8a2c140/re35723.pdf, accessed 6 August 2019.

Delzell C. F. (1971), *Mediterranean fascism 1919-1945: selected documents edited by Charles F. Delzell*, Macmillan, London.

ERA (1939a), *Vabariigi Presidendi juhend noorsoo organiseerimise alal no. 2* [Guidelines No. 2 of the President of the Republic on Organisation of the Youth], not signed, 16 February, 1108.7.219, l. 237-38.

ERA (1939b), Noorsoo-organisatsiooni "Eesti Noored" seadus [Act that amends the Youth Organisation Estonian Youth Act], not signed, 25 May, 1108.7.219, l. 359-62.

Flunser Pimentel I. (2006/2007), "Influências internas e externas na Obra das Mães e na Mocidade Portuguesa Feminina" [Internal and External Influences on the Work of Mothers and Portuguese Female Youth], *Campus Social* Vol. 3-4, pp. 19-43, available at http://revistas.ulusofona.pt/index.php/campussocial/article/view/222/131, accessed 6 August 2019.

Hünerson J. (1926), "Skoutlus ja riigikaitse ülesanded. Noorsoo rahvavaimustus" [Scouting and the tasks of national defence. Folk spirit and enthusiasm of the youth], *Kaitse Kodu* No. 12, pp. 487-90.

Kadak E. (1935), "Noorsoo organiseerimine – päevaprobleem" [Organisation of young people – a hot issue], *Kaitse Kodu* No. 22, p. 743.

Kaitse Kodu (1928), "Kaitseliit asutab noorte rühmad" [The Defence League is establishing youth groups], *Kaitse Kodu* No. 6, pp. 371-72.

Kaitse Kodu (1933), "Meie noored: Noorte pere tuleb ühendada ühiseks tööks" [Our youth: young people need be united for our common work], *Kaitse Kodu* No. 17, p. 493.

Kaitse Kodu (1934), "Meie noorte organiseerimisest" [On organising our young people], *Kaitse Kodu* No. 23/24, pp. 737-38.

Kaitse Kodu (1935), "Eesti noorsooliikumine vajab ühtlustamist" [Youth movement in Estonia is in need of unification], *Kaitse Kodu* No. 1, p. 14.

Krentz N. (2002), *Der Bund Deutscher Mädel (BDM)* [The League of German Girls], Deutsches Historisches Museum, available at www.dhm.de/lemo/kapitel/ns-regime/ns-organisationen/bund-deutscher-maedel.html, accessed 6 August 2019.

Lee S. J. (2002), *European dictatorships, 1918-1945*, Routledge, London and New York.

Manrique Arribas J. C. (2011), "Juventud, Deporte y Falangismo. El Frente de Juventudes, la Sección Femenina y los Deportes del Movimiento" [Youth, Sports and Falangism. The Youth Front, the Feminine Section and the Sports of the Movement], in Piujadas X. (ed.), *Atleta y ciudadanos. Historia social del deporte en España. 1870-2010 [Athletes and citizens. Social history of sport in Spain 1870-2010]*, pp. 233-272, available at www.researchgate.net/publication/265514767_Juventud_Deporte_y_Falangismo_El_Frente_de_Juventudes_la_Seccion_Femenina_y_los_Deportes_del_Movimiento, accessed 6 August 2019.

Mauri Medrano M. (2015), *Frente de juventudes y escuela: la construcción del imaginario social de la juventud durante el franquismo (1940-1960) [Youth and School Front: the Construction of the Social Imaginary of Youth during the Franco Regime]*, available at www.researchgate.net/publication/322562238_Frente_de_juventudes_y_escuela_la_construccion_del_imaginario_social_de_la_juventud_durante_el_franquismo_1940-1960, accessed 6 August 2019.

Meakin T. (2007), "Mussolini's Fascism", *History Review* No. 59, pp. 40-44.

Miller J. W. (1938), "Youth in the dictatorships", *American Political Science Review* Vol. 32, No. 5, pp. 965-70.

Neggo V. (1928), "Noored Kotkad", *Kaitse Kodu* No. 7/8, pp. 379-81.

Neggo V. (1930), "Missuguseks peaks kujunema "Noorte kotkaste" organisatsioon" [What should be the organisational form of "Young Eagles"?], *Kaitse Kodu* No. 1/2, pp. 32-34.

Orlando Queirós J. (2014), *History of youth work and youth policies in Portugal*, Council of Europe, Strasbourg, available at https://pjp-eu.coe.int/documents/42128013/47262055/H4_Portugal.pdf/d7a1f14a-dd00-4890-90b7-ee7b1bac0bb4, accessed 6 August 2019.

Pasqualini M. (2013), *Mente sana en cuerpo sano: Raza, juventud y cultura física en una publicacion del fascismo italiano (1930-1937) [Healthy Mind in Healthy Body: Race, Youth and Physical Culture in a publication of Italian Fascism (1930-1937)]*, XIV Jornadas Interescuelas/Departamentos de Historia, Departamento de Historia de la Facultad de Filosofía y Letras, Universidad Nacional de Cuyo, Mendoza, available at http://cdsa.aacademica.org/000-010/914.pdf, accessed 6 August 2019.

Payne S. G. (1987*), The Franco regime, 1936-1975*, The University of Winsconsin Press, Madison WI.

Petrov L. (1925), "Kaitseliit ja skoutlus" [The Defence League and Scouting], *Kaitse Kodu* No. 1, pp. 17-19.

Riigi Teataja (RT) (1936), *1936, 82, 655,* Noorsoo organiseerimise seadus [Youth Organisation Act], 7 October.

Riigi Teataja (RT) (1938), *1938, 33, 262,* Noorsoo organiseerimise seaduse muutmise seadus [Law on the Amendment of the Youth Organisation Act], 1 April.

Sanz Fernández F. (2000), "Las otras instituciones educativas en la Postguerra Española" [The other educational institutions in the Spanish post-war period], *Revista de Educación*, No. Extra 1, pp. 333-358.

Sauerwein T. (2006), *Hitlerjugend (HJ), 1926-1945*, available at www.historisches-lexikon-bayerns.de/Lexikon/Hitlerjugend_(HJ),_1926-1945, accessed 6 August 2019.

Stellavato O. (2008), "Gioventù fascista: l'Opera nazionale balilla" [Fascist youth: the Opera Nazionale Balilla], PhD thesis, Università degli Studi "Roma Tre", Faculty of Political Science, available at http://dspace-roma3.caspur.it/bitstream/2307/180/1/Gioventu_fascista._LOpera_nazionale_balilla.pdf, accessed 6 August 2019.

Tilk M. (1991), *Skautluse ajaloost* [History of Scouting], Tallinna Pedagoogiline Instituut, Tallinn.

Vaan L. (2005), *Propagandatalitus Eesti Vabariigis autoritaarsel ajajärgul*, MA thesis, University of Tartu, Tartu.

Vahtre S. (ed.) (2005), *Eesti ajalugu VI: Vabadussõjast taasiseseisvumiseni* [Estonian history VI: from the War of Independence to regained independence], Ilmamaa, Tartu.

Chapter 11

The Komsomol and youth organisations in Belarus

Olga Khabibulina

Introduction

In late September 2018, an announcement was circulating the internet in Belarus informing about the plans that month for celebrating the centenary anniversary of the Komsomol within the country. Some historical facts will help us discover why that date is important in understanding the current political and social situation and the history of the organisation, which was founded in the Russian Communist Republic in 1918 and still exists in the independent (since the collapse of the USSR in 1991) Republic of Belarus.

The Komsomol stands for the All-Union Leninist Young Communist League (Kommunisticheskiy soyuz molodyozhi). It was officially established in 1926 as a step towards the reform of the Russian Leninist Young Communist League. This raises the question of what the connection was between Russian communist youth and Belarusian communist youth in the 1920s.

The formation of the Komsomol

After the communist revolutions of 1917, the political dimension had also been brought into the youth sphere. Previously, in the time of the Russian Empire, youth work was mainly concentrated within volunteering activities and was closely connected with the system of formal education at its different levels of primary, secondary and, for those who were granted it, higher education.

If the upheavals of the early 20th century are examined more closely through the lens of youth affairs, it is important to mention that the revolutions that had shaken the system of absolute monarchy in the Russian Empire were also about establishing agency for promoting youth in the political sphere. The political arena both at legislative and executive levels, was closed for young people prior to the revolutions. Consequently, after the revolution period of February to October 1917, there was a much wider involvement of youth in the political and social spheres of life. In theory, youth should have been playing an important role in the USSR, which was formed officially in 1922, but in practice the role of youth had been limited to various executive missions concerned with fulfilling a variety of aims targeted by the Communist Party. At the same time, throughout the period of the USSR's existence, pragmatic use was made of the youth resource by the political authorities in supporting the execution and propagandising of their aims, and there was a total lack of any real involvement of youth in the policy-making process.

From its existence until its collapse in 1991, the Communist Party and state bodies, with the help of the Komsomol, sought to ensure a cheap and massive workforce that should have guaranteed an intensive solution for either rapidly reconstructing the damaged economy after any war, or supplying itself with arms and concomitant goods.

Komsomol membership requirements

As defined in its statute, the age of prospective members of the Komsomol was defined as 14-28 years old. During the Soviet era, it was expected that all young people within this age range who applied to join the Komsomol should have membership status. However, within the internal ideological transformations of the Soviet political system, membership of the Komsomol had become a type of privilege and a guarantee of a positive career-building process for young people. The opposite applied to those young people who did not or were not allowed to become members of the Komsomol. If a young person was not a member of the Komsomol, then he or she would definitely experience ideological difficulties in job promotion, securing awards for free apartments or prestigious resort opportunities during summer breaks.

In fact, this policy of discrimination towards applicants for membership of the Komsomol had already existed almost from the start when, in the 1920s and 1930s, there was a formal requirement prescribed: non-proletarian (for example, non-working) youth were not accepted. Therefore, the number of members during the first decades of the organisation's existence was only about 0.2% of the total youth population inhabiting all 15 Soviet socialist republics that were finally gathered under the name of the USSR. It is important to underline that 70 years later, the number of members had increased to approximately 40 million[71] (in 1984, the highest number), whereas by 1991 it had dropped off to approximately 26 million, bringing the proportion to 7.5% of the total youth population. The requirement of work experience for applicants, which had to be from at least six months to two years, had been enforced since the 1920s until the collapse of the USSR. By 1990, it was impossible to leave the Komsomol voluntarily. In many countries that had obtained sovereignty and independence after the collapse of the USSR, the Komsomol organisations were liquidated.

Early history, aims and ideology

In Belarus, on 24 September 1924, the First All-Belarusian Plenary (the legislative body of the Communist Party in the Soviet Belarus) accepted the idea of establishing the Communist Union of Belarus Youth (KSMB, Kommunisticheskiy soyuz molodyozhi Bielarusi). By that time, the Belarusian Soviet Socialist Republic had been officially formed on 31 July 1920 and in December 1922 it became one of the constituent members of the USSR along with Russia, Ukraine and Transcaucasia, which had chosen, dependently or independently, the political rule of state socialism. The

---

71.   Encyclopaedia Britannica: www.britannica.com/topic/Komsomol.

plenary session outlined that KSMB had become an undivided part of the Russian Communist Union of Youth. In 1926, this would be transformed into the Komsomol, merging the youth communist leagues in all the socialist republics.

The overall aim of the Komsomol was then not disputed for well over half a century and was formulated as follows: to prepare youth for the defence of the socialist motherland by training them to become self-sacrificing patriots ready to resolutely repel attack by any enemy.

While subscribing to its overall aim, the Komsomol also developed quite effectively more direct and short-term strategies that defined its goals within the prevailing political situation of the USSR at both internal and international levels. As an example, there was a goal of fighting against "non-Bolshevik elements" and of recruiting soldiers to fight at the side of the Red Army in the civil war. Another example is that in the 1920s and 1930s youth in the Komsomol became involved in the processes of industrialisation, collectivisation and eliminating illiteracy across the rural areas of the USSR. During the Second World War, it was quite a privilege to apply for recruitment on a voluntary basis, rather to be recruited systematically for military actions involving the Russian Army.

The level of Soviet propaganda steadily increased as part of reinforcing the building of ideology, but it is important to note that this still met some of the expectations of young people: being involved politically and benefiting from some economic advantages. For example, it was a matter of honour to serve in the Soviet army. Another example of the rewards available was that the most active Komsomol members were granted accommodation, in the form of apartments. This was for the duration of their service in the executive or nominally representative structure bodies, or with professional promotion and/or reserved places at specially designated departments of state universities under the name, Department for Working Class Representatives. Education was free, part-time and its schedule met the needs of working youth members of the Komsomol.

After the Second World War

In his analytical article on the political education of youth in the USSR, Ploss (1956: 490) notes, "The strenuous effort to indoctrinate Komsomol and Soviet youth which has been witnessed in the past decade may be traced to the months immediately preceding V-E Day". Indeed, it can be seen that immediately after the Second World War, the Central Communist Party, the executive body of the Soviet system, had put much more endeavour into youth involvement in the communist agency through their participation in the largest and most central youth organisation in the Soviet Union. After the end of the Second World War, the Komsomol witnessed a considerable increase in its membership, mainly due to the fact that young people were looking for new possibilities for their professional and economic advancement. They had come to the conclusion that membership of the Komsomol was worthwhile and likely to be rewarded. Consequently, the number of Komsomol members had been rapidly increasing from the end of the 1940s until the mid-1980s. It seems to have been the best match of the target group's expectations with the political agency's need for the implementation of ideology.

As a result, the Komsomol had become the most popular youth organisation in the USSR among those that existed in the areas of culture, sport and science.[72] This was not only due to its strong, multifaceted propaganda tools but also because of its response to the needs of the young people who had formed the Komsomol. Both aspects had made the Komsomol prestigious and popular. Consequently, the more specific goals of the Komsomol for the period from the end of the 1940s until 1991 were concentrated on activities such as construction (Baikal–Amur Mainline) and education (extracurricular activities on a so-called voluntary basis in the formal education system). Only members of the Komsomol could rely on promotion in the spheres of science or sport.

Logically, only members of the Komsomol could be applicants to the Communist Party, however Komsomol membership did not guarantee automatic membership. The party's governing body selected members carefully, seeking to eliminate the entry of young people with potentially oppositional views. Moreover, exclusion from both the Komsomol and the Communist Party was a kind of rejection of those people with different views from the official ideological point of view. The Komsomol also served as a mobile pool of labour and political activism, with the ability to relocate people to geographic and economic areas of high priority at short notice.

At the same time, the Komsomol was used by the Communist Party of the USSR as a tool for political influence and propaganda throughout the whole population. Possessing and using its media resources such as the newspaper *Komsomolskaya Pravda* (The Komsomol Truth), the organisation played an important role as a mechanism for communicating the values of the Communist Party to young people. It is important to underline, however, that in fact the Komsomol had little direct influence on the Communist Party or on the government of the Soviet Union, but served like a nomenklatura[73] pool.

Belarusian independence and the establishment of new youth organisations

Just before the USSR collapsed in 1991, various independent youth organisations were established in Belarus with the support of Western youth organisations with their patterns of youth work (UNESCO Clubs, Belarusian Scout and Guide Girls organisations, Red Cross Society, Voluntary Service Organisations). It is worth mentioning that several youth organisations were rooted in intellectual pro-national circles and planned to support the aim of supplying the government bodies of the independent country with youth brought on by the ideas of national identity (Shukan 2003: 109-44). At the same time, many of those who kept their membership in the Komsomol and never left it officially, were later able to reconvert easily to the reality of civil society

---

72. The Komsomol was the dominant and largest youth organisation, although rightfully there were several youth and children organisations that constituted the membership of the Committee of Youth Organisations, a kind of umbrella youth organisation representing Soviet youth mainly at international level.

73. Nomenklatura – the ruling elite at national and local level in the Soviet governance system. Encyclopaedia Britannica: www.britannica.com/topic/Soviet-law#ref749933.

organisations and pluralist initiatives and tended to incorporate methods and tools of youth work entertained in the Komsomol to the newly established organisations.

Over the next decade in Belarus there was a boom in establishing new youth organisations. Within that boom the Belarusian Youth Union, which was nominally the successor of the Belarusian Branch of the Komsomol, started officially in the 1990s. Also, there was still the Belarusian Pioneer Organisation, which had inherited the symbols and statute documents from the Pioneer Organisation of the USSR.

Meanwhile, however, there were consultations with the Council of European National Youth Councils (CENYC) on forming and transforming the national umbrella youth organisation, including the potential leading role of the newly established independent organisation – the Belarusian Youth National Council "Rada", which was formed in 1993 (Zinchenko 2016:131). At the same time, the acting Committee of Youth Organisations that had been founded in the late 1980s was also playing the umbrella role for youth organisations.

However, the "Rada" had been co-chaired by three heads of youth organisations in Belarus: the Association of Young Politicians, the organisation Next Stop – New Life, and the Belarusian Youth Union. Many experts consider the time during the 1990s as the "golden age", when youth organisations had the opportunity for defining their own cross-sectoral strategy and fundraising management, acting independently at international levels and seeking youth promotion and inclusion in various spheres.

A short while later, in 2002, the Belarusian Youth Union left the "Rada" and merged with the Belarusian Patriotic Youth Union. Shortly after that, the Belarusian Republican Union of Youth (BRUY) acted as an initiator for creating an "updated" version of the Belarusian Committee of Youth Organisations (BCYO), which had also been formed in 1993. In fact, the BCYO tended to act as the national umbrella organisation following close co-operation with state bodies and getting sound funding for its activities from the state budget. For several years there were two national umbrella organisations in Belarus that represented youth organisations with different ideological positions.

Both processes of youth policy making and implementation were rather thin, due to the changes in the executive bodies of the Belarus government that was reforming and delegating the issues of youth from one department to another. This influenced youth organisations' unity regressively.

The break in the youth sector was, as a result, unavoidable. Many youth organisations that, at the time, decided on closer co-operation with the government decided to leave the "Rada" and join the Belarusian Committee of Youth Organisations, of which BRUY was a member.

BRUY was the main pro-government youth organisation in Belarus and since the establishment of the Belarusian Committee of Youth Organisations has aimed, in accordance with its statute documents, at creating conditions for the diverse development of youth by supporting young people's creative potential, and enabling them to contribute to civil society based on the patriotic and moral values of the Belarusian nation. The organisation today also acts as the major partner for youth policy implementation in Belarus, with more than 500 000 members, which is approximately one quarter of the youth population of Belarus.[74] One particular issue is that the BRUY, which receives the major part of the state budget granted to youth organisations at national and local levels, also benefits from close co-operation with national and local state authorities, which allows it to reach larger numbers of young people.

Conclusion

In summary, with regard to the history of the Komsomol organisation and its influence on the present situation and youth policy in Belarus, it is worth underlining that a system with one leading youth organisation, with a huge membership, under the direct influence of the prevailing political ideology still exists in Belarus. That situation causes fragmentation in the youth sector, diminishing the role of other actors, denying them the opportunity of active participation, and isolating them from the policy-making processes.

References

Ploss S. I. (1956), "Political education in the postwar Komsomol", *The American Slavic and East European Review* Vol. 15, No. 4, p. 490.

Shukan I. (2003), "Les recettes d'une reconversion réussie: étude de cas des Komsomols ukrainien et biélorussien à la fin des années 1980" [The recipes of successful reconversion: case study on the Ukrainian and Belarusian Komsomols in the late 1980s], *Revue d'études comparatives Est-Ouest* Vol. 34, No. 2. pp. 109-44.

Zinchenko Y. (2016) *Rada: moepokolenie* [Rada: my generation], Kovcheg, Minsk.

---

74. Statute of the Belarusian Republican Youth Union: http://brsm.by/about/info/statute/.

Chapter 12

The turbulent history of youth work in Bosnia and Herzegovina

Lana Pasic

Introduction

Youth work in Bosnia and Herzegovina has existed in different forms since at least the beginning of the 20th century. Youth work is an activity carried out by young people, civil society, policy makers, researchers, youth workers, parents and other social professionals during informal learning and leisure time, to discuss young people's needs and reflect on their lives. Due to its complexity, youth work can be defined and examined in a broader sense than we perceive it today.

At the end of the 1800s and turn of the century, youth work was taking place within traditional education settings, carried out by private educational and religious institutions, and within youth activism movements related to the pro-independence resistance movement with pan-Slavic sentiments.

Following the Second World War, youth work became more structured and organised, with the state socialist government actively engaging young people in the system. This was through the Union of Pioneers and activities such as youth work actions, which relied on young people's volunteerism and participation in infrastructure projects, as well as political activity, cultural events, sports and youth clubs. State control over young people's leisure time subsided in many parts of Yugoslavia over the decades. In contrast, there was a boost in youth engagement in Bosnia and Herzegovina during the 1980s due to the organisation of the 1984 Winter Olympic Games in Sarajevo.

In the early 1990s, due to rising ethno-nationalism, youth engagement was focused on political advocacy and peace protests. This quickly changed in 1992, as the four-year long armed conflict put a stop to much of the structured practice of youth work. During this 1992-95 period, most of the youth work and youth club work that took place was ad hoc, conducted by individuals on a pro bono basis, or by humanitarian organisations. On the other hand, the formal structures that persisted focused on the political and military engagement with young people and promoted ethno-nationalism and hatred.

Following the signing of the Dayton Peace Agreement[75] in November 1995, the structural vacuum in youth work was filled by civil society (local and international) and foreign donors. Thus, in the late 1990s and early 2000s, youth work focused on topics of reconciliation, peace building, dialogue and tolerance. Even 20 years after the conflict, the youth sector is still largely influenced by international actors and foreign donors, operating with a European outlook, particularly during the last decade. Youth organisations and the youth sector continue to look towards Europe for guidance, structural support, networking and funding, with a clear focus on skill development, employability and mobility of young people.

At the institutional level, however, youth work and the youth sector have not yet achieved their full potential. Due to the specificities of Bosnian institutional arrangements,[76] the relevant youth ministries, policies and laws exist only at the entity levels, with cantons and municipalities also lagging behind when it comes to youth strategies. In the future, a lot still remains to be done to align institutional and civil society sector engagement with expertise on youth work.

Bosnian youth at the turn of the century

At the end of the 1880s and turn of the century, young people in Bosnia and Herzegovina were mainly engaged by educational and religious institutions. The multi-ethnic nature of the Bosnian state at the time, comprising Muslims, Orthodox, Catholics and Jews, and the social, cultural and political influences from the occupying Ottoman and Austro-Hungarian empires, shaped young people's sentiments and type of engagement.

During the Ottoman times, schools and religious institutions worked closely together on influencing personal development and value systems of young people through religious and private educational institutions. Changes in the geopolitics of Europe in the late 1800s resulted in the demise of the influence of the Ottoman Empire in the Balkans. At the Berlin Congress in 1878, the Austro-Hungarian Empire, aspiring to have a greater role in the region, gained the right to administer Bosnia and Herzegovina, eventually annexing it in 1908, resulting in the Bosnian crisis.[77]

In parallel, the emergence of the pan-Slavic movement in the 19th century and the ideas of a common state free from both Eastern and Western influences was gaining ground among intellectual elites in the region, and Bosnia and Herzegovina was no exception.

---

75. The General Framework Agreement for Peace in Bosnia and Herzegovina was initialled in Dayton, Ohio on 21 November 1995 and formally signed in Paris, France, on 14 December 1995, ending a four-year conflict in Bosnia and Herzegovina.

76. According to the Dayton Peace Agreement, Bosnia and Herzegovina is composed of two entities: Federation of Bosnia and Herzegovina, which further consists of 10 cantons, and Republika Srpska, as well as a self-governing District Brčko. The highly decentralised nature of the Bosnian state means that there is a limited jurisdiction at the state level.

77. The Bosnian crisis was a state of international tension between Austria-Hungary, Germany, Russia and Serbia over a final annexation of Bosnia and Herzegovina by the Austro-Hungarian Empire in 1908. Although it was resolved diplomatically, it is considered to have contributed to the start of the First World War.

The change in political and administrative influence on the country, and the independence of the neighbouring states and pan-Slavic sentiments, also influenced Bosnian youth and led to the formation of youth movements. Young people, disillusioned with their socio-economic status, were becoming more interested in politics.

High school and university student movements were active in the country, and were particularly influenced by young Bosnians abroad. In 1910-11, a first meeting of Slavic and Bosnian youth took place in Vienna, setting the grounds for the intellectual pan-Slavic orientation of young people. Their revolutionary and militant attitudes gave rise to attempted assassinations of important figures (Grgić 2007).

In 1910, an attempted assassination of one of the Austrian representatives in a Bosnian village by a young peasant, and the 1912 student and youth protests in Sarajevo, set the scene for the emergence of one of Bosnia's most prominent youth movements – Young Bosnia (Mlada Bosna) (Masleša 1945). Due to its loosely ideological, but largely unorganised, nature, the movement was open to a range of intellectual influences, student groups and pan-Slavic movements from neighbouring and European centres: Belgrade, Zagreb, Vienna and Prague. It is believed that with the help of radical groups and organisations in Belgrade members of Mlada Bosnia planned and executed the Sarajevo assassination of Archduke Franz Ferdinand and his wife Sophia on 28 June 1914, which is considered to be the trigger for the First World War.

Following the First World War, Bosnia and Herzegovina was incorporated into the Kingdom of Serbs, Croats and Slovenes, later known as the Kingdom of Yugoslavia. The period between the two wars saw a range of youth movements and ideologies in the country, either with a strong pro-Yugoslav and pan-South-Slavic focus, or with clear anti-Yugoslav and nationalist sentiments (Škulj 2017). A few attempts at establishing Woodcraft youth organisations related to Boy Pathfinders and Girl Hikers of the Kingdom of Yugoslavia were recorded in Sarajevo and youth were also influenced by the Young Communist League of Yugoslavia (SKOJ) (Škulj 2017).[78]

The Second World War and the roots of new forms of youth work

During the Second World War, the occupation of Bosnia and Herzegovina by the military forces of the Independent State of Croatia (NDH), an ally of Germany, resulted in the emergence of resistance movements in the multi-ethnic country. An uprising started on 27 July 1941 in Drvar, with large numbers of young people joining the partisans. The Young Communist League of Yugoslavia (SKOJ) played an important role in organising armed resistance. The United Association of Anti-Fascist Youth of Yugoslavia (USAOJ) was established in Bihać in northern Bosnia in 1942 and co-operated with SKOJ. The two merged into one organisation – People's Youth of Yugoslavia[79] in 1946 (Škulj 2017).

---

78. The Young Communist League of Yugoslavia (SKOJ) had already been established in 1919 but it was declared an illegal organisation through the Protection of the State Act in 1921 and it operated underground after that. Its members set up cultural and educational societies in order to be able to undertake public activities (Škulj 2017).
79. In 1951, the Union of Students of Yugoslavia was established and it also merged with the People's Youth of Yugoslavia. The final name of the organisation was the League of Socialist Youth of Yugoslavia, which ceased to exist at its last congress in Ljubljana in 1991.

During this time, young people participating in the anti-fascist and liberation struggle also had special privileges. In July 1944, the Declaration of the rights of citizens of Bosnia and Herzegovina was passed during the second meeting of the National Anti-Fascist Council for the People's Liberation of Bosnia and Herzegovina (ZAVNOBiH) which, among other rights, including equal treatment of men and women in politics and all other aspects of life, also granted the right to vote to all citizens over 18. However, young men and women in the partisan forces were granted this right regardless of their age, which gave youth a direct vote (Arnautovic 2013). This was symbolically an important step in acknowledging the role young people played in the anti-fascist movement.

Youth work in the socialist Yugoslavia

Following the Second World War, with the creation of the new state – Yugoslavia – youth work became more structured and organised. The socialist government actively encouraged young people's participation in politics and all aspects of life, under the auspices of the party. Due to the anti-fascist movement and ideological influences of the party, youth work was also heavily influenced by values such as collectivism, international solidarity, liberty, brotherhood, unity, equality, social inclusion and cohesion (Krnjaic 2012). Important measures were also taken on youth education, vocational training, employment and housing.

Young people were celebrated as a resource. Youth Day was marked on Josip Broz Tito's birthday (25 May) and the President himself was actively involved in celebrations which involved young people from all Yugoslav republics performing various cultural, artistic and sports activities and ended with them presenting a final torch to Tito himself. Tito and the party repeated his famous mantra, restated during his last appearance at the Youth Day in 1979: "A nation with these young people does not need to worry about its future".

Youth work was integrated within the state education and social welfare system, and comprehensive structures for youth engagement were introduced, including policies and activities which relied on young people's volunteering and engagement in political activities, cultural events, sports and youth clubs (Petkovic 2014). The most widespread and structured methods of youth participation were through the Union of Pioneers and Socialist Youth of Yugoslavia.

Union of Pioneers of Yugoslavia

The Union of Pioneers of Yugoslavia was the main youth body responsible for entrenching collective identity and socialist values in children and youth. Established in 1942, during the Second World War, it played an important role in the post-war state construction of Yugoslavia.

Its activities were based in primary schools, with symbolic rituals such as uniforms and anthems being used to create social connections among young people, emphasising collective spirit and allegiance to the state (Krnjaic 2012). Every child became a "Tito's pioneer" at the age of 7, in the first grade of primary school. The mentors were teachers and older pupils, which meant that an early form of peer-to-peer learning and mentoring was practised. After graduating from primary school, young people were encouraged to join the Socialist Youth of Yugoslavia.

Socialist Youth of Yugoslavia

Socialist Youth of Yugoslavia had been established in 1919, and existed until 1948 as the Young Communist League of Yugoslavia, a youth wing of the Communist Party. After the Second World War, it merged with the Unified League of Anti-Fascist Youth of Yugoslavia, eventually becoming the Socialist League of Youth of Yugoslavia, which existed until 1991 (Krnjaic 2012).

Socialist Youth of Yugoslavia organised various activities in schools, including debating clubs, science groups, cultural, arts and sports activities and youth work actions. It promoted socialist ideology in society, at the same time upholding youth participation and volunteering, building social cohesion and social capital and bridging the ethnic differences in society. These structures created an important base for youth work in the country (Kovačić and Ćulum 2018). Socialist Youth of Yugoslavia was also involved internationally, to a lesser extent, through the former Communist Youth International's (CYI) membership of the World Federation of Democratic Youth and International Union of Students. It organised various international youth events over the decades, with young people from around the world coming to Yugoslavia to participate. As part of these activities, Sarajevo hosted the first International Youth Congress of Esperanto in 1973 (Škulj 2017).

Youth work actions

Some of the best-known youth work practices in the former Yugoslavia were youth work actions, public initiatives and voluntary youth labour camps conducted by young people and organised by the Communist League of Yugoslavia in order to build public infrastructure (roads, bridges, hospitals, railways), organise sports and cultural activities and build trust and collective identity in the multi-ethnic post-conflict country (Krnjaic 2012). More than a quarter of a million young people from Yugoslavia and abroad participated in the volontary construction work between 1945 and the 1970s (Škulj 2017).

The motto of the public work activities – "We are building railways – railways are building us" – implied that these activities contributed on the one hand towards the collective development of the country and on the other hand to the development of young people as human beings and responsible members of society (Krnjaic 2012). Besides providing cheap and fast labour, they helped to build social capital and develop skills and the personal and professional capacities of young people before they entered the labour market (Kovačić and Ćulum 2018).

The works were launched in Bosnia and Herzegovina with the construction of the Brčko–Banovići railway that created transport links to the coal mine. It was followed by the construction of the Šamac-Sarajevo railway, which was completed in seven months with 217 000 young people from Yugoslavia and 6 000 young people from other countries. Other important projects included the Brotherhood and Unity Highway from Zagreb to Belgrade, which by 1963 linked the entire country from

Ljubljana to the Greek border. It also included the construction of large factories, such as the steel factory in Zenica near Sarajevo, and the hydropower plant in Jablanica, Herzegovina. Smaller-scale local work activities in towns was then implemented over the years (Škulj 2017).

An additional positive aspect of the youth work actions was that they were also managed by youth. Even if young people did not have professional training, they built their skills through non-formal education, vocational training and practical work, and acting at times as youth workers (Kovačić and Ćulum 2018).

These activities were a crucial stepping stone in working with young people, although they differed from the contemporary understanding of youth work in several important aspects: they were not co-created with youth but rather planned in advance, participation was voluntary (though still expected and encouraged), the non-formal vocational training offered in the process was focused on building the skills which were required by Yugoslav industry and the activities in which young people participated were often gender-specific (Kovačić and Ćulum 2018). The main criticisms of the youth work actions were that the voluntary nature of the activities was not truly voluntary. Although many young people participated with enthusiasm, in projects whose aim was to reconstruct and industrialise the country, Škulj (2017) argues that a lack of co-operation was unlikely, as it would have been viewed as resistance.

Olympic Games and the revival of the spirit of volunteerism

The 1980s saw the decline of the voluntary youth work actions in Yugoslavia, but the award of the 1984 Winter Olympic Games to Sarajevo boosted volunteerism and youth engagement in Bosnia and Herzegovina, and particularly in the capital city. The Winter Games marked a turning point with regard to Olympic volunteerism, with 10 450 volunteers making a contribution (Panagiotopoulou 2010). The spirit of youth involvement in the Olympic Games continues today, with over 750 volunteers involved in the European Youth Olympic Festival in Sarajevo in February 2019 (EYOF 2019).

Turbulent 1990s: from peace protests to war

During the late 1980s and beginning of the 1990s, rising nationalism was slowly leading to the disintegration of Yugoslavia. In Bosnia and Herzegovina during this time, citizens, including large numbers of young people, took part in the peace protests, anti-war campaigns and petitions for peace. At the same time, nationalist and right-wing political parties exerted their own influence over young people in Bosnia and Herzegovina, shaping their values and belief systems in a different direction.

After the referendum and a declaration of independence on 1 March 1992, and the failure of negotiations and political dialogue, the four-year-long conflict began, displacing over 2 million people (Malcolm 1996). Conflict and insecurity made it very difficult to conduct traditional youth work activities which had taken place in the country until then (World Bank and UNICEF 2003). Youth work was largely influenced and conducted by foreign donors, humanitarian organisations and NGOs, which were catering for displaced children and youth and children in the conflict zones, organising schools and extracurricular activities focused on humanitarian issues (Krnjaic 2012). At the same time, youth work was conducted informally during the conflict by various educators through different types of activities and clubs. However, more formal, organised and structured ways of working with young people only started being put into place after the conflict.

The signing of the Dayton Peace Agreement in November 1995 meant that the structures and institutions were slowly to be re-established. Yet the youth sector was not one of the main priorities for the state. In similar vein to the rest of the region, young people in Bosnia and Herzegovina found themselves marginalised socially, politically and economically (Petkovic 2014). The European Youth Forum (2000), the World Bank and UNICEF (2003) emphasised that the entire South-East Europe region was practically left without a youth policy during this time. Political and social changes created a vacuum not only in terms of policy but also of structures and organised activities of the various states, while youth organisations and civil society were not sufficiently developed as independent actors to fill this gap (World Bank and UNICEF 2003).

From war to reconciliation: youth and peace building

Towards the end of the 1990s, with the focus moving towards peace building and reconciliation, the international sector and non-governmental organisations started organising non-formal education and training aimed at developing young people's personal, professional and social skills. Their work was centred around topics of tolerance, conflict prevention, non-violent communication, conflict resolution, peace building and active citizenship (Kovačić and Ćulum 2018). The international community aimed, through the youth sector, to promote human rights and conflict transformation, and address discrimination and hate speech. This has remained one of the key areas of youth work in Bosnia and Herzegovina until today.

Youth work in the post-conflict era was very much independent from the state system. Young people were seen as having important potential for stability, peace building and conflict prevention. Thus, in many small towns, youth centres and youth organisations were established to address hostility and mistrust, and to organise exchanges and training for young people. Neutral, non-political activities such as music, arts, sports and ecology were promoted in order to overcome prejudices among youth of different ethnicities (World Bank and UNICEF 2003). Some of the examples of the activities in the region included the School of Peace study camp for Youth and the SEE Youth Network volunteer exchange programme to other countries in the Balkan region (World Bank and UNICEF 2003).

Contemporary context

The population of young people in Bosnia and Herzegovina between the ages of 15 and 29 numbers 950 000, or about a quarter of the total population of the country (World Bank 2013). It ranks 80 out of 183 countries on the Youth Development

Index.[80] Out of five indicators (health and well-being, education, employment and opportunity, civic participation and political participation), it ranks lowest in the areas of employment and opportunity (116 out of 183), civic participation (144 out of 183) and political participation (125 out of 183) (The Commonwealth Secretariat 2016).

Civic and political participation are limited because young people have no trust in political institutions, and they are further discouraged by the complex governance system, segregation and corruption. Young people consider their level of influence in schools, the workplace and political organisations to be limited, and they have an insignificant role in decision making (United Nations 2016). Only one third of young people in Bosnia and Herzegovina vote, and less than 3% are members of legislative institutions (World Bank and UNICEF 2003).

The most important concerns for young people in Bosnia and Herzegovina are sustainable livelihoods, education quality, employment and emigration, opportunities for decision making, [not] being in control of their own lives and making their own choices (United Nations 2016). There are large disparities in terms of socio-economic groups and between rural and urban areas, and, particularly for youth belonging to minority groups, the education system is outdated and mobility is limited (Žiga et al. 2015).

The state perceives young people as a problem rather than a solution. Young people are seen as a passive, vulnerable group, with limited social and political rights, strong nationalism, high ethnic mistrust and vulnerability to radicalisation and extremism, high unemployment rates, violence, and lifestyle risks (Žiga et al. 2015). Despite such worrying statistics and perspectives, youth work in Bosnia and Herzegovina is steadily being established, though it is still in a developmental stage.

Institutional and policy framework

The complex administrative structure of Bosnia and Herzegovina means that policy is often fragmented and difficult to co-ordinate. In spite of the commitment to raise the quality of education, training, youth policy and youth work through the Stabilisation and Association Agreement (SAA) that Bosnia and Herzegovina signed in 2015 with the "European Communities and their Member States", young people in Bosnia and Herzegovina still lack a structured system of care (European Commission 2015).

Youth policy is under the jurisdiction of the entity and cantonal level, and relevant ministries only exist at these levels, which means that there is no national-level policy. At the national level, in 2009, the Ministry of Civil Affairs of Bosnia and Herzegovina established a standing body – a Commission for Co-ordination of Youth Issues in Bosnia and Herzegovina – in order to co-ordinate approaches to youth. The Commission has nine members: four members from the government institutions – one representing each of the entities – two from the Ministry of Civil Affairs of Bosnia and Herzegovina, and five representatives from the youth NGO sector. Considering that

---

80. The Commonwealth, "Global Youth Development Index and Report 2016", pp. 118-28. Note: rankings and scores compiled by the Institute of Economics and Peace are on the basis of data available in the 18 indicators of the YDI.

there is no national youth council, the goal of the commission is also to promote youth participation in decision making, as well as to co-ordinate activities related to youth, harmonise entity plans and strategies, analyse problems and co-ordinate youth projects (Ministry of Civil Affairs of Bosnia and Herzegovina 2019).

In 2014, the Agency of Statistics of Bosnia and Herzegovina introduced for the first time the "associate expert on youth work" in its occupational classification (KULT 2014). This is an important step towards recognising youth work, but there are still no educational opportunities or training courses, quality assurance or monitoring system, nor ethnic codes of conduct for youth workers or those working with youth in other sectors, such as health, education or employment. Youth work is financially supported in part by the local and regional governments, but mostly via international donors.

At the entity level, the Ministry of Family, Youth and Sports of Republika Srpska and the Ministry of Culture and Sports in the Federation of Bosnia and Herzegovina are responsible for youth policy and youth work (Jasarevic 2017). Both entities have youth policies focusing on employment, housing, education, youth work, society, information, leisure, participation and culture (Youthpolicy.org 2014). Likewise, there are youth councils active at both these levels.

Federation of Bosnia and Herzegovina

The Federation of Bosnia and Herzegovina has a Youth Law (2010) explaining young people's rights, youth work and youth councils. A Youth Strategy (2016-2020) is still under development, driven by the Federal Ministry of Culture and Sport. As part of the preparation for the Youth Strategy, an Analysis of Federation Bosnia and Herzegovina Youth Conditions and Needs was produced in 2013 and a Draft Youth Strategy was adopted by members of the Working Group in 2015.

Youth work is defined by the Law on Youth of the Federation of Bosnia and Herzegovina as a "planned, purposeful and conscious support to young people through their volunteer participation", including extracurricular education, creative, arts, sports and cultural youth activities, all of which are aimed at developing young people's abilities, skills and knowledge, and are related to the well-being, social and health protection of young people and communities. It also encompasses youth counselling, youth tourism, intercultural co-operation and exchange, and all other models of creative and planned leisure time for youth (Federation of Bosnia and Herzegovina 2010).

Republika Srpska

In Republika Srpska there is a Law on Youth Organisation (2008 and 2011) and a Law on Volunteering (2013). The third youth policy of Republika Srpska (2016-2020) was developed through a highly participatory and consultative process, organised by the Ministry of Youth, Family and Sport in co-operation with the Youth Council of the Republika Srpska, Youth Communication Centre Banja Luka and the United Nations Population Fund (UNFPA), involving over 300 experts and young people (Jasarevic 2017).

The Law on Youth Organisation of Republika Srpska defines youth work as "a part of youth activities organised with and for young people within their leisure time, with the goal of improving conditions for personal and social development of young people together with the general benefit. Youth work is voluntary and it is based on needs and opportunities of young people". Based on this law, government and local communities are expected to adopt youth strategies which include youth work, mobility, information and counselling (Republika Srpska 2012).

Other structures

In District Brčko, a draft Law on Youth was adopted in 2017 (Government of Brčko District 2017). At the cantonal level, youth policies are largely awaiting adoption and implementation, with Canton Sarajevo adopting its first Draft Youth Strategy in 2018 (Canton Sarajevo 2018).

At local level, youth work has been more tangible, although policies and strategies have been influenced by international agencies. Youth councils started developing in the late 1990s and early 2000s (World Bank and UNICEF 2003). Today, youth councils, youth centres, youth clubs and the Association of High School Students serve as forums for youth voices and their activities, and are important autonomous spaces for youth, where young people undergo training and organise various initiatives (Schuler Helfen Leben 2018).

Municipalities have various budgets for youth, including Novo Sarajevo, Jablanica, Gračanica, Banja Luka, Prijedor and Trebinje (KULT 2019). Yet only 10% of municipalities across Bosnia and Herzegovina have a municipal officer in charge of youth. Likewise, only 47% of municipalities have adopted any kind of strategy on youth, of which very few are implemented (Žiga et al. 2015).

Civil society and youth organisations

As contemporary youth work in Bosnia and Herzegovina started developing independently of the educational and welfare state systems, it is to be expected that the non-formal sector continues to have a large influence on its functioning. The youth NGO sector, think tanks and youth workers have become more numerous over the past few years and their capacities have also been strengthened through various European programmes and donors.

It is estimated that there are between 250 and 300 youth organisations in Bosnia and Herzegovina and they are the main providers of youth work in the country. Their portfolios include the provision of non-formal education, organising initiatives, projects, information services, opportunities for volunteering, and also serving as training centres for new youth workers (Jasarevic 2017).

At national level, various organisations have been influencing the youth field. The KULT Institute for Youth Development has been operating in Bosnia and Herzegovina since 2011. The institute aims to co-operate with authorities at all levels and with local and international organisations, and it has initiated the draft youth legislation in the Federation of Bosnia and Herzegovina and in Brčko District. KULT conducts non-formal education through seminars and courses, workshops and round tables, and it publishes materials and supports youth organisations and informal groups through their activities (KULT 2019). KULT has lobbied for the recognition of youth work as an occupation, and since the incorporation of youth work in the occupational classification, it has been working on providing training and capacity building for youth workers through one-year courses (KULT 2014).

The youth sector operates with a clearly European perspective – youth organisations and the youth sector are looking towards European initiatives for guidance, networking and funding, with a clear focus on skills development, employability and mobility of young people. The range of activities varies from education to social work, particularly in the area of prevention, countering radical influences and nationalism, and promoting reconciliation and peace building. Unfortunately, the values promoted through non-formal education by the civil society sector are largely in contrast to formal education in the country. The Bosnian education system is segregated, with separate curricula for young people from different ethnic groups, and physical segregation in schools.[81] This division remains in spite of Bosnia and Herzegovina's commitment through the Stabilisation and Association Agreement to ensure "that access to all levels of education and training in Bosnia and Herzegovina is free of any discrimination on the grounds of gender, colour, ethnic origin or religion." This means that there are two very different, competing influences on young people (European Commission 2015).

The European and international dimension

European and international actors have invested in strengthening the youth sector in Bosnia and Herzegovina through various initiatives and programmes, developing volunteering, and European and inter-regional youth exchange in the Western Balkans. The European Union, Switzerland and the USA prioritise youth issues in their strategic documents, and the Council of Europe makes an important contribution to young people in the country.

The Council of Europe started its programme aimed at youth policy development in the region in 2002 (Siurala 2006). It has since implemented a variety of projects targeting youth leaders and youth workers, and initiatives such as the Youth Peace Ambassadors project and the involvement of youth organisations in conflict transformation processes. The Council of Europe Action Plan for Bosnia and Herzegovina 2015-2017 also defines specific aims for youth, including their greater involvement in the promotion of human rights, and work against discrimination and segregation. Youth groups in Bosnia and Herzegovina were also encouraged to take part in the No Hate Speech Movement campaign (Council of Europe 2015).

The European Union's project, EU Support to the Coordination and Implementation of Bosnia and Herzegovina's National Youth Policy (2012-2014) (European Union 2012), was meant to jump-start youth policy development processes in the country,

---

81. "Two schools under one roof" is a term used for schools in parts of Bosnia and Herzegovina based on the ethnic segregation of children who attend two distinct schools in one building.

delivering training programmes and providing support to the development of local youth policies at municipal level.

The agreement on the establishment of the Regional Youth Cooperation Office (RYCO) of the Western Balkans (signed on 4 July 2016 in Paris during the Western Balkans Summit) helped to strengthen the regional dimension of youth work, ensure institutional support, promote exchange of youth and prioritise the values of human rights and tolerance (RYCO 2016).

Conclusion

Youth work in Bosnia and Herzegovina has evolved over the last century from revolutionary, militant, pro-independence and anti-fascist youth movements to firmly state-controlled youth work structures after 1945. The 1990s saw a collapse of youth work in the country, with a subsequent revival in the late 1990s influenced largely by foreign donors.

The complex structure of the Bosnian state also translates to the youth field, resulting in highly decentralised approaches to working with young people. The lack of youth policy and youth strategies at national level means that limited focus and priority is given to young people. While youth policies, laws and strategies at entity, cantonal and local levels have been developing, largely advocated for by civil society, their implementation still requires state support.

Contemporary youth work in Bosnia and Herzegovina is far from European youth work standards, such as co-management and the structured dialogue. Furthermore, the fact that institutions responsible for youth are poorly functioning, and the non-existence of an Erasmus+ national agency, means that Bosnia and Herzegovina is not able to take advantage of all the co-operation programmes young people could benefit from at European level.

In the meantime, civil society and youth organisations, supported by international and European donors, continue to pursue European values of democracy, human rights and tolerance through their youth work activities. What is needed, however, for a sustainable and long-term approach to youth work is to bridge the gap between institutions and civil society and ensure better co-ordination among the sectors, in order to have a more inclusive and relevant youth policy and meaningful involvement of youth in decision-making processes at all levels.

References

Arnautovic S. (2013), "The electoral system in Bosnia and Herzegovina according to the declaration about the rights of the citizens of Bosnia and Herzegovina." *Historical searches*, No. 12, pp. 1-302, Institute for History, Sarajevo.

Canton Sarajevo (2018), Nacrt strategije prema mladima Kantona Sarajevo za period 2018.-2022. godina [Draft Strategy on Youth 2018-2022, December 2017, Sarajevo, adopted at 38th Working Session of the Assembly of the Canton Sarajevo], available in Bosnian/Croatian/Serbian at: http://skupstina.ks.gov.ba/nacrt-strategije-prema-mladima-kantona-sarajevo-za-period-2018-2022-godina-0, accessed on 16 July 2018.

Council of Europe (2015), Council of Europe Action Plan for Bosnia and Herzegovina 2015-2017, GR-DEM(2015)4, 17 February 2015. Document approved by the Committee of Ministers of the Council of Europe on 4 March 2015 [CM/Del/Dec(2015)1221].

Dayton Peace Agreement (1995), General Framework Agreement for Peace in Bosnia and Herzegovina, initialled in Dayton, Ohio on 21 November, 1995 and signed in Paris on 14 December 1995, available at www.refworld.org/docid/3de495c34.html, accessed 8 August 2019.

European Commission (2015), "Stabilisation and Association Agreement between the European Communities and their Member States, of the one part, and Bosnia and Herzegovina, of the other part", 30 June 2015, *Official Journal of the European Union*, Brussels, available at https://europa.ba/wp-content/uploads/2008/06/SAA-EU-BiH-eur-lex.europa1.pdf, accessed 11 August 2019.

European Union (2012), IPA-EU support to the coordination and implementation of Bosnia and Herzegovina's National Youth Policy, Inception report, March 2012, available at https://pjp-eu.coe.int/documents/42128013/47262055/Montenegro.pdf/b9164413-e04d-4162-963a-9d56fdd2a42b, accessed 11 August 2019.

European Youth Forum (2000), Development of Youth Work in South Eastern Europe, for a coordinated approach. Position paper adopted by the Executive Committee at Ponta Delgada, Azores, Portugal, 14-15 April 2000.

EYOF (2019), European Youth Olympic Festival 2019. Sarajevo and East Sarajevo, available at https://eyof2019.net/ba/, accessed 8 August 2019.

Federation of Bosnia and Herzegovina (2010), Youth Law of the Federation of Bosnia and Herzegovina, [Zakon o mladima Federacije Bosne i Hercegovine, Službene novine Federacije BiH broj 36/10, 16 June 2010], available at www.fbihvlada.gov.ba/bosanski/zakoni/2010/zakoni/22hrv.html, accessed 11 August 2019.

Government of Brčko District (2017), Zakon o mladima Brčko distrikta BiH [Law on Youth, adopted at the 12th regular session of the Parliament Brčko District on 24 May 2017], available in Bosnian/Croatian/Serbian at https://skupstinabd.ba/ba/zakon.html?lang=ba&id=/Zakon%20o%20mladima%20Brc--ko%20distrikta%20BiH, accessed on 15 July 2018.

Grgić S. (2007), Mlada Bosna i sarajevski atentat 1914. godine. Detaljan pogled na sarajevski atentat. [Young Bosnia and Sarajevo assassination in 1914. Detailed analysis of Sarajevo assassination], Available in Bosnian/Croatian/Serbian at www.povijest.net/2018/?p=1808, accessed 8 August 2019.

Jasarevic J. (2017), *Contribution of non-programme countries to EU Youth Wiki. Chapter I Bosnia and Herzegovina: youth policy governance*, Partnership between the European Commission and the Council of Europe, Strasbourg.

Kovačić M. and Ćulum B. (2018), "A new kid on the block: youth work meets youth policy in Croatia", in Williamson H., Basarab T. and Coussée F. (eds), *The history of youth work in Europe. Connections, disconnections and reconnections – The social dimension of youth work in history and today*, Vol. 6, Council of Europe Publishing, Strasbourg.

Krnjaic Z. (2012), "The history of youth work and its relevance for youth policy in Serbia today", in Coussée F., Williamson H. and Verschelden G. (eds), *The history of youth work in Europe: relevance for today's youth work policy*, Vol. 3, Council of Europe Publishing, Strasbourg.

KULT: Institute for Youth Development (2013), Towards a Youth Policy in FBiH. Survey on the Position and Needs of Youth in the Federation of BiH in 2013, available at http://mladi.org/v2/en/projects/3/support-to-youth-in-fbih/7556-promotion-of-analysis-of-states-and-position-of-youth-in-fbih-in-2013 , accessed on 7 June 2018.

KULT: Institute for Youth Development (2014), Youth workers, available at http://mladi.org/v2/en/projects/2/youth-workers/177-youth-workers, accessed 15 September 2018.

KULT: Institute for Youth Development (2019), History, available at http://mladi.org/v2/en/about/history, accessed 11 August 2019.

Malcolm N. (1996), *Bosnia: a short history*, Macmillan, London.

Masleša V. (1945), *Mlada Bosna*, Kultura, Beograd.

Ministry of Civil Affairs of Bosnia and Herzegovina (2019), Commission for Coordination of Youth Issues in Bosnia and Herzegovina, available at www.mladi.gov.ba/index.php?option=com_content&task=view&id=35&Itemid=35, accessed 11 August 2019.

Ministry of Family, Youth and Sports of Republika Srpska (2016), Prijedlog omladinske politike Republike Srpske [Youth Policy of the Republika Srpska], available at www.omladinskisavjet.org/wpcontent/uploads/2016/07/Prijedlog-omladinske-politike-RS-od-2016.-do-2020.- godine.pdf, accessed 11 August 2019.

Panagiotopoulou R. (2010), *Citizen participation in the Olympic Games*, University Lectures Series No. 20, Centre d'Estudis Olimpics, Barcelona, available at https://ddd.uab.cat/pub/worpap/2010/181095/panagiotopoulou_eng.pdf, accessed 8 August 2019.

Petkovic S. (2014), "History of youth work in Montenegro", Draft paper, Council of Europe, Strasbourg, available at https://pjp-eu.coe.int/documents/42128013/47262055/montenegro.pdf/b9164413-e04d-4162-963a-9d56fdd2a42b, accessed on 8 August 2019.

Republika Srpska (2012), The Law on Youth Organisation of the Republika Srpska (ЗАКОН О ОМЛАДИНСКОМ ОРГАНИЗОВАЊУ, „Службени гласник Републике Српске" бр. 98/04, 119/08 и 1/12 Available at: www.pm.rs.ba/wp-content/uploads/2016/01/Zakon-o-omladinskom-organizovanju-RS.pdf , accessed on 6 June 2018.

RYCO (2016), RYCO-Agreement signed during the Western Balkans Summit in Paris on July 4th, 2016!, available at https://rycoblog.wordpress.com/2016/07/05/ryco-signed-at-paris-balkans-2016-conference/, accessed 11 August 2019.

Schüler Helfen Leben (2018), Youth policy, available at www.shl.ba/lat/omladinska-politika, accessed on 5 June 2018.

Siurala L. (2006), *A European Framework for Youth Policy*. Directorate of Youth and Sport, Council of Europe Publishing, Strasbourg.

Škulj J. (2017), Contributions to the history of youth sector in Slovenia, Partnership between the European Commission and the Council of Europe in the field of youth, Council of Europe, Strasbourg, available at https://pjp-eu.coe.int/documents/42128013/47262055/Slovenia_EN.pdf/177d96b1-7e86-4901-bd16-7ab5407331f6, accessed 8 August 2019.

The Commonwealth Secretariat (2016), *Global Youth Development Index and Report*, available at: http://cmydiprod.uksouth.cloudapp.azure.com/sites/default/files/2016-10/2016%20Global%20Youth%20Development%20Index%20and%20Report.pdf, accessed 11 August 2019.

United Nations (2016), *Voices of Youth, Research into youth in BIH, Consolidated report on the quantitative and qualitative research*, United Nations, Sarajevo. Available at: www.worldbank.org/en/news/feature/2013/02/14/improving-opportunities-young-people-Bosnia-Herzegovina.

World Bank (2013), Improving opportunities for young people in Bosnia and Herzegovina, available at www.worldbank.org/en/news/feature/2013/02/14/improving-opportunities-young-people-Bosnia-Herzegovina, accessed 11 August 2019.

World Bank and UNICEF (2003), *Youth in South Eastern Europe: report of the Rome Conference on Participation, Empowerment, and Social Inclusion, June 2002*, World Bank and UNICEF, Washington and Geneva.

Youthpolicy.org (2014), Bosnia and Herzegovina factsheet, available at: www.undp.org/content/dam/unct/bih/PDFs/UNICEF%20pics%20for%20publications/VoY2016/VoY2016.pdf, accessed 11 August 2019.

Žiga J., Turčilo L., Osmić A., Bašić S., Džananović Miraščija N, Kapidžić D. and Brkić-Šmigoc J. (2015), *Youth study Bosnia and Herzegovina*, Faculty of Political Sciences and Friedrich Ebert Stiftung, Sarajevo, available at www.youthpolicy.org/factsheets/country/bosnia-herzegovina/, accessed 11 August 2019.

Chapter 13

Youth work in Ukraine: from Soviet model to international integration

Yevgeniy Borodin

Introduction

Youth work first appeared in Ukraine in the mid to late 19th century. Ukraine, whose history dates back to Kyivan Rus (since the 9th century), was subsequently deprived of its statehood and youth work changed accordingly. The short existence of the Ukrainian People's Republic and the Western Ukrainian People's Republic after the First World War was replaced by the emergence of the Ukrainian SSR, which was part of the USSR until the 1990s. Modern Ukraine proclaimed its independence on 24 August 1991.

The essence of youth policy and youth work over the past quarter of a century was the reformation of thΩe Soviet inheritance and implementation of innovations reflecting national traditions and international experience in this field. This chapter covers both issues regarding the Soviet system of youth work and its development and provision within independent Ukraine.

Youth work in Soviet Ukraine

Soviet system of youth work

Youth work in Ukraine during the Soviet era did not differ much from other republics, as the highly centralised political system of the USSR defined the unification of all processes in the national republics. All significant innovations needed approval from Moscow. In the years 1920-30, the structures entrusted to work with youth were formed and strengthened. At the same time, all non-communist youth organisations were formally abolished, leaving room only for the Komsomol and its child branch, the Pioneer organisation. The work of religious organisations with young people suffered severe restrictions. However, the introduction of totalitarian ideology did not prevent the use of some practices of youth work that had been devised by organisations that were subject to prohibition in the USSR. In particular, there was the borrowing of Scouting methods by the Pioneer movement, which resulted in a specific symbiosis of communist slogans and non-communist forms and methods of youth work.

Under the conditions of Stalin's regime, any deviation from the established dogmas and rituals that informed youth work, educational, social pedagogical and upbringing work, and other activities was rigidly repressed. At the same time, young people were offered new opportunities for leisure-time activities, recreation, self-development and self-management, but only within the ideology of the Communist Party of the Soviet Union (CPSU).

The liberalisation of the Soviet authoritarian regime that took place in the post-Stalinist period contributed to the fact that in certain areas of youth work the ideological component could be minimised or even could be avoided.

In the terminology of the Soviet society of the 1960s and 1980s, the following concepts were among those used to define youth work: "work with young people", "upbringing work", "extracurricular activities", "organisation of meaningful leisure activities" and "struggle with neglect".

Traditionally, the main providers of youth work in the USSR were the Komsomol, the Pioneer organisation, education institutions, cultural programmes, physical education and sports, leisure and recreation activities. It is important to remember that the ruling Communist Party took a leading interest in this work. For example, not long before the fall of communism in the late 1980s, in February 1986, at the 27th Congress of the Communist Party of Ukraine, one of its leading functions was underlined: "In work with young people, party committees should closely unite the efforts of the Komsomol and trade union, Soviet and economic, cultural and educational, arts, sports and mass defense organizations".[82]

The main structures for youth in the USSR were the Komsomol (for those aged 14 to 28) and the Pioneer organisation (from age 7 to 13). The Komsomol had the status of a non-governmental organisation but in fact it was a part of the state administration. Many Komsomol organisers combined their official positions with direct youth work. In each administrative-territorial unit and within large institutions, organisations and establishments, there was a Komsomol Committee with paid employees, and in all small structures, the Komsomol work was carried out on a voluntary basis. Each school had a paid senior *vozhatyi* (Pioneer leader), who organised extracurricular activities.

The important tools of youth work in the USSR were various clubs and their sections, which were organised by paid adult leaders, with premises and the necessary funding provided by the state. Pioneer Houses (Palaces) functioned within the education system, with their official purpose defined as "assistance to the school, the Komsomol and the Pioneer organisation in the communist education of pupils, their comprehensive development, in preparing them for [adult] life and work" (Yakovleva 1964).

Particular attention should be given to the concept of "out-of-school work" in the USSR, which defined educational and upbringing work. It was a form of organisation of leisure activity and was carried out "on the basis of voluntary participation, active involvement and self-determination of children taking into account their interests" (Kairov and Petrov 1964). In addition, "extracurricular work" was conducted in schools,

---

82. Communist Party of Ukraine (1986), 27th Congress of the Communist Party, verbatim report, p. 54.

within which school clubs, school parties, disputes, contests, quizzes, excursions and individual classes were organised.

There were numerous out-of-school establishments for young people, most of which operated within the system of education and culture, trade unions and voluntary sports associations. These included children's parks, railways, libraries, theatres, sports academies, centres for young technicians and naturalists, excursion and tourist centres, and clubs of young motorists.

From around 1971, children's and youth clubs became another tool for working with children and youth aged from 7 to 17 years old (school age). The clubs were maintained and funded by housing and utilities organisations. They appeared to be based on children's clubs in housing administrations that acted on a volunteer basis. The main activities of those clubs were sports activities and upbringing work.

Children and youth camps, which combined educational work and healthy recreation for children, were widespread in the USSR. The most famous were the country's Pioneer children camps belonging to various enterprises, institutions, organisations (including educational authorities, trade unions, factories, *kolkhoz* (collective farms) and *sovkhoz* (state farms)). They had their own infrastructure (with dormitories, sports grounds, summer theatres, dining rooms and beaches) and the necessary funding. The activities of those camps were based on the Pioneer methodology.

To work in Pioneer camps in the position of *vozhatyi* (the youth worker of that time), students (either as part of their compulsory pedagogical practice in higher educational institutions or in their spare time), teachers and employees of enterprises, institutions and organisations were involved. This paid summer seasonal work was continued, after the end of communism, in volunteer work with children and youth. The All-Union Children's Centre Artek (near the village of Gurzuf in the Crimea region) and the Molodaya Gvardiya (Young Guard) Pioneer Camp were located in the territory of the Ukrainian SSR. There were also labour and recreation camps set up for the senior schoolchildren from the 1970s. These combined work on agricultural enterprises with leisure activities.

The network of centres, clubs and sections of adult organisations developed for youth of school age was complemented by a network of institutions for young people who studied in higher educational institutions or worked after school. Each higher educational institution had its own Students' House of Culture, gyms, sports camps, infrastructure and other resources for the work of clubs, sections, scientific student societies and other associations. The ideological control and organisational work relied on the Communist Party and the Komsomol.

Under Komsomol control from the 1960s, the movement of student detachments had developed. The most famous were students' building units (brigades) formed on a voluntary basis, and in addition to the construction of new buildings, they participated in youth work in those areas where they worked. The inclusion of disadvantaged adolescents into students' building and agricultural units was the other important form of youth work delivered by students. However, the most striking manifestation of youth work were the student pedagogical units that worked out the forms and methods of voluntary involvement of adolescents in activities based on the principles of "non-formal pedagogy".

In this Soviet youth work, a large number of restrictions and prohibitions were placed on student associations related to those whose ideas or actions ventured beyond political loyalty to the regime. As a result, many initiatives for the non-formal organisation of student youth did not find support, and the activists themselves turned into dissidents (as participants in political opposition movements). Young workers in various enterprises were also involved in youth work through the activities of the Komsomol and trade union organisations, Houses of Culture, and recreational institutions. Some of them became youth workers taking part in the organisation of leisure activities for schoolchildren in sections, clubs and working in summer Pioneer camps.

One important feature of youth work in the USSR was its professionalisation. Positions of paid youth workers at different levels, in different sectors and with different titles were introduced. They included the "professional Komsomol workers", *vozhatyi* in schools; and heads of centres, clubs and sections in institutions of education, culture, physical education and sports, trade union organisations and non-governmental organisations. There were also schoolteachers engaged in non-formal education; deputy head teachers of schools, vocational and technical schools and vice-rectors of higher education institutions responsible for upbringing work; full-time and seasonal *vozhatyi* of children's camps (in particular Artek and Molodaya Gvardiya) and others.

In the meantime, a large number of people carried out volunteer work with youth. This was expressed in the official language of the time as a "public duty". These volunteers included teachers from educational institutions, students, workers, representatives of scientific and technical intelligentsia, artists and scientists. The main method of their becoming involved in this way was through election to positions as leaders within the Komsomol organisations, or appointment as *vozhatyi* in schools. Besides public duties, some volunteers initiated the establishing of youth clubs and sections.

The system for the training and professional development of youth workers in the Soviet era included pedagogical institutes, higher educational establishments of sport, culture and education, and classical universities. There were also higher party, Komsomol and trade union educational institutions, as well as various advanced training courses that operated at Houses of Pioneers and higher education institutions. For students in higher educational establishments, there were faculties of public professions that had elements of curricula on both non-formal and additional education. They provided the opportunity to obtain the competences necessary for youth work. Nevertheless, despite this range of training provision, a significant proportion of those involved in working with young people did not receive the necessary education. Those from Ukraine, however, had the opportunity to study at the Higher Komsomol School in Moscow and the Republican Komsomol School in Kyiv, receiving higher education that combined the features of management training and specialist in youth work.

The Komsomol had a big budget and a solid logistics base. It was the founder of youth newspapers and magazines, the pages of which covered the best practices of working with youth; discussions on relevant topics were organised. The All-Union newspaper was *Komsomolskaya Pravda*, and in Ukraine at the republican level the Ukrainian-language *Youth of Ukraine* and the Russian-language *Komsomolskoye znamya* were published. Each oblast (municipality) had its own Komsomol newspaper. There were also newspapers and magazines for children. The activities of Komsomol publishing houses Molodaya Gvardiya in Moscow (the same name as the All-Union Pioneer Camp in the Ukrainian SSR) and Molod in Kyiv allowed the publication of methodological materials for specialists who worked with children and young people.

Understanding of the special, informal nature of youth work encouraged Soviet theorists and practitioners in this area of activity to attempt to introduce new concepts to determine its essence. In the late 1960s and 1970s, a conceptual study was carried out among Western professionals who in fact proposed the concept of "non-formal education" (Blakey 2015; Smith 2001). In the USSR, at the same time, S. Soloveichyk, I. Ivanov, M. Kordonsky and V. Lantsberg went their own way, which was too close to the Western approach. In the 1960s to 1970s, the notion of "non-formal pedagogy" emerged among Soviet educators engaged in extra-curricular education. It was based on the principles of free choice for children and youth of relevant associations, common interests, joint activities and self-governance. A Ukrainian member of the movement of non-formal pedagogy from the city of Odessa, M. Kordonsky, said that in order to ensure the participation of children in extracurricular activities "there was nothing left for the teacher as to become an informal leader of the children's team" (Kordonsky n.d.). As a researcher of the Soviet era noted, the process of educating the creative personality was taking place, but "such a person was needed for the System, but in small quantities, because, on a mass scale, creative, harmonious, humane and educated people destroy the industrial society" (Shubin 2008).

Influence of perestroika on youth work

From the spring of 1985 to the summer of 1991, one of the main Communist Party slogans of that time entered Soviet history under the name of "perestroika". Gradually, the division of power branches, the multi-party system, private property, the privatisation of enterprises, and freedom of speech and religion were introduced in the USSR. Ukraine remained in the Soviet Union until the last days of its existence, but it was already an increasingly different country in comparison with each preceding year.

Important changes took place in the youth field. The deprivation of the CPSU and the Young Communist League of its special constitutional status put on the agenda the issue of state youth policy, which required the creation of appropriate legislation and authorities. In August 1990, the State Committee on Youth, Physical Education and Sports was created in the Ukrainian SSR. In April 1991, the USSR Law on General Principles of State Youth Policy in the USSR appeared. Youth units appeared in oblast and city governments. They actively engaged in the organisation of youth work, competing with the Komsomol, which supported the establishment of these structures.

During perestroika, even the CPSU took a new look at youth work. In 1990, at the 28th Congress of the CPSU, a resolution on youth policy was adopted in which communist upbringing work was no longer mentioned, and party structures undertook to work directly with youth themselves. In addition, it was claimed that youth should take an active part in the development and implementation of youth policy (Communist Party of the Soviet Union 1990).

The Komsomol of Ukraine in 1986-91 slowly lost the status of the communist-led organisation, trying to defend the right to ideological choice and self-rule. At first, its leaders believed that the organisation would still be able to subordinate all other initiatives that young people took. After all, for a long period, only one youth organisation had been allowed and the only way to act within the framework of the law was for young activists to agree that they could create the so-called self-ruled association (samodeyatelnye) only under the aegis of the Komsomol. Examples of such self-ruled associations, during the 1960s to 1980s, were nature protection groups and amateur singing clubs. They were often called non-formal associations in official documents. The activities of these associations were allowed by the authorities. Along with this, the representatives of various youth subcultures (hippie, punks, yoga followers and rockers) were also named as non-formal associations but these were banned.

During the period of perestroika, the Komsomol committees supported various clubs and enterprises engaged in youth leisure activities (in particular breakdancing, skateboarding, songwriting, rock music, military-patriotic education, physical training, educational and cultural activities). Over time, these structures demanded their own independence and formalisation. This was facilitated by the adoption of Soviet legislation on public associations in October 1990.

The creation of Tovarystvo Leva by youth in Lviv was a vivid example of this trend in Ukraine. It arose in 1987 with the support of the city Komsomol Committee. Concentrating first on issues of national consciousness, the Ukrainian language, the preservation of cultural and historical monuments and nature protection, the organisation eventually shifted to political activity. It opposed the communists and put forward its representatives to the Verkhovna Rada of the Ukrainian SSR (highest legislative body of public power), the regional and city councils. The activities of the Tovarystvo Leva extended to all Western Ukraine.

The appeal to national issues resulted in a number of youth organisations moving in this direction (the Union of Ukrainian Students, the Union of Independent Ukrainian Youth, the Ukrainian Student Union). They worked with young people towards gaining independence for Ukraine.

The Ukrainian Komsomol, influenced by the mood within the youth environment (its number decreased from 6.7 million in 1986 to 3.4 million in 1991), took tentative steps towards reform. An attempt to rebrand through the addition of a new word in its title, Youth for Democratic Socialism, did not succeed. The regional Komsomol organisations changed their names to democratic ones in Lviv, Ivano-Frankivs'k and Vinnytsia regions in autumn 1990. But neither separation from the Communist Party, nor actions in support of the Ukrainian national culture, among which the most notable was the song festival, Chervona Ruta, helped the Komsomol.

Some of the Komsomol activists did, however, see the prospect of applying foreign experience in working with youth in those circumstances. The Komsomol borrowed the US experience of creating programmes for young astronauts. It founded the

All-Union Youth Aerospace Society "Soyuz". In 1989, in Dnipropetrovs'k, the Ukrainian space and rocket centre of the USSR, they established an office that organised work in Ukraine. After the proclamation of Ukraine's independence, it was a platform for the creation of the youth aerospace association "Suzir'ia" in 1991. The second President of Ukraine, L. Kuchma, has been the honorary chairman of this organisation since its foundation.

In 1989, the Student Forum of the USSR was held. It resulted in the formation of a Student Committee of the country that would work under the aegis of the Komsomol on the development of pupils and students' self-government.

Democratic changes in the Soviet Union led to the restoration of the activities of organisations associated with the world history of youth work. Initially, this concerned the Scouting movement. In 1989, the process of revival of the national Scout organisation, Plast, began in Lviv. It was founded in the territory of Western Ukraine, which had been part of the Austro-Hungarian Empire in 1911. However, the restored Plast operated not only within the lands of its creation, but also in other regions of Ukraine, including Kyiv and Donetsk.

In October 1990, youth organisations such as the Ukrainian Student Union and Student Brotherhood organised a protest action against the communist authorities of the Ukrainian SSR, demanding democratic change. Representatives of Kyiv, Lviv and Dnipropetrovs'k attended the mass hunger strike in the capital of Ukraine, and there were strikes in many universities. The authorities agreed to their demands.

Youth work in independent Ukraine

Youth policy and recognition of youth work

Since the proclamation of its independence, Ukraine has developed new opportunities for youth policy and youth work. Ideological restrictions that had been in force under the USSR were rejected and new ideas and practices that previously had been forbidden have been adopted. Questions of national identity, as with most former Soviet republics, were of particular importance for the provision of new forms of youth work.

The state youth policy developed in Ukraine has been quite dynamic. During the first decade, the parliament adopted the Declaration on the General Principles of State Youth Policy in Ukraine (1992), the Laws of Ukraine on Facilitating Social Formation and Development of Youth in Ukraine (1993), on Youth and Children Non-Governmental Organizations (1998), and on Social Work with Children and Youth (2001). As a result, conditions for the activities of youth units of the authorities at all levels, the development of youth organisations, the establishment of youth centres, the financing of youth work, the implementation of non-formal education, and the development of competences of youth workers have been created.

In 1998, the government adopted a national youth programme for the first time. In 2003, the National Youth Support Programme was approved by the parliament. The government in 2009 and in 2016 again approved the next two programmes, Youth of Ukraine.

In 2013, the Strategy for the Development of State Youth Policy in Ukraine for the Period up to 2020 appeared for the first time. At national, regional and local levels, there were units on youth issues that at different times derived from policy areas such as sport, family and children, tourism and education. From 1991 to 2013, the ministry responsible for youth policy was restructured nine times, which adversely affected the continuity of activities.

In Ukrainian public policy, the issues of citizenship and patriotism have been separated from each other. Patriotic education of children and youth was defined as one of the priorities of government youth policy and it was approved in official documents in the 1990s to 2000s. However, following the change of power in 2014 it obtained a greater significance under external aggression, strengthening of national identity and decommunisation. In 2015, the President of Ukraine, P. Poroshenko, adopted The Strategy of National and Patriotic Education of Children and Youth for 2016-2020.

To implement youth work in educational institutions, and in public and private enterprises, from the beginning of the 1990s, appropriate structures have been established replacing the liquidated committees of the Komsomol. At universities, there were two processes at work at the same time: student self-governing bodies, and units or assistants of university rectors on youth issues.

Over time, the emphasis has shifted to student self-government. At national level, there were co-ordination bodies called the All-Ukrainian Student Council (in 2001-2008 under the president, in 2009-2010 under the government, and under the Ministry of Education and Science since 2005). Various public initiatives operated, including the Ukrainian Student Self-Government Association (founded in 1999), which joined the European Students' Union.

The management of large associations and some enterprises quite actively promoted or initiated the emergence of youth organisations among its employees and at the same time established units for work with youth, which developed their own programmes of activities. Trade unions have also been involved in youth work. In 2004, the Federation of Trade Unions of Ukraine approved its own concept of youth policy.

Many political parties tried to influence youth policy by introducing their drafts to parliament. Their participation in youth work was mainly through the creation and support of their youth organisations (the youth wings of different political parties). A political party's entry into the parliament meant the intensification of its youth work, and the loss of parliamentary status usually led to a dramatic reduction in its youth work. Thus, in the 1990s, the People's Democratic Party, the Social Democratic Party of Ukraine (united), the People's Rukh, the Socialist Party, and the Communist Party of Ukraine all influenced youth policy. Accordingly, the People's Democratic Youth League, Young Rukh, Ukrainian Social Democratic Youth, the Young Socialist Congress, and the Komsomol of Ukraine were active. Between 2010 and 2014, the Young Regions (youth wing of the Party of Regions) became more active. Today (2019), all these organisations have disappeared from the political scene. The political influence on youth is reflected in its active participation in political confrontation with the government during the Orange Revolution (late 2004 to the beginning of 2005) and the Revolution of Dignity (late 2013 to the beginning of 2014).

In the post-Soviet period in Ukraine, the deployment of diverse youth work by religious organisations developed. Before that, the atheistic communist state limited the opportunities for different churches to work with youth. Since the beginning of the 1990s, youth structural units have been created, strategic documents have been developed, youth publications and internet resources of various religious organisations have been founded. Separately, there was a task for churches to establish clubs, centres and courses for their youth organisations. Different denominations started youth volunteer movements. They established their summer camps and Scout formations, and festivals for young people under the auspices of different denominations became a normal routine. The fact that the priests managed Scout groups, youth clubs and children's camps was unusual at first, but then it gradually became commonplace to Ukraine. For a quarter of a century now, a dialogue between the Church and the authorities in the youth field has evolved, which eventually allowed a multilateral exchange of views and co-operation. In March 2017, for the first time in many years, the Ministry of Youth and Sports of Ukraine organised a joint meeting of representatives of Orthodox, Catholic, Greek Catholic, Protestant and Muslim communities responsible for youth work. They agreed to develop co-operation, among other things, on volunteering, the promotion of healthy lifestyles and the establishment of an interfaith forum on youth issues.

Many official documents have used the concept of "work with youth". This has often had a broader understanding than "youth work", because it did not always involve the voluntary participation of young people. In my own scientific publications from the 2000s, attention was drawn to the fact that the use of the concept of "youth work" is urgent for Ukraine (Borodin 2008, 2009). However, the practical implementation of this idea has been delayed for many years.

The initial lack of preparation of the authorities to include the concept of "youth work" in the legislation and other normative legal documents showed that for a long time it was mistranslated. In 2008, on the website of the Ministry of Ukraine for Family, Youth and Sport, there was a translation of the Declaration of the 8th Council of Europe Conference of Ministers responsible for youth "The future of the Council of Europe youth policy: AGENDA 2020" from English into Ukrainian, where the term "youth work" was translated as "work of youth".[83] In the first government decision on the implementation of the Agreement between Ukraine and the European Union (September 2014), a similar mistake occurred when the term was translated as "young workers" (Cabinet of Ministers of Ukraine 2014).

Such errors around the understanding and translation of the concept of youth work is not an issue just for Ukraine. In 2001, researchers on youth policy and youth work in Europe also drew attention to the same issue: "interlocutors in Southern European countries didn't understand – or misunderstood – the English term 'youth work'. Many of the first answers referred to the labour market conditions of young people ('working youth')" (Schizzeretto and Gasperoni 2001).

Steadily, however, the wider European understanding of youth work was acknowledged in Ukraine. The youth sector of Council of Europe and the EU–Council of Europe

83. http://dsmsu.gov.ua/index/ua/material/36, but page only accessible in Ukrainian.

youth partnership subsequently provided opportunities for Ukrainian policy makers, youth workers and youth researchers to study the experience of youth work in other countries. And the international review by the Council of Europe of youth policy in Ukraine contains recommendations on youth work and non-formal education for Ukrainian authorities (Krzaklewska and Williamson 2013).

In 2015, the draft Law of Ukraine on Youth included the definition of the concepts of "youth work" and "youth workers", but this document has not yet been approved by parliament. In the governmental programme Youth of Ukraine for 2016-2020 (approved in February 2016) along with the words "workers working with youth" stands the name of the training programme, Youth Worker.

The situation is somewhat better with the implementation of the concept of "non-formal education". In the programme Youth of Ukraine in 2016-2020 the task of "non-formal education development" was set in the context of the implementation of the Youth Worker programme. There are now definitions of non-formal and informal education in the new Law on Education (2017).

Until recently, the training of youth work specialists was carried out mainly through training delivered through international organisations and foreign funds. In the 1990s, the preparation of bachelors and masters in the fields of social pedagogics (until 2015) and social work (up to now) was introduced at classical and pedagogical universities. In 2014, the State Institute of Family and Youth Policy, with the support of UNDP and UNICEF, launched the Youth Worker programme. This provides youth worker training at both basic and specialised levels, as well as training for trainers in which equal numbers of public authorities and public-sector representatives participated. In 2014-2018, more than 1 500 people of all levels took part in the training courses and obtained the relevant certificates.

In November 2017, the First All-Ukrainian Forum of Youth Workers took place in Kharkiv. Leading foreign experts in youth policy and youth work, including Prof. H. Williamson and Prof. A. Crowley, participated. The forum identified the best practices of Ukraine. In September 2018, the Youth Workers group on Facebook numbered 4 190 participants. In November 2018, the Second All-Ukrainian Forum of Youth Workers was held in Dnipro.

Youth centres

The development of youth centres took place when the contradictions existed between, on the one hand, the need to keep the network of existing out-of-school educational institutions within the system of education, culture, physical education and sports departments and, on the other hand, the need for the establishment of new (in form and content) structures in the youth sector.

In the spring of 2016, there were 4 053 state and communal out-of-school educational institutions functioning in Ukraine, the activity of which was directed by several ministries, including 1 395 integrated educational institutions (1.23 million pupils), 1 295 cultural institutions (301 700 pupils), 545 sports institutions from the educational sector (243 900 pupils) and 818 (251 800 pupils) sports institutions from the sports sector.

In the independent Ukraine, the system of summer country children's recreation camps was preserved, though the number has been gradually decreasing. In 2010 there were 815 camps, but in 2012 only 784. During the privatisation of industrial enterprises, these out-of-school institutions closed. At the same time, however, private children and youth camps were established.

In the early 1990s, former clubs in children's neighbourhoods, which in Soviet times had belonged to housing and utilities services, quickly transferred to the youth sector in most cities and towns. They represented, as before, a union of clubs for school-age children. As a result, for a long time, there was an unresolved issue as to the appropriate youth work provision for the older age group. The youth sector demanded new forms of youth centres.

Since 1992, the state system of centres for social services for young people began to develop in the youth sector, which initially focused on the social aspects of youth work. In 2010, there were 27 regional, 484 district, 170 municipal, 40 district in cities, 581 rural, 88 village and 510 branches of district centres. However, their activities gradually refocused on the work with families, and in 2010, they were withdrawn from the youth sphere.

From the late 1990s until the late 2000s, there was an attempt to develop a network of youth employment centres in the youth sector, but the lack of sources for stable funding led to the abandonment of this project.

At the end of 2000s, the network of patriotic education and military-patriotic education centres for children and youth was created. After 2015, the attention of the authorities and NGOs on the centres of national and patriotic education has been strengthened and increased. The network of centres was extended at regional, subregional and local levels.

On the policy agenda by the beginning of 2010, however, was the issue of the creation of fundamentally new youth centres, which would become the venues for the implementation of the initiatives proposed by the youth themselves. Between 2015 and 2018 there were significant positive changes on this front, as regional youth centres in Luhans'k, Cherkasy, Zaporizhzhia and Dnipropetrovs'k became the seeds of change. These centres paid much attention to civic engagement and youth participation.

In 2017, the regulations on youth centres and its expert council were approved, with a National Quality Label and Quality Criteria for Youth Centres. The innovative approach was to create centres with their infrastructure and locate them in libraries, out-of-school educational institutions, schools, universities, clubs and Palaces of Culture. In a decentralisation reform, the establishment of youth centres has become a popular trend in local government activity. It has been successfully combined with the organisation of training for youth workers throughout the country.

The Council of Europe, the organisations of the UN system and the representatives of foreign funds have joined to support the development of youth centres in Ukraine. In November 2017, the Association of Youth Centres of Ukraine was formed. The founders were the representatives of 42 centres of different levels and activities. In December of the same year, the Budget Code of Ukraine introduced changes that for the first time in the history of independent Ukraine allowed the financial support from local budgets of youth centres within the youth sector.

Youth organisations

Initiated during the period of perestroika, the diversity of the youth movement has gradually expanded. The Komsomol was reorganised, having become the Union of Ukrainian Youth Organizations in October 1991. Instead, the representatives of the restored Communist Party used the name of the Komsomol and gave it to their youth organisation.

In the first period after independence, the most active were youth organisations of a political nature. So, at the beginning of the 1990s, the Union of Ukrainian Students, the Ukrainian Student Union, the Union of Independent Ukrainian Youth and the Association of Young Ukrainian Political Scientists and Politicians were most often mentioned.

At the beginning of 2010, researchers and experts portrayed the most active youth organisations as the following: the Regional Initiative Fund, the Democratic Alliance, the Public Network "Opora" ("Support"), the Christian Democratic Youth of Ukraine and the Ukrainian Student Union (Borenko 2011).

The national Scout organisation, Plast, rapidly became an important site of youth work in Ukraine as it expanded its activities throughout the country. In 2017, the organisation consisted of 137 divisions (in 1992, there were 36) and 8 238 participants (in 1992, there were 1 652). Plast organises summer camps for volunteers, children and youth, nationwide youth events and training for educators. The organisation receives financial assistance from the Ministry of Youth and Sports (in 2017, 3.8 million Ukrainian hryvnia (UAH) for 60 events) (Herus and Andriichuk 2017). In March 2008, President Yushchenko issued a special decree "On measures to promote the development of the Plast (Scout) Movement in Ukraine", which instructed the government, central and regional authorities to contribute fully to this organisation. Plast has a distinctive Ukrainian identity and operates in diasporas (the USA, Canada, Great Britain, Argentina, Australia, Germany, Poland and Slovakia). For a long time, the Scout Movement in Ukraine was characterised by both diversity and institutional fragmentation, which for some time hindered its integration into international structures. Only in 2007, the National Scout Organization of Ukraine arose, which in 2008 joined the World Organization of the Scout Movement. At the same time, the Association of Ukrainian Guides, YMCA Scouts in Ukraine, the Catholic Scouts of Europe in Ukraine, the Orthodox Scouts of Ukraine, the Student Association of Scouts of Ukraine and other structures emerged in the 2000s.

The revival of activities in Ukraine of international youth organisations and movements took place with the support of foreign partners. In 1992, thanks to the representatives of the United States and the Czech Republic, the Ukrainian YMCA resumed its activities. This organisation had operated in the Ukrainian territories (Kyiv) of the Russian Empire since 1913. Currently, the YMCA of Ukraine has 25 local organisations in 16 oblasts. In February 1992, a member of the Norwegian Association of Scouts and Guides, having visited Ukraine, contributed to the development of the Guide Movement in Ukraine. In 1995, representatives of Norway and the United Kingdom attended the constituent conference of the Association of Ukrainian Guides, bringing together representatives from 13 oblasts.

Perhaps the best illustration of the establishment of an effective network of an international youth organisation has been AIESEC activity in Ukraine since 1994. AIESEC established its offices in the 14 main university cities of Ukraine, which maintain their performance and regularly renew their members and leaders. New teams of students and graduates of the higher educational establishments succeed each other in providing the activity of AIESEC in Ukraine. In 2011-12 the representative of Ukraine held the position of president of this international organisation.

Among the main areas of activity of youth organisations in Ukraine, the following became popular: involvement in political activity and support of certain parties; solution of social problems; leisure organisation; economic activity; promotion of employment and entrepreneurship development; social and psychological assistance; popularisation of a healthy lifestyle and counteraction of negative phenomena; civil and patriotic education; and creativity.

Most studies indicate that the participation of youth in non-governmental organisations does not exceed 5% (Bielyshev 2011). However, the organisations themselves are working closely with those young people who are not their members. In 2015, during the sociological survey "Youth of Ukraine", 2% of respondents confirmed their membership of youth organisations. Meanwhile, three and a half times more survey participants (7%) reported that they took part in different events of the youth organisations (Yarema 2016).

In the youth work of public organisations, a wide range of activities has developed such as festivals, contests, hiking, camps, campaigns and competitions. Various educational activities for activists and target groups of young people (seminars, training courses, schools) also became important. Thanks to the direct connection of many Ukrainian youth organisations with European partners, it is within their environment that approaches to the recognition of various forms of youth work, volunteering and non-formal education have been accelerated. The financial support of Ukrainian youth organisations from international and foreign funds has been instrumental in these developments.

At the same time, the development of the youth movement and youth advisory bodies in Ukraine has confirmed the warnings of those researchers who foresaw the emergence of "a two track policy, where relatively privileged young people can enjoy the forum function of youth work, adapting society to their needs, while disadvantaged young people are targeted in transit youth work, adapting young people to the needs of society" (EU–Council of Europe n.d.).

In 2015, a UNICEF expert expressed his grounded opinion about members of youth parliaments, youth NGOs, student councils and other advisory bodies: "the young people sitting in these groups are aligned with political parties. They are the elite: well qualified, they speak English, they know what they want. There is no one living with HIV, no poor youth, no disabled youth" (Anderson 2015: 67).

In 1992-2018, different "umbrella" youth organisations sat on the national youth council. From 1992 to 2001, the Ukrainian National Committee of Youth Organisations played a role on the national youth council and it was also a full member of CENYC (the Council of European National Youth Committees). After that, the Ukrainian Youth Forum then occupied this position. Today, the National Youth Council of Ukraine is a Candidate Member of the European Youth Forum. Since 2002, youth organisations at national level have received financial support from the state budget based on project contests.

Conclusions

Youth work during the years of Ukraine's independent history is based both on previous traditions shaped under the Soviet system and more contemporary national and international innovations.

The preservation of some approaches of the Soviet era was due to the fact that during the period of perestroika the ideological colouring of work with young people was substantially mitigated, and the concept of "state youth policy" was introduced and put into practice. The traditional approaches include the efforts to regulate the youth sphere in detail (as a result of which a large number of normative legal acts appeared), to keep an extensive network of state and municipal institutions, and to institutionalise youth work in educational establishments, institutions and enterprises.

Innovation in youth work in Ukraine has been the development of a truly diverse youth movement, the involvement of third-sector organisations in youth work, the funding of non-governmental organisations from state and local budgets, the application of instruments approved by the Council of Europe, the European Union and foreign countries, and the use of financial and intellectual resources of international and foreign institutions.

A positive aspect is the fact that the scope of youth work in Ukraine has significantly expanded through public initiatives, which has led to a real dialogue between government and non-governmental organisations. However, there have also been negative aspects when parity and dialogue between the authorities and public associations was not ensured. Substantial harm was caused by efforts to politicise the youth sphere and to subordinate youth work to narrow party political interests. There were also attempts to limit youth work only to leisure activities, to shift the focus towards gifted youth, to restrict the participation of young people in social life and to direct youth work to ensure active citizenship of youth. An emphasis has been put on patriotic education.

Nowadays, youth work and non-formal education of young people are on the agenda of the authorities, a position that is being strengthened by the state's international commitments in the context of European integration processes. A strong reason for this is the experience gained in the third sector.

The immediate tasks for the development of youth work include, in particular, the following: the integration of the concepts of "youth work" and "non-formal education of youth" in a legal framework; the promotion of the professionalisation of youth work; the training of youth work specialists on the basis of domestic and foreign experience; updating the content of state, regional and local youth programmes;

intensifying co-operation with international and foreign organisations that have extensive experience in the field of youth work; an increase in funding and search for new sources of financing; and the strengthening of research support for the process of the establishment and recognition of youth work and non-formal education.

References

Anderson K. (2015), *Gap analysis of Ukrainian youth legislation in relation to recommendations of the EU-Ukraine association agreement and other relevant EU policies*, Final report, Coram Children's Legal Centre, available at https://coraminternational.org/wp-content/uploads/Gap_Analysis_of_Ukrainian_Youth_Legislation.pdf, accessed 13 August 2019.

Bielyshev O. (ed.) (2011), *Молодь в умовах становлення незалежної України (1991-2011): щорічна доповідь Президенту України, Верховній Раді України про становище молоді в Україні* [Youth in the context of the formation of an independent Ukraine (1991-2011): annual report to the President of Ukraine, the Verkhovna Rada of Ukraine, the Cabinet of Ministers of Ukraine on the situation of youth in Ukraine], p. 265, available at https://dismp.gov.ua/downloads/dopovid-molod-v-umovakh-stanovlennya-nezalezhnosti-ukrayini-1991-2011-roki, accessed 13 August 2019.

Blakey B. (2015), *Nonformal education*, available at http://etec.ctlt.ubc.ca/510wiki/Nonformal_Education, accessed 13 August 2019.

Borenko Y. (2011), Reviews on youth policies and youth work in the countries of South East Europe, Eastern Europe & Caucasus: Ukraine, available at www.academia.edu/1252963/Review_on_youth_policy_and_youth_work_in_Ukraine, accessed 13 August 2019.

Borodin Y. (2008), *Державна молодіжна політика в Україні: процес формування та розвитку (1991-2004)* [State youth policy in Ukraine: the process of formation and development (1991-2004)], Porogy, Dnipropetrovs'k, pp. 17, 253.

Borodin Y. (2009), "Молодіжна політика" [Youth policy], in Poltorak V. A., Petrov O. V. and Tolstoukhov A. V. (eds), *Соціологія політики: енциклопедичний словник* [Sociology of politics: encyclopedic dictionary], Видавництво Європейського університету [European University Publishing House], Kyiv, pp. 249-50.

Cabinet of Ministers of Ukraine (2014), The order "On the implementation of the Association Agreement between Ukraine of the one part and the European Union, the European Atomic Energy Community and their member states of the other part" [розпорядження No. 847-р "Про імплементацію Угоди про асоціацію між Україною, з однієї сторони, та Європейським Союзом, Європейським співтовариством з атомної енергії і їхніми державами-членами, з іншої сторони], dated 17 September 2014, available at https://zakon.rada.gov.ua/laws/show/847-2014-p, accessed 12 August 2019.

Communist Party of the Soviet Union (1990), Материалы XXVIII съезда Коммунистической партии Советского Союза [Materials of the 28th Congress of the Communist Party of the Soviet Union], Издательство политической литературы [Publishing house of political literature], Moscow, pp. 172-76.

Communist Party of Ukraine (1986), XXVII съезд Коммунистической партии Украины: стенографический отчет, [27th Congress of the Communist Party of Ukraine: verbatim report, 6-8 February 1986], Издательство политической литературы Украины [Publishing house of political literature of Ukraine], Kyiv, p. 54.

Council of Europe (2008), 8-а Європейська міністерська конференція з питань молоді Київ, Україна, 10-11 жовтня 2008 року "Майбутнє молодіжної політики Ради Європи: ПОРЯДОК ДЕННИЙ 2020", [8th Council of Europe Conference of Ministers responsible for youth, "The future of the Council of Europe youth policy: AGENDA 2020", 10-11 October 2008], available at https://rm.coe.int/1680702428 [http://dsmsu.gov.ua/index/ua/material/36], accessed 13 August 2019.

EU–Council of Europe (n.d.) *History of youth work*, youth partnership, available at https://pjp-eu.coe.int/en/web/youth-partnership/history-of-youth-work, accessed 13 August 2019.

Herus O. and Andriichuk S. (eds) (2017), Річний звіт Пласту за 2017 [Plast Annual Report for 2017], available at www.plast.org.ua/about-plast/annual-report-2017/, accessed 13 August 2019.

Kairov A. I. and Petrov F. N. (eds) (1964), "Out-of-school work" [Внешкольная работа], *Pedagogical Encyclopedia* [Педагогическая энциклопедия], Soviet Encyclopedia [Советская энциклопедия], Moscow, Vol. 1, p. 347.

Kordonskyy M. (n.d.), *Что такое неформальная педагогика?* [What is non-formal pedagogy?], available at www.altruism.ru/sengine.cgi/5/28/4, accessed 13 August 2019.

Krzaklewska E. and Williamson H. (2013), Youth policy in Ukraine, Strasbourg, pp. 123-34.

Schizzeretto A. and Gasperoni G. (2001), Study on the state of young people and youth policy in Europe, Milano, p.124., available at https://history.wikireading.ru/251063, accessed 13 August 2019.

Shubin A. V. (2008), Диссиденты, неформалы и свобода в СССР [Dissidents, non-formal groups and freedom in the USSR], available at https://history.wikireading.ru/251092, accessed 13 August 2019.

Smith M. K. (2001), "What is non-formal education?", The encyclopaedia of informal education, available at http://infed.org/mobi/what-is-non-formal-education/, accessed 13 August 2019.

Yakovleva A. P. (1964), "*Дворцы и дома пионеров и школьников*" [Palaces and houses of Pioneers and schoolchildren], in Kairov A. I. and Petrov F. N. (eds), *Педагогическая энциклопедия* [Pedagogical encyclopedia] Советская энциклопедия [Soviet encyclopedia], Moscow, Vol. 1, p. 648-51.

Yarema O. (ed) (2016), Ціннісні орієнтації сучасної української молоді: щорічна доповідь Президенту України, Верховній Раді України про становище молоді в Україні (за підсумками 2015 року) [Valuable orientations of modern Ukrainian youth: Annual report to the President of Ukraine, the Verkhovna Rada of Ukraine, the Cabinet of Ministers of Ukraine on the situation of youth in Ukraine (in 2015)], p. 115, available at http://dsmsu.gov.ua/media/2016/11/03/22/Shorichna_dopovid.pdf, accessed 13 August 2019.

Chapter 14

Reflective trialogue: conclusions from the history project – 12 trilemmas for youth work

Howard Williamson and Filip Coussée

Introduction

The simplicity of youth work belies its complexity. Within and behind the seemingly rather straightforward practice of "working with young people" there are multiple layers and levels of tensions, contradictions and dilemmas, making youth work arguably the "hardest job in the world" (Coussée and Williamson 2011). Sometimes these are presented as binary options and tensions, such as having to look simultaneously to the agendas and expectations of those funding work with young people and to the expressed needs and wants of young people; or both winning space for the contemporary "associative life" of young people while simultaneously building bridges for young people's transitions towards the future (the very heart of the Declaration from the 2nd European Youth Work Convention[84]). However, the challenges presented to youth work are often more usefully framed within triangles of reflection. These triangles present themselves at many levels – politics, policy, methods and practice – demanding what we are calling, in a nod to the heartbeat of a great deal of youth worker training that seeks to cultivate the "reflective practitioner" (see Schön 1983), the reflective trialogue. The triangles that are debated below have emerged firmly and forcefully from the 10-year History of Youth Work in Europe project, which has interrogated both country (hi)stories of the evolution of youth work and more overarching and sometimes more conceptual themes. In sum, the project has sought not only to capture youth work's largely hidden history but also to consider wider lessons and learning for today's youth policy in Europe and the place of youth work within it.

We are, of course, now routinely familiar with what has become known as the "magic triangle" of youth research, youth policy and youth practice (see Milmeister and Williamson 2006), with youth work sitting somewhere within it. The Partnership

---

84. https://pjp-eu.coe.int/documents/42128013/47262187/The+2nd+European+Youth+Work+Declaration_FINAL.pdf/cc602b1d-6efc-46d9-80ec-5ca57c35eb85.

between the European Union and the Council of Europe in the field of youth (here-after the "youth Partnership") has not only developed its own recurrent work plans within this particular triangle but has also been a central driver behind the history project, anchoring seven history seminars over 10 years that have produced seven volumes of material.[85] It is important to acknowledge, however, that the triangle of research, policy and practice in the youth sector has often been manipulated further into many other shapes and formations in order to stimulate debate on a variety of issues and relationships that prevail when seeking to understand developments in the field of youth (see Zentner 2016). For this reason, we are aware that the projection of our cluster of triangles may leave us open to accusations of being too simplistic, perhaps even too contrived, but nevertheless we maintain that they do derive from the core of the history project and are worthy of reflection and deeper interrogation at we look to the future.

The History of Youth Work in Europe project

Youth work is a polyvalent and multifaceted practice. It takes place in a wide range of settings, it varies from unstructured activities to fairly structured programmes, it reaches a large diversity of young people, touches a lot of different themes and is on the interface with many other disciplines and practices (Coussée 2009: 7).

This perspective on youth work was the basis on which the History of Youth Work in Europe project was cemented, conveying a willingness to explore the spectrum of activities, movements, organisations, issues and ideas that have come under the banner of youth work across Europe over the past century and a half. As Williamson (2006) has noted, all youth work encapsulates a journey over time as it engages with different groups of young people, invokes different methods, addresses different issues and operates in different settings. Every journey is, in some respects, distinct, even though there will, inevitably, be common patterns. Similarly, every country story of the development of youth work is distinct. Part of the challenge for the history project was, therefore, to draw out the elements of shared trajectories and to reconfigure them to inform contemporary debate around youth work policy and practice, and indeed the contribution to be made by youth work to the wider canvas of youth policy in today's Europe.

A very short account of the unfolding place and position of youth work on the European map is provided in #27 of the European youth work magazine *Coyote*, which celebrates 20 years of the youth Partnership (see Vanhee and Williamson 2018). For half of those 20 years (2008-18), the youth Partnership supported the History of Youth Work in Europe project, in collaboration with a number of countries that hosted the sequence of seminars from which subsequent publications were drawn.

Originating as the modest idea of emulating the UK's "Durham history project", which had, over a number of years and through a sequence of conferences and publications, drilled deep into the annals and archives of youth work throughout the UK, a small seminar in Blankenberge in Belgium considered some of the country

---

85. See https://pjp-eu.coe.int/en/web/youth-partnership/the-history-of-youth-work-in-europe-volume-1.

(hi) stories of youth work throughout Europe. A second seminar, also in Blankenberge, did much the same. The third was a larger event that was organised to precede the 1st European Youth Work Convention, which celebrated awareness of the diversity of youth work across Europe. The fourth seminar, held in Estonia, acknowledged the powerful political influences on the trajectories of youth work in different European countries, notwithstanding the grounded challenges facing young people and the professional principles that often sought to be the compass for youth work practice. The fifth seminar, in Finland, then considered the strengths and weaknesses of, and for, youth work through its alignment with the broader canvas of youth policy priorities and pressures, such as formal education, vocational training, employment initiatives, health imperatives and other policy domains. Youth work routinely proclaimed its historical roots and routes as an educational practice and its central place within the framework of non-formal education, yet the sixth seminar, held in Malta, explored its equally influential antecedents in social work. The final seminar took place in Slovenia, discussing the varied histories of transnational and pan-European youth organisations.

The body of knowledge accumulated through the history project is both phenomenally diverse and, at the same time, strikingly integrated. Lines of connection can be drawn within it in so many different ways. Country differences often conceal important shared points of influence in the development of youth work, whether political change or the pioneering work of charismatic individuals. Unexpected positions are revealed, such as progressive alliances with fellow travellers (in both formal education and social work, particularly), despite forthright proclamations of the distinctiveness, and indeed distinction, of youth work as a separate profession and practice.

An internal evaluation[86] of the work of the history project itself produced some interesting and important observations. Predictably, these included an acknowledgement of the diversity of youth work and appreciation that the history project had covered this spectrum without simplification, generalisation or reductionism. The report noted that "there has previously been no comparable attempt in Europe to portray this field and this profession so comprehensively, internationally and from an historical perspective". It went on to confirm a central contention of the history project: that youth work is embedded in the lifeworlds of young people but intersects constantly with "political and organisational structures, power interests and programmes". In that respect, youth work always needs to be seen as a *relational activity*, one that at the same time is essentially about "fostering relationships among young people *and* between them and society" (emphasis added).

Three key messages were drawn from this internal evaluation about the "basic and transversal features" of youth work in relation to the countries of modern Europe. First, youth work is always walking a line between an agenda of working for the emancipation and autonomy of young people on the one hand and promoting the conformity and integration of young people on the other, sometimes through some level of regulation and control (though few self-respecting youth workers would wish to concede that!). Second, as has always been the case, youth work continues to be

---

86. Walter Lorenz (2018), The History of Youth Work in Europe – an evaluation of the publications and contributions from the series of seven European exchange workshops.

delivered through three channels – the state, the market and civil society. Each has different expectations of youth work and exerts different forms of influence on youth work delivery and practice. Third, where state involvement in youth work is more prominent, this often carries the benefits of strengthened resources and recognition for youth work and youth workers but can produce a distortion of the principles of youth work, a risk of subservience to wider public policy agendas and a loss of professional independence. When youth movements become youth programmes, one is reminded of a question posed by the authors of a history of youth in Australia (see Irving, Maunders and Sherington 1995): are they still "heads of a movement" or "arms of the state"? Clearly some forms of youth work in Europe have close and mutual relationships with established political and policy-making processes, at national and, indeed, European Union and Council of Europe levels, while other forms of youth work remain more critical and sometimes even oppositional.[87]

Youth work has, indeed, emerged from many quarters and corners. The internal evaluation records a number of key historical strands that have combined in myriad ways to form the particular character of youth work in different countries and across Europe. These have included:

▶ the provision of education and learning beyond school;

▶ the need to strengthen the protection and welfare of young people;

▶ a commitment to develop constructive leisure activities and opportunities;

▶ the desire to promote citizenship at national and international levels;

▶ an explicit political agenda.

Embedded within each of these strands have been further differentiations and calibrations – leisure activities, for example, can embrace everything from sports clubs, to hiking and summer camps. Indeed, the mosaic of elements of youth work traverses political, physical, social and cultural dimensions, producing puzzlement and confusion about its core identity, as the American youth work academic Joyce Walker pondered at the fifth history workshop:

> Is youth work a social service delivery mechanism, an allied educational system, a community recreation programme, a problem prevention scheme, a client service system of case management, an intervention unit to pull out when something goes wrong, or a service on the side of young people? (Walker 2016: 14)

What is rarely disputed is that youth work needs to be significantly about "meeting young people where they are at", whatever other agendas are at play or at stake. As the Declaration of the 2nd European Youth Work Convention[88] asserts, youth work takes place on young people's terms and on their turf. It builds on and from their expressed and identified needs, is anchored in their rights, seeks to construct holistic and person-centred opportunities, and supports and endeavours to strengthen young people's sense of agency. As the first seminar and publication from the history project

---

87. The position of national youth councils, as one form of "youth work" is particularly interesting in this regard: see Holtom et al. 2016.

88. https://pjp-eu.coe.int/documents/42128013/47262187/The+2nd+European+Youth+Work+Declaration_FINAL.pdf/cc602b1d-6efc-46d9-80ec-5ca57c35eb85.

registered, youth work constantly and consistently is characterised by its juggling of providing a "forum" and producing a "transit zone", ideas that subsequently became pivotal themes, as "spaces" and "bridges" within the Council of Europe Recommendation on Youth Work.[89] Indeed, the internal evaluation confirmed the interplay between the two as a central thread in the subsequent history seminars, concluding that "only authoritarian or anarchic approaches [to youth work] deny the value of this dialectic".

Youth work would be lost, or would lose its way, if it manifestly failed to maintain these two key characteristics in some reasonable balance, however much they may often appear to be in tension with each other. A retreat into the splendid isolation of simply providing space (a forum) for young people would abdicate youth work's social responsibility. Conversely, the full embrace of a transitions (transit zone) agenda by youth work would be a denial of its commitment to young people. Such transitory work is, of course, a commitment to young people, but it is not the *raison d'être* of youth work, even though youth work can, and should, find ways of working in co-operation with more explicitly focused transitory actors, such as schools, employment agencies and even social work. But the history project points to a cycle that constantly needs renewal: what may start as transitory work tends to flounder as it becomes apparent that young people need another kind of (compensatory or complementary) education and learning, a third educational environment that is less focused on transitions and more focused on being together, the development of social skills, the cultivation of democratic attitudes, having fun and learning by experience. Sometimes these are put in place, one way or another, but routinely the pendulum moves back towards transition priorities, at least for the youth work that can be instrumentalised in that way. Future-focused youth work then becomes subjected to targets and outcome-driven practice, before the importance of relationships, time, trust and patience reassert themselves as critical for successful youth work in the present (see Coussée and Williamson 2012). And so the circle turns.

Spaces and bridges are not, however, the only tensions that youth work has to seek to balance and keep in balance. Indeed, as youth work gets buffeted by wider social and political pressures at national and European levels – in relation to, for example, the re-engagement of young people not in education, employment or training (NEET), the promotion of employability, the cultivation of healthy lifestyles and well-being, or the combating of radicalisation – finding an appropriate position and place within and between all of the following triangles becomes an increasingly demanding professional challenge.

Triangulations – 12 trilemmas from the history project

The following trilemmas emerged very clearly and forcefully from the history project. They surfaced as inherent tensions, contradictions and paradoxes for both thinking about youth work and its actual practice. They are not for resolution and indeed many, by their very nature, cannot be resolved. Rather, and the reason they are presented diagrammatically in the form of triangles, they provide the terrain (within the triangle) within which youth workers and policy makers (both politicians and civil

---

89. https://rm.coe.int/1680717e78.

servants) have to make (professional) decisions as to how to (a) position youth work, (b) manage the circumstances that derive from that positioning, and (c) negotiate and justify the position they have taken. Youth work has always been a practice of co-creation and co-management between policy makers and youth workers. In some practice, young people have also been central players in the shaping of youth work, not in the very early days but, over the years, the voice of young people has become increasingly important, not only within self-governed youth organisations but across the whole spectrum of youth work practice. Others will, almost always, be seeking to reposition the place of youth work within the framework of public policy directed towards young people, and youth workers will need a robust defence for the stance they have elected to take.

1. Roots: what is youth work? Education, social work, counselling

Social work

Education   Counselling

Youth work has routinely proclaimed that it is an educational practice, lying firmly within an activity also portrayed as non-formal education or non-formal learning. Yet, as Volume 6 in the history series demonstrated forcefully, there is a long tradition and trajectory of forms of youth work that are embedded in social work and therapeutic conceptualisations of practice.

Youth work also often asserts that it is essentially about some kind of collective, experiential practice but others sometimes see it as concerned with lending more individual and individualised support to young people, arguably through the provision of information and advice, or what might be construed as a low-level form of counselling. Though such a view is frequently rebutted by the youth work profession, there is no doubt that within the wider practice of youth work, youth workers do extend a great deal of support to individual young people. Indeed, a popular element in many definitions of youth work is that it is concerned with the personal development of young people.

Recognising these different traditions should help youth work and youth workers to argue that they draw on all three traditions but combine them differently according to different contexts of practice – youth work within an "open" youth centre or through self-governed youth organisations, in contrast to youth work in a hostel for homeless young people or on the street, is and should be differently conceived and constituted.

2. Method: how is youth work done?

Advice and Information

Education/learning   Coaching/training

Youth work may routinely claim to be primarily engaged in non-formal education but this is another simplicity that belies more empirical complexity. The cycle of experiential learning (do, review, learn, apply) does not take place organically but through skilled and timely interventions that may involve elements of formal education (more akin to schooling, though not in school; didactic teaching rather than active learning), considerable advice and information, and sometimes specific coaching and training.

The typical youth work outdoor pursuits menu of rock climbing, abseiling, caving and canoeing could not take place without this methodological blend, nor could a youth work sporting event or, indeed, a routine evening youth club activity.

Many activities undertaken by youth workers need not be youth work. Without the non-formal educative and experiential learning focus, they would remain as leisure-time trips, a sporting tournament or an outdoor adventure, contributing very possibly to informal, but not non-formal,[90] learning. Youth workers have a job to do to explain how their core methodological approaches combine with those of others to produce a distinctive youth work outcome.

3. Delivery: who does youth work? The practitioners

Volunteers

Paid workers　　　Young people
(all professional?)

The debate about youth work often lurches clumsily over very different ground. Nowhere is this more apparent than in discussions of who does it and how it is done – the question of professionalisation and the question of professionalism. Three points are, however, crystal clear. One is that most youth work, in all parts of Europe, continues to be done by volunteers, both adults and young people themselves. The second is that where there are paid, professionalised youth workers, there are other – arguably higher – expectations of what youth work can achieve and should be expected to do. The third is that whoever is providing youth work offers and experiences (voluntarily or paid), this should be done in a reflective and professional manner, in terms of adherence to agreed ethical standards and codes of conduct, as well as proper attention to issues such as health, safety and protection.

This debate raises a set of questions about the education and training of all youth workers. The history project conveyed graphically the very patchy nature of such provision, if it existed at all, and certainly the absence for the most part of any progression routes within coherent thinking about "workforce development". This has

---

90.　For a short illustration of how a "hike in the hills" becomes a platform for non-formal education, see www.worldready.org/news/howard-williamson/.

recently become a matter of attention for the youth Partnership and is a central issue within the Council of Europe's Recommendation on Youth Work.

There are many levels to be addressed here, not least questions concerning "licence to practice" in youth work, the kind of content and curriculum that needs to be enshrined in youth worker training, and the location(s) in which such education and training should take place. There are always "chicken and egg" questions within the professionalisation debate, which itself is closely linked with youth work's desire and claim for greater recognition (and reward). Youth work has thrived, in many places for over a century, on voluntarism, which has not always equated to amateurism (self-governed youth organisations, youth movements and enterprising youth work projects are excellent examples of this point), but there is little doubt that youth work practice is enhanced when there is at least some level of paid professional activity within the triangle – to oversee or underpin its quality and development.

4. Pressures: why youth work? Policy, principles, priorities

Principle/philosophy

Policy   Priorities of young people

Youth work typically proclaims that it exists to "meet the needs of young people". Needs, or wants? Sometimes the wording is adapted to talk about "responding to the priorities of young people". Clearly it would not be youth work if the agendas of young people were ignored, but that is not the only pressure on, or indeed *raison d'être* for, youth work.

Youth work is also guided and governed by its own principles and philosophy. Most commonly expressed are treating young people "holistically" and that all forms of youth work are premised on a "voluntary relationship" but these are not completely cast in stone. There are, furthermore, value-based positions such as ensuring "anti-oppressive practice", a commitment to equalities, and the promotion of human rights and democracy. Volume 7 of the history project talks about youth work being laboratories for democracy, yet some youth workers would claim that part of their role is to defend the minority of one or challenge the tyranny of the majority. The value base of youth work is not completely fixed, though some core principles would probably secure a reasonably broad consensus.

Yet youth work is also subject to considerable policy pressures. Volume 4[91] of the history series showed clearly how youth work is routinely harnessed by governments to address issues of concern to them. There may not always been a need for resistance to such pressures. Youth unemployment is no doubt as much of a concern to young people as it is to public authorities! The question for youth work is then not whether to engage with public policy initiatives on this front, but how.

---

91. https://pjp-eu.coe.int/en/web/youth-partnership/the-history-of-youth-work-in-europe-volume-4?inheritRedirect=true.

Youth work is not an outcome-focused practice, but an open practice. Youth work is not about equipping young people with qualifications and skills that may strengthen their position in the labour market; that is the task of the formal educational system, vocational training and careers agencies. Youth workers may, of course, inadvertently support young people's employability, refer them to relevant transitory agents, and encourage young people to make full use of them. The aim of youth work, however, is *Bildung*; as the 2nd history workshop argued, youth work was not about learning to earn a living, but learning about fully living a life. One component of that is, of course, to address social problems such as high youth unemployment. Youth workers may well work with young people (and indeed other stakeholders) on such matters, through discussing issues such as barriers to the labour market, the creation of better and alternative opportunities, or innovative projects that may strengthen young people's positive opportunities and experiences in that policy domain. But youth work is not a supplementary labour market preparation or placement agency.

Indeed, striking the balance between responding to public (youth) policy priorities, maintaining fidelity to youth work principles and meeting the needs of young people is a paramount, ever-present challenge for youth work. Getting sucked into any one corner of this triangle is a recipe for paralysis – enslavement by government, purist ideologies that simply do not connect with the real world, or an uncritical compliance with the demands of young people. Sliding towards any corner of the triangle will attract accusations and negative criticism from the other two.

5. Space: where does youth work happen? Street, building, online

Buildings

Street   Digital

Youth work has classically taken place in dedicated physical spaces, albeit often shared with others (community centres, cultural centres, churches/mosques) though sometimes exclusively for the use of young people (youth centres). For some time, however, there has also been an incremental growth in street work, whether as a form of outreach designed to make contact with young people in order to attract them to projects or centres, or as detached work with young people wherever they are to be found. More recently, there has also been the emergence of "virtual" youth work, most lately manifesting itself in the form of "digital" youth work (see Kiviniemi and Tuominen 2017), though this is still in its infancy. Nonetheless, as we all increasingly inhabit a digitalised world, youth work will have to look deeply into how it makes appropriate connections.[92]

---

92. See the youth Partnership's *Perspectives on youth: young people in a digitalised world*, Vol. 4, 2018; see also Theben et al. 2018.

The history project dwelt largely on youth work that has taken place in defined spaces, including of course volunteering programmes and summer camps. For the future, however, it is likely that youth work will increasingly have to connect and combine physical, virtual and undefined (uncontrolled) space in pursuit of relevant youth work practice. Indeed, the loss of buildings – whether the hobby education centres favoured under state socialism, or the Albemarle dedicated youth centres in England and Wales – means that youth work will need to think more creatively than ever about the location, as well as the methodology of its practice.

6. Rationale

Recreation

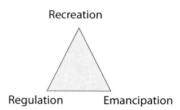

Regulation   Emancipation

Youth work has often been perceived, from the outside, as little more than recreation – the classic allegation, certainly in some parts of Europe, remains that it is largely about table tennis and pool. Of course, it could be argued that youth work is most definitely about "re-creation", providing young people with associational space within which positive activities (including table tennis and pool!) take place. Youth work has certainly always claimed that it is, one way or another, about emancipation – through the provision of developmental experiences and opportunities. However, as Coussée (2008), *inter alia*, has argued recurrently, youth work has historically always had a strong regulatory dimension, particularly for some groups of young people. He makes the point that while youth movements for students were emancipatory, youth programmes for working-class youth (boys) were far more concerned with regulation – nipping trouble in the bud and promoting behaviourally acceptable and more healthy lifestyles.

This is an old debate, but it remains pertinent today. Youth workers are neither exclusively agents of social change nor agents of social control: they are some mix of the two, though quite how they determine that mix is a matter for professional judgment. The mix will undulate over time, in the context of different activities and in relation to different (groups of) young people. For young people themselves, knowing when to display more autonomous self-direction and enterprise and when to be more acquiescent and compliant to authority is arguably a critical contemporary competence, and it is also arguably a contemporary responsibility for youth work.

7. Focus of attention

Groups

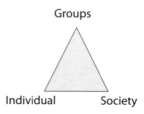

Individual   Society

Youth work, as is often claimed by its exponents, is essentially a group activity. The argument is often then developed to assert that, through the group work that is central to youth work, the individual is connected to society.

Yet, building in particular from two of the previous trilemmas (1 and 4: historical roots and contemporary pressures), there are always demands on youth work that take the focus of attention away from group work to the provision of individual support on the one hand and the delivery of societal agendas on the other. These may not necessarily, as also already noted, be incompatible or in conflict with each other: helping individual young people to manage anger may have a valuable youth crime prevention outcome; advising on exercise has health policy benefits; assisting with job applications supports the employability agenda. But, critically, they take youth work away from group work.

Whether it is casual conversations, games or sporting activities, summer camps or environmental projects, youth work typically takes place together. It has been described by Rogers and Smith (2010) as "journeying together". Done in isolation or at the direction of wider policy imperatives – however much both may have a case – defeats the central objective of youth work: to engage in a shared and mutually agreed practice. Maintaining the primary (though not always exclusive) focus of attention on young people as a group remains a paramount responsibility for youth work.

8. Style of practice

Negotiated/exchange

Proactive   Reactive

Just as youth work is not only about meeting the needs of young people (see tri-lemma 4, the recurrent pressures on youth work), so youth work is not only about responding to the needs and wants expressed by young people. It is also about, to some extent, making (pro)active interventions in young people's lives, whether in terms of ideas (through conversation), relationships (through constructed activities) or experiences (through planned opportunities). Indeed, it would be an abdication of a youth work role if practitioners did not find ways of moving young people from their comfort zones into circumstances that stretched their imaginations, perspectives and horizons. Young people can always retreat from such contexts (and will do so if the youth work is done badly) but it is contingent on youth work to try.

And the best way for youth work to try is, of course, not through imposition but through negotiation, exchange and persuasion. There may, however, be times when more forceful cajoling and encouragement is desired, even required (who, after all, really likes to be jerked out of their comfort zone?), though this should fall short of a compulsion that jeopardises the "voluntary relationship". (This is part of a huge current policy debate about how youth work is conducted within semi-coercive environments, such as schools or young offender institutions.)

Youth work functions most effectively within a culture of mutuality and reciprocity. Where youth work responds well to the expressed wishes of young people (and that may well often be around leisure and recreational aspirations), there is a much greater possibility of persuading young people to try out new experiences and contemplate new ideas. In short, the quality of the relationship developed between youth workers and young people will invariably be the weathervane of what can be attempted within the framework of youth work practice.

9. Locus of practice

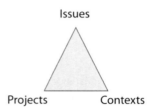

The framework of youth work practice, alluded to above, prospectively extends far and wide, over time and space. This presents another challenge for youth work, when everything attached to "working with young people" can be viewed by others and indeed claimed by those involved to be "youth work".

Youth work can, however, certainly embrace myriad projects (such as volunteering or environmental work, or intergenerational support), give attention to a host of issues in young people's lives (interpersonal relationships, living healthy lifestyles, racism, intercultural tolerance and understanding, political literacy, or moral responsibility), and take place in many different contexts, both close to home and further afield.

Explaining to others quite how such hybrid activities (doing a project on a particular issue in a particular context) constitutes a form of youth work rather than something else (such as a tourist offer or an evangelical mission) remains a significant challenge for youth workers.

10. Target of practice

Youth work is also ill-defined when it comes to the target of its practice. Notwithstanding the age question (not just definitions of "young people" but also the age range most appropriately addressed by "youth work", from around 11 to up to 30), there is always the "target" question in terms of the type of young people who should be the priority for youth work.

Youth workers themselves are usually reluctant to classify and categorise young people (in part because of the holistic principle – seeing young people in the round and not on the basis of any particular presenting attitudes or behaviour); instead, they favour the adoption of a more open-door philosophy, and not just in relation to the classical open youth centre (or youth club) approach that has prevailed in some parts of western and northern Europe.

Yet such universality is increasingly difficult to sustain, certainly in terms of public support for youth work. Indeed, public authorities have often leaned towards supporting forms of youth work directed at either the spotting and development of talent (certainly in eastern Europe and the Caucasus, even now) or the prevention of deviance and the containment of disadvantage. Clever words have sometimes been adopted to try to accommodate all of this under one umbrella, such as a "universal service differentiated according to need",[93] but all youth work has to continue to reflect on the balance it strikes between engaging with more privileged and included (the "valued") young people on the one hand, more disadvantaged and excluded (the "villains" and the "vulnerable") young people on the other, and the vast majority of "ordinary" young people in between: those whose names are neither inscribed on the honours' boards of their schools nor scratched into the desks (see Brown 1987) – those who are often the "invisible".

11. Making the connections

Justice

Health   Employment

Youth work has often bemoaned its existence in the shadows and on the margins of stronger professional practice (such as school teaching and social work). From those sidelines, however, it has also argued that – given the chance – it can make a significant contribution to those more powerful and pressing youth policy agendas. Youth work can, some claim, promote the health of young people, strengthen their employability and prevent their propensity to offending. Volume 5[94] of the history project put some of this to the test, arguing that there is a paradoxical prospect of youth work securing greater autonomy through the dependencies it may establish with wider public services and public policy priorities.

There is, of course, a risk of youth work being subordinated to the agendas of others, enslaved rather than empowered through partnership. There are no easy answers. Multi-agency practice invariably rests on a "precarious equilibrium" of organisational, professional and personal relationships (see Williamson and Weatherspoon 1985; Williamson 2017). Youth work – or rather youth workers, when presented with specific contextual scenarios – has to consider what concessions it is willing to make. Independent youth work carries the risk of being considered irrelevant by society, but dependent youth work, whatever the promise of greater autonomy, risks being

---

93. This was the mantra of the Connexions service in England, a new "youth support service" in 2000.
94. https://pjp-eu.coe.int/en/web/youth-partnership/the-history-of-youth-work-volume-5.

compromised to the point where it is considered irrelevant by young people. There is a tightrope to be walked, but it cannot, and should not, be avoided.

12. The value of youth work

Outcomes and impact have become critical concerns in relation to all public services. Youth work is not immune from the challenge of demonstrating the return it provides (produces) as a result of investment in it. Yet youth work is premised, as reported above, on the journey it takes with young people; part of the strapline of the radical British campaign, In Defence of Youth Work, is that youth work is "conversation without guarantees".[95]

Would, we have to ask, the youth work process in fact be pointless if there were no outcomes or wider impact? Perhaps. But the pervasive claim by youth workers is that, beyond the value of the process, there are multiple benefits derived from youth work, not only for young people involved but for the communities in which they live and for society at large. The list advanced is endless, from numerous soft skills and competencies developed by individuals, through social inclusion and civic and community responsibility, to wider social and political participation.

Demonstrating such impact and outcomes is, however, rather more difficult. Quite how they accrue from youth work, over what period of time and precisely in what way, is currently exercising the minds of many in the youth work sector. Retreating back to assertions of the value of process, relationships and the centrality of time, patience and trust is no longer an acceptable position to adopt (if it ever was).

However, as Coussée and Williamson (2012) have argued, both process and outcomes have to be scaled appropriately. If youth work becomes too heavily preoccupied with outcomes and impact, at the expense of process factors, then it will cease to be youth work. Equally, if youth work is dismissive of demands to "prove" its effects, it will fail to secure public recognition and support and be sidelined in favour of other public service priorities. It is for youth work to balance its arguments accordingly.

Youth work and youth policy

All of these triangles reveal and reflect the challenge for formulating and activating youth work policy. The great beauty of the Declaration arising from the 2nd European Youth Work Convention[96] and the subsequent Council of Europe Recommendation on

---

95. The full strapline of In Defence of Youth Work is: "that is volatile and voluntary, creative and collective – an association and conversation without guarantees".

96. https://pjp-eu.coe.int/documents/42128013/47262187/The+2nd+European+Youth+Work+ Declaration_FINAL.pdf/cc602b1d-6efc-46d9-80ec-5ca57c35eb85.

Youth Work[97] was their essential simplicity: the idea that all kinds of youth work share the common ground of winning space and supporting bridges for young people. This is achieved through the careful and considered weighing and balancing – never resolution – of all of the trilemmas outlined above: within each of them and between all of them. What such documentation does not do, however, is to assert, with any precision, what that balance should be. If this was to be done – and some youth work policy at certain times has sought to be prescriptive in this way – this would prohibit the great reflexivity of practice (praxis) that is the very soul of youth work. Yet it is this need to ensure the maintenance of the possibility of reflective practice, allowing youth workers to reconcile the corners of these triangles according to the specific realities and demands of the contexts within which they are working, that makes the shaping of youth work policy all the more problematic. Indeed, there was no youth work policy in the beginning; as youth work became entangled with wider dimensions of public policy directed towards young people, so it became subject to the same public policy frameworks and expectations, including the increasing pressure to delineate and deliver specific outcomes.

Though some crumbs of public resources may have been thrown at youth work in the past, in the belief that democracy and social learning need what have been called "wild zones" – free spaces for additional, non-formal learning – public institutions are less and less willing to simply write a blank cheque in the blind faith that youth work will deliver. "Deliver what?" is invariably an opening question. But further questions immediately arise: where should it take place, who should provide it, how and where should youth work happen? In many related areas of public policy and professional activity directed towards young people (education/schooling, social work, vocational preparation, health promotion, crime prevention), the answers to such questions may still be difficult but they are not so hard to conceptualise: teachers work in schools, social workers have caseloads and clients, vocational training instructors impart skills, health advisers manage diets, supervisors regulate activity. The conceptualisation of youth work is, by contrast, considerably more fluid and loose-knit, and arguably opaque, even though it could accommodate all of the actions listed above, or none of them. And that is the conundrum facing those seeking to articulate and advocate the case for youth work to those with responsibility for policy making. The ultimate paradox (and the history project has been full of them) is that the very *raison d'être* at the heart of youth work – to have space for exploration and experience – seems to be, simultaneously, the reason to doubt the legitimacy of youth work. If young people are "doing nothing" (just hanging around), how can they be learning anything!

A further paradox is that many, probably most, of those making policy have them-selves participated in and experienced youth work provision and practice. They should be well aware that, at least implicitly, youth work is always striving to move along a path that exists beyond the individual (as noted above, youth work is essen-tially a practice of working with groups, however much some level of individual support and guidance may be provided) but falls short of what might be called the "institutional", in that it serves the expressed needs and wishes of young people as much as those of the state and society. Finding this line between individualisation

---

97.   https://rm.coe.int/1680717e78.

and institutionalisation is but one of the challenges for, and indeed skills of, those involved in youth work.

Looking forward – towards a youth work policy agenda for the next decade

The History of Youth Work in Europe project has spent the past decade looking back at both national and thematic histories of youth work and considering elements that remain pertinent for a contemporary consideration of youth work policy. This chapter has sought to consolidate those elements into discrete themes and issues for the future. In terms of shaping a future for youth work through robust youth work policy advocacy, three lines of further development stand out.

The first is concerned with the conceptualisation of youth work. Though often depicted in more recent youth policy documentation as a key platform for supporting a range of wider challenges experienced (and sometimes caused) by young people, its capacity and capabilities are often, at least implicitly, overstated: to what extent can (or should) youth work be expected to address youth radicalisation, tackle the European refugee crisis, or deal with the rise in serious violence among the young? Working out the realistic boundaries of youth work as well as the potential within which it can deliver its promise will be an essential task if it is to make a plausible argument about its place and value within the wider canvas and framework of youth policy.

The second, related, issue lies in the competence of those engaged in youth work. It is related because the more competent the practice, the broader the canvas on which youth work can stake its claim for relevance and recognition. This generates questions that are already being addressed around the education and training paths for youth workers and the kind of curricula that is needed to shape the learning and professional development of youth workers. If youth work is as complex as is often asserted, demanding carefully calibrated reflection, judgment and intervention, then presumably even its army of volunteers need well-honed professional skills.

Third, and once again related, is the question of the credibility of youth work, which clearly rests on its ability to demonstrate that there are real outcomes to the practice that it preaches. The evidence base, to date, remains thin. There is a paucity of knowledge as to what really goes on within a youth work setting, project or programme. Output can often be quite readily mapped but understanding the process and/or gauging the impact and outcomes is more elusive. There have been some commendable recent stabs at this (see Ord et al. 2018), beyond rhetorical proclamations, but even these research findings are vulnerable to "being dismissed as the self-indulgent ramblings of those already inside the youth work bubble, who have found a methodology to suit their case and cause" (Williamson 2019). It may appear critical to produce evidence about youth work process and "product" that is persuasive and plausible beyond the youth work sector. But whether from within or without the youth work sector, this may be a quest for the holy grail: the history of youth work tells us very clearly that youth work works precisely because of the room and space it makes accessible to young people, physically and intellectually, as they explore and learn from the world (and the youth workers) around them. Youth work is, by definition, loose-knit and flexible; when it is regimented, harnessed, institutionalised in one way or another, it ceases to be youth work. Youth work may have to find ways of securing credibility other than through outcomes.

Conclusion

This chapter has sought to distil some of the core conclusions arising from the extensive findings, arguments and perspectives produced by the History of Youth Work in Europe project. It has endeavoured to look forward through having looked back, in order to consider the ongoing and future challenges for youth work and the place of youth work within the broader youth policy context in Europe.

In sum, the youth work history that has been explored and documented through this project has conveyed that youth work cannot be defined separately from other fields and methods of social and pedagogical work, nor can it be discussed in any detail as if abstracted or divorced from its social, cultural and political context. There are, of course, some constants, irrespective of context. The question of social cohesion (how to shape society) is always there, as is the question of what counts as good education (how to shape young people). Both questions relate to political issues concerned with democracy, diversity, equality, solidarity and liberty (though in some historical moments in some European countries so-called youth work has been far from a proponent of these concepts). Both questions address balances of power, between the haves and the have-nots, on the one hand, and between the old and the young on the other. Throughout history there were periods when the youth question dominated the social question and vice versa. Policy makers have frequently displayed an intention to use youth work as a weapon or vehicle for very different, often externally defined, targets. The history project perhaps does not give enough exposure to ways in which youth workers and young people themselves reacted to those instrumental intentions, but it does reveal a clear tendency among youth workers to concentrate on a third question, one concerned with method (how to organise youth work), not least because that feels like safer and more familiar ground. Strangely enough, after all the probing and debate, and despite a multiplicity of perspectives, youth work still lacks a solid theory to which most of those involved can subscribe, firmly grounded in practice and enabling youth workers to define their own targets in an open and constructive dialogue with policy makers and offering a valid alternative to the introduction and sometimes imposition of neoliberal and managerialist logic to youth work policy and practice.

Youth work is therefore arguably one of the hardest jobs in the world: making connections to the life of young people (making them feel at home) while enlarging their lifeworlds (challenging them to meet new people and do things they do not do at home). The challenge for youth work is not guidance towards smooth social integration, labour market insertion or an ideal-typical adulthood. Youth work is more than the management of growing up. The youth work challenge is to keep open identity development so as not to let it be prematurely constrained and corralled within a standard set of expectations. To achieve that without generating estrangement or anxiety in young people is a huge challenge. Having fun and being in a group is therefore quintessential to youth work in all its facets. The practice of youth work is critical within a dynamic democracy. Indeed, youth clubs and youth projects have been depicted as mini-democracies. This may not always be strictly true, but they are platforms for the learning of democracy one way or another. Youth workers need the resources to offer a safe harbour to young people, from which they can set sail: somewhere to go, something to do, a place of their own where they can experience and exercise autonomy, and where they find friends and role models. The quartet of association, activities, autonomy and advice. And youth workers also need the social pedagogical space to move forward with young people, from bonding to bridging, from consuming to producing and from participation in youth work to participation through youth work into their wider worlds.

References

Brown P. (1987), *Schooling ordinary kids: inequality, unemployment and the new vocationalism*, Tavistock, London.

Coussée F. (2008), *A century of youth work policy*, Academia Press, Gent.

Coussée F. (2009), "The relevance of youth work's history", in Vershelden G., Coussée F. and Williamson H. (eds), *The history of youth work in Europe – Relevance for today's youth work policy*, Council of Europe Publishing, Strasbourg.

Coussée F. and Williamson H. (2012), "In need of hydration", proceedings of European youth workers conference Vulnerable Youth in the City (Antwerp 8-10 June 2011), Uit de Marge, Brussels, pp. 44-54.

Coussée F. and Williamson, H. (2011), "Youth worker, probably the most difficult job in the world", *Children Australia* Vol. 36, No. 4, pp. 224-28.

Holtom D., Williamson H. and Watkins J. (2016), *Key issues in developing and implementing youth policy strategic documents*, Mreža mladih Hrvatske, Zagreb, available at www.mmh.hr/files/ckfinder/files/Key%20issues%20in%20developing%20and%20implementing%20youth%20policy%20strategic%20documents(1).pdf, accessed 14 August 2019.

Irving T., Maunders D. and Sherington G. (1995), *Youth in Australia: policy, administration and politics; a history since World War II*, Macmillan Education, South Melbourne.

Kiviniemi J. and Tuominen S. (eds) (2017), *Digital youth work – A Finnish perspective*, Verke, Helsinki.

Milmeister M. and Williamson H. (eds) (2006), *Dialogues and networks: organising exchanges between youth field actors*, Youth research monographs Vol. 2, Editions Phi, Luxembourg.

Ord J. with Carletti M., Cooper S., Dansac C., Morciano D, Siurala L. and Taru M. (eds) (2018), *The impact of youth work in Europe: a study of five European countries*, Humak University of Applied Sciences Publications, Helsinki.

Rogers A. and Smith M. (2010), *Journeying together: growing youth work and youth workers in local communities*, Russell House Publishing, Lyme Regis.

Schön D. (1983), *The reflective practitioner: how professionals think in action*, Basic Books, London.

Theben A., Porcu F., Peña-López I. and Lupiáñez Villanueva F. (2018), *Study on the impact of the internet and social media on youth participation and youth work – Final report*, Publications Office of the European Union, Luxembourg.

Vanhee J. and Williamson H. (2018), "Putting youth work throughout Europe on the map", *Coyote* 27, available at https://pjp-eu.coe.int/en/web/coyote-magazine/putting-youth-work-throughout-europe-on-the-map, accessed 14 August 2019.

Walker J. (2016), "Crafting the space between either and or: attending to the role of words, young people and public will", in Siurala L., Coussée F., Suurpää L. and Williamson H. (eds), *The history of youth work in Europe: autonomy through dependency – Histories of co-operation, conflict and innovation in youth work*, Vol. 5, Council of Europe Publishing, Strasbourg.

Williamson H. (2006), *Youth work and the changing policy environment for young people*, National Youth Agency, Leicester.

Williamson H. (2017), "A precarious equilibrium – Working together in youth policy and practice", in Nico M., Taru M., Potočnik D. and Salikau A. (eds), *Needles in haystacks: finding a way forward for cross-sectoral youth policy*, Council of Europe Publishing, Strasbourg.

Williamson H. (2019), "Review of *The impact of youth work in Europe: a study of five European countries*, Ord J. with Carletti M., Cooper S., Dansac C., Morciano D., Siurala L. and Taru M. (eds) (2018)", In Defence of Youth Work, available at www.indefenceofyouthwork.com, accessed 14 August 2019.

Williamson H. and Weatherspoon K. (1985), *Strategies for intervention: an approach to youth and community work in an area of social deprivation*, University College Cardiff Social Research Unit, Cardiff.

Zentner M. (2016), "Observations on the so-called 'magic triangle' or: where has all the magic gone?", in Siurala L., Coussée F., Suurpää L. and Williamson H. (eds), *The history of youth work in Europe: autonomy through dependency – Histories of co-operation, conflict and innovation in youth work*, Vol. 5, Council of Europe Publishing, Strasbourg.

Notes on contributors

Tanya Basarab is Youth Policy and Research Officer at the EU–Council of Europe youth partnership, where she works on the European Knowledge Centre on Youth Policy, youth work and social inclusion of young people. Having studied international relations with a focus on development, she has been engaged with civil society organisations in youth, community development, active citizenship, social and anti-poverty fields. Her contributions have focused on governance, civil dialogue and participatory democracy, social inclusion and rights-based policy processes. She has been involved in the editorial work of the Youth Knowledge Books 23 and 24.

Yevgeniy Borodin is a doctor of historical sciences and professor of public administration and local self-government. His doctoral degree dissertation was on the issues of youth policy formulation and development in modern Ukraine (2007). He is the author of three monographs and many articles on youth policy. He has rich experience in the youth sphere as an activist with NGOs, as a youth worker, public official and youth policy researcher. He has been involved as an expert on youth policy and programmes design at national and regional levels, as a national youth policy expert for UN entities and different projects. He is currently working as First Deputy Director, Professor in Dnipropetrovs'k Regional Institute for Public Administration.

Elisa Briga is Head of Advocacy at the European Federation for Intercultural Learning (EFIL), the umbrella of AFS Intercultural Programs organisations in Europe, where she has worked for eight years. In EFIL she has worked on profiling the organisation towards youth and school education policy stakeholders, and lately has followed closely the developments related to Erasmus+ and the European Education Area. In the past, she worked as a trainee and staff member at the EU–Council of Europe youth partnership. She has been volunteering for CISV International for 18 years and is currently the President of CISV Italy. She holds a master's degree in International Relations and Diplomacy with a thesis on information on youth mobility opportunities.

Filip Coussée is a researcher at Ghent University and co-ordinator of a local centre for special youth care. His focus is on social pedagogy as a perspective on social work and on youth and community work. He has studied the history of youth work in Flanders and its connections to developments in the other social professions and in other European countries.

Melek De-Wint has been leading the research team at The Duke of Edinburgh's International Award Foundation in London since 2017 following her five-year role as the Regional Director for Europe, Mediterranean and Arab States (EMAS). Prior to starting to work for the Foundation in late 2011, she worked in management consultancy, sales, market research, human resources and project management jobs in the private sector. Melek was born and brought up in Ankara, Turkey. She completed a BSc degree in Business Administration at the Middle East Technical University in Turkey and an MSc degree in Social Psychology at the University of Surrey in the UK.

Tanja Dibou is curator and lecturer on the youth work programme at the College of Educational Sciences, Tallinn University, Estonia. Her research interests are youth policy, youth work and non-formal education, youth career counselling and intercultural learning in youth work. Tanja is also a PhD candidate in Political Science at Tallinn University and her PhD research is "Youth policy in Estonia: addressing challenges of joined up working in the context of multilevel governance". In the practical youth work field, Tanja has been working since 2009 as a youth worker, youth project manager, youth information and career specialist. Currently, Tanja is an active member of the Estonian Association of Youth Workers and contributes as an international consultant to the adolescent development programmes at UNICEF.

Vesselina Valcheva Dimitrova has been active in the youth field since 2006, taking up different roles as a youth leader, trainer and co-ordinator, mainly working on youth projects in an international setting. She hold a master's degree in Organisation of Youth Work and has been involved in several research projects exploring educational programmes, career opportunities for youth workers and competence models for youth workers, existing in different countries across Europe. Vesselina was an active volunteer and a member of the Bulgarian Red Cross Youth from 2006 to 2012, which inspired her to research the history of the organisation and prepare the text for this book.

Olga Khabibulina has been researching eastern European youth and culture issues since 2013, contributing to local, national and international reports, drawing on her knowledge and experience working in Belarus youth NGOs since 2006. Since 2018, she has been co-operating with SALTO EECA Resource Centre and the European Cultural Foundation, particularly in the areas of youth volunteer projects and intercultural dialogue between migrant and local communities. She holds MA degrees in Eastern European Studies from the University of Warsaw and one from the Institute of Philosophy and Sociology of the Polish Academy of Sciences. Her academic and civic interests are in discovering the issues of tolerance and social equality, intercultural communication and human dignity within both historic discourse and current policy making in the countries of eastern Europe.

Rein Meus is Policy Officer for Social Tourism at the Flemish Tourism Office. Until 2018 he worked as General Secretary of Don Bosco Youth-Net ivzw, steering the organisational development from 2004. He has lengthy experience in European youth work, working with the European Union's youth sector and the Council of Europe's youth department. He is an experienced trainer in European youth work. He has published several educational resources for European youth work from the perspective of Don Bosco's educational methodology.

Petre Mrkev became involved in the international youth work hosting and sending of the first EVS volunteers in/from North Macedonia in 2002 on behalf of his native organisation the Council for Prevention of Juvenile Delinquency – SPPMD from Kavadarci, North Macedonia. He has co-ordinated one of the Contact Points for the YOUTH/Youth in Action programme in North Macedonia on behalf of the SALTO SEE Resource Centre. Since 2006 he has been a member of the pools of accreditors and trainers of the SALTO SEE RC. Between 2012 and 2016 he volunteered as Vice-President of the International Young Nature Friends – IYNF based in Prague. He is co-author of several publications addressing the situation of volunteerism and volunteering opportunities in North Macedonia and the Balkans.

Lana Pasic holds an MPhil in Development Studies from the University of Oxford, UK (2013), a Joint European Master Degree in Comparative Local Development from the University of Trento, Italy (2011) and a BAdmin (Hons) in International Relations from the University of Pretoria, South Africa. She has been working in the development sector since 2007, in the area of civic participation and activism and youth participation. Lana worked and consulted with a number of local and international NGOs, research institutes and international organisations in Bosnia and Herzegovina and internationally, including UNICEF, UNDP, Oxfam and Save the Children. She was a contributor to Balkanalysis.com, Al Jazeera English, Open Democracy and Café Babel, and she also published Forced Migration Review and Academia journals. In 2015 she published a Kindle edition of her e-book "Twenty Years After Dayton: Where is Bosnia and Herzegovina Today?". Lana was a member of the Pool of European Youth Researchers from 2017 to 2019. She currently works as Youth Research and Policy Officer with the Partnership between the European Commission and the Council of Europe in the field of youth.

Amy Pearce is a research officer at The Duke of Edinburgh's International Award Foundation, based in London. She manages large-scale international research projects which include outcomes and impact measurement, social value research, and monitoring and evaluation research within quality assurance processes. Amy completed her BA (Hons) degree in Social Anthropology from Durham University, UK, in 2015. Amy is also a Gold Award Holder.

Eli Pilve holds an MA in History from the University of Tallinn (1982). Her main research topics are Estonians migrating from Soviet Russia in the 1920s, ideological pressure in the Soviet school system, youth organisations in Estonia and Estonian land reform in 1919. Eli has been employed at the Estonian Institute of Historical Memory since 2006 – from 2008 as a researcher and from 2017 onwards as a researcher and project manager. She has co-authored a book on the history of youth work in Estonia and a chapter in volume 4 of *The history of youth work in Europe*.

Hanjo Schild studied social affairs with a special focus on social pedagogy and social work in Frankfurt and Wiesbaden, Germany. After some years as a social worker, trainer and project manager, he was a consultant in national and international projects, before joining the Youth Policy Unit of the European Commission (2001-2005). Later he joined the team of the Partnership between the European Commission and the Council of Europe in the field of youth (2005-2016). Before his retirement in late 2017, he joined INBAS, the Institute for Vocational Education, Labour Market and Social Policy.

Simona Sglavo holds an MA in Political Science from MIREES (Master of Interdisciplinary Research and Studies on Eastern Europe), University of Bologna. She obtained her bachelor degree at the Università per Stranieri di Siena, Department of Human Science, in 2015. Currently, she is working at the Eesti Mälu Instituut (Estonian Institute of Historical Memory). She previously collaborated with the Cold War History Research Center, Corvinius University of Budapest. Her academic interests are mostly related to Russian foreign and security policy, security issues in the post-Soviet space, energy security, minority issues, historical memory and information warfare.

Ioana Șurubaru is Vice-President of the European Confederation of Youth Clubs (ECYC). She became active at her local youth centre at the age of 7 and while in high school began working at the same youth centre as a youth worker. She is studying educational sciences at Vrije Universiteit Brussel, with an interest in research on the topic of education of youth workers and youth work as embodied knowledge.

Marti Taru is a researcher at Tallinn University in Estonia. He has a background in research on young people – youth work, youth and public policy, participation in society – and his current interests are in youth, youth work, public policy and evaluation. Within the wider youth, youth policy and youth work framework, he works on youth and employment and the role of youth work in supporting young people's personal development and integration into society. Marti Taru was national correspondent to the European Knowledge Centre for Youth Policy until 2017 and is a member of the Pool of European Youth Researchers.

Sabine Troitzsch went on summer camps with the Catholic and Protestant youth movements as a child and teenager. She became politicised during her studies in Magdeburg and Leipzig through a trade union and in SJD-Die Falken, a socialist educational youth movement in Germany. From 2009-16 Sabine was a member and later head of the international committee of SJD-Die Falken and co-ordinated seminars, campaigns, international camps and SJD's work in YES, IFM-SEI and IUSY. From 2015-17 she represented the German Youth Council internationally and worked as an educator in a small archive on the history of youth labour in Germany. Since 2017, Sabine has worked in the federal office of SJD-Die Falken in the sector on child policy and international work. She aims to educate children, young people, other educators and herself on the causes and consequences of inequalities in the world and to empower everyone to stand up for a society where co-operation, democracy, diversity and good living conditions for all are more important than profit and competition.

Eduard Vallory chairs the UNESCO Centre of Catalonia and leads the alliance for educational change, Escola Nova 21. He holds a PhD in Social and Political Sciences, has been Director of the Barcelona Graduate School of Economics, Visiting Scholar at New York University and Research Fellow at the University of Cambridge. He was also Chief of Staff of the Ministry for Universities, Research and the Information Society at the Government of Catalonia. He has been Chairman of the National Youth Council of Catalonia (CNJC) and Vice-President of Catalan Scouting and Guiding.

Jan Vanhee works on European and international youth policy in the Knowledge & Policy Division at the Department for Culture, Youth and Media in the Flemish Community of Belgium. He is EU Youth Affairs Attaché with the Permanent Representation of Belgium to the EU (General representation of the Government of Flanders), represents Belgium (Flanders) in the EU Youth Working Party and on the Council of Europe's Intergovernmental Steering Committee for Youth (CDEJ) and CMJ (Joint Council on Youth), and tries to follow all major political developments and debates on youth (work) issues in Europe and beyond. His special interests include EU relations, the Council of Europe, the United Nations, civil society policy, youth (work) policy, human rights, democracy, youth mobility, co-operation on youth issues with South Africa, social work, young refugees and extreme poverty reduction.

Howard Williamson CVO CBE FRSA FHEA is Professor of European Youth Policy at the University of South Wales in the United Kingdom. Previously he worked at the Universities of Oxford, Cardiff and Copenhagen and has held visiting positions in Hong Kong, Malta, Zagreb, Beijing, Rennes, Tehran and Melbourne. He is a nationally qualified youth worker and ran a youth centre for 25 years in parallel with his academic research that spanned issues such as youth crime, youth unemployment, vocational training, enterprise and entrepreneurship, substance misuse, homelessness, school curricula and youth work. He conducted the original "status zer0" research that attracted political attention to young people not in education, employment or training (NEET) and has followed the lives of a group of men (The "Milltown Boys"), now reaching the age of 60, whom he first met when they were young offenders in the 1970s. He has advised many levels of governance on youth policy issues, from the Welsh and UK governments, the European Commission, the Council of Europe and the United Nations. He is a trustee of Grassroots – the Cardiff City Centre Youth Project, the European Forum Alpbach Foundation, and The Duke of Edinburgh's International Award for Young People. In 2002, he was appointed a Commander of the Order of the British Empire (CBE) and, in 2016, a Commander of the Royal Victorian Order (CVO). In 2019, he was presented with an "Outstanding Contribution to Youth Work" Excellence Award by the First Minister of the Welsh Government.

Sales agents for publications of the Council of Europe
Agents de vente des publications du Conseil de l'Europe

BELGIUM/BELGIQUE
La Librairie Européenne -
The European Bookshop
Rue de l'Orme, 1
BE-1040 BRUXELLES
Tel.: + 32 (0)2 231 04 35
Fax: + 32 (0)2 735 08 60
E-mail: info@libeurop.eu
http://www.libeurop.be

Jean De Lannoy/DL Services
c/o Michot Warehouses
Bergense steenweg 77
Chaussée de Mons
BE-1600 SINT PIETERS LEEUW
Fax: + 32 (0)2 706 52 27
E-mail: jean.de.lannoy@dl-servi.com
http://www.jean-de-lannoy.be

CANADA
Renouf Publishing Co. Ltd.
22-1010 Polytek Street
CDN-OTTAWA, ONT K1J 9J1
Tel.: + 1 613 745 2665
Fax: + 1 613 745 7660
Toll-Free Tel.: (866) 767-6766
E-mail: order.dept@renoufbooks.com
http://www.renoufbooks.com

CROATIA/CROATIE
Robert's Plus d.o.o.
Marasoviçeva 67
HR-21000 SPLIT
Tel.: + 385 21 315 800, 801, 802, 803
Fax: + 385 21 315 804
E-mail: robertsplus@robertsplus.hr

CZECH REPUBLIC/
RÉPUBLIQUE TCHÈQUE
Suweco CZ, s.r.o.
Klecakova 347
CZ-180 21 PRAHA 9
Tel.: + 420 2 424 59 204
Fax: + 420 2 848 21 646
E-mail: import@suweco.cz
http://www.suweco.cz

DENMARK/DANEMARK
GAD
Vimmelskaftet 32
DK-1161 KØBENHAVN K
Tel.: + 45 77 66 60 00
Fax: + 45 77 66 60 01
E-mail: reception@gad.dk
http://www.gad.dk

FINLAND/FINLANDE
Akateeminen Kirjakauppa
PO Box 128
Keskuskatu 1
FI-00100 HELSINKI
Tel.: + 358 (0)9 121 4430
Fax: + 358 (0)9 121 4242
E-mail: akatilaus@akateeminen.com
http://www.akateeminen.com

FRANCE
Please contact directly /
Merci de contacter directement
Council of Europe Publishing
Éditions du Conseil de l'Europe
F-67075 STRASBOURG Cedex
Tel.: + 33 (0)3 88 41 25 81
Fax: + 33 (0)3 88 41 39 10
E-mail: publishing@coe.int
http://book.coe.int

Librairie Kléber
1, rue des Francs-Bourgeois
F-67000 STRASBOURG
Tel.: + 33 (0)3 88 15 78 88
Fax: + 33 (0)3 88 15 78 80
E-mail: librairie-kleber@coe.int
http://www.librairie-kleber.com

NORWAY/NORVÈGE
Akademika
Postboks 84 Blindern
NO-0314 OSLO
Tel.: + 47 2 218 8100
Fax: + 47 2 218 8103
E-mail: support@akademika.no
http://www.akademika.no

POLAND/POLOGNE
Ars Polona JSC
25 Obroncow Street
PL-03-933 WARSZAWA
Tel.: + 48 (0)22 509 86 00
Fax: + 48 (0)22 509 86 10
E-mail: arspolona@arspolona.com.pl
http://www.arspolona.com.pl

PORTUGAL
Marka Lda
Rua dos Correeiros 61-3
PT-1100-162 LISBOA
Tel: 351 21 3224040
Fax: 351 21 3224044
E mail: apoio.clientes@marka.pt
www.marka.pt

RUSSIAN FEDERATION/
FÉDÉRATION DE RUSSIE
Ves Mir
17b, Butlerova ul. - Office 338
RU-117342 MOSCOW
Tel.: + 7 495 739 0971
Fax: + 7 495 739 0971
E-mail: orders@vesmirbooks.ru
http://www.vesmirbooks.ru

SWITZERLAND/SUISSE
Planetis Sàrl
16, chemin des Pins
CH-1273 ARZIER
Tel.: + 41 22 366 51 77
Fax: + 41 22 366 51 78
E-mail: info@planetis.ch

TAIWAN
Tycoon Information Inc.
5th Floor, No. 500, Chang-Chun Road
Taipei, Taiwan
Tel.: 886-2-8712 8886
Fax: 886-2-8712 4747, 8712 4777
E-mail: info@tycoon-info.com.tw
orders@tycoon-info.com.tw

UNITED KINGDOM/ROYAUME-UNI
The Stationery Office Ltd
PO Box 29
GB-NORWICH NR3 1GN
Tel.: + 44 (0)870 600 5522
Fax: + 44 (0)870 600 5533
E-mail: book.enquiries@tso.co.uk
http://www.tsoshop.co.uk

UNITED STATES and CANADA/
ÉTATS-UNIS et CANADA
Manhattan Publishing Co
670 White Plains Road
USA-10583 SCARSDALE, NY
Tel: + 1 914 472 4650
Fax: + 1 914 472 4316
E-mail: coe@manhattanpublishing.com
http://www.manhattanpublishing.com

Council of Europe Publishing/Éditions du Conseil de l'Europe
F-67075 STRASBOURG Cedex
Tel.: + 33 (0)3 88 41 25 81 – Fax: + 33 (0)3 88 41 39 10 – E-mail: publishing@coe.int – Website: http://book.coe.int